CLIFTON
THROUGH TIME
Will Musgrave

AMBERLEY PUBLISHING

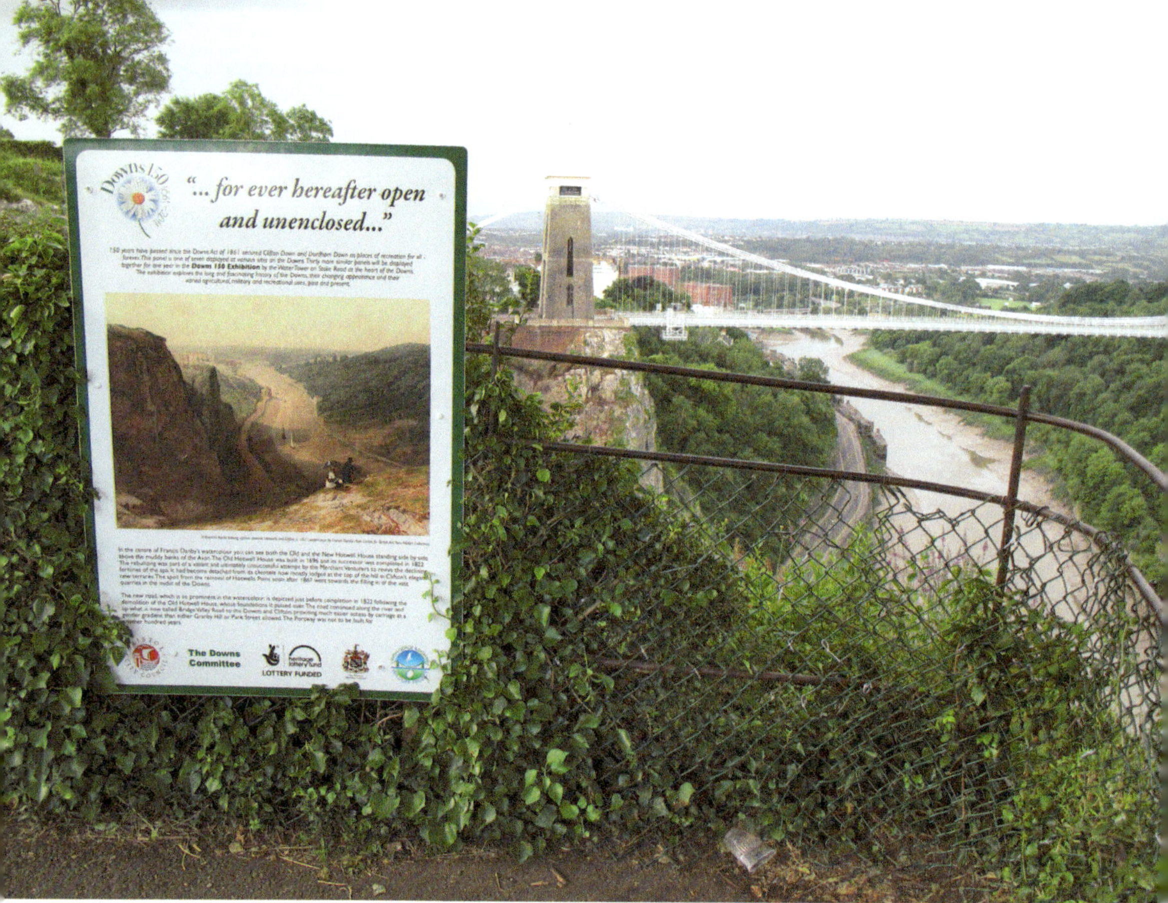

Clifton Suspension Bridge

A view of Brunel's Suspension Bridge taken from St Vincent's Rock, looking up the River Avon towards Bristol docks. In the foreground is a display board, erected by Bristol City Council and The Downs Committee in 2011, showing a watercolour by Francis Danby, painted in the early 1820s before the Suspension Bridge was built.

First published 2012

Amberley Publishing
The Hill, Stroud, Gloucestershire, GL5 4EP
www.amberley-books.com

ISBN 978 1 4456 1141 9 (print)
ISBN 978 1 4456 1165 5 (ebook)

British Library Cataloguing in Publication Data.
A catalogue record for this book is available from the
British Library.

Typesetting by Amberley Publishing.
Printed in Great Britain.

Introduction

Standing in a prominent position overlooking the River Avon and the Bristol basin, Clifton has been an important site for habitation for a long time. The remains of an Iron Age fort at the top of The Promenade, leading to Clifton village (and where the Observatory now sits), and the evidence of two other forts across the Avon Gorge at Burwalls and Leigh Woods are reminders of its early origins. Roman activity in the area can be found just along the River Avon at Sea Mills, where the small settlement of Abona acted as a trading post for the occupying forces.

In the Middle Ages Bristol became an important maritime port, trading in goods such as wool, wine, grain and fish with a number of Western European countries including Ireland, France, Spain and Portugal. Clifton, however, remained predominantly a pastoral backwater. The Age of Exploration during this period (John Cabot sailed from Bristol to Newfoundland in 1497 aboard his worryingly small vessel, *The Matthew*) largely passed Clifton by, and the most exciting discovery to be made in its vicinity were the herds of grazing livestock. Bristol continued to prosper in the seventeenth and eighteenth centuries, mainly through the glass, sugar, wine, shipbuilding and mining industries, but it wasn't until the beginning of the nineteenth century that Clifton really came into its own.

The healing waters of the Hotwells spa, just below Clifton, had been popular for the previous century (it had become the summer vacation venue for the prosperous classes, who then travelled on to Bath for the winter season), but the outbreak of the Napoleonic Wars and the dubious medicinal benefits of 'taking the waters' led to its decline. What was Hotwells' loss was Clifton's gain, and the upper classes began to flock uphill to enjoy the more impressive natural setting. Clifton has always profited from its fine geographical location: its sweeping vistas along the Avon Gorge, across to Leigh Woods and Dundry, have long attracted poets and artists, and a panoramic view over the Cumberland Basin (and its floating harbour) and central Bristol completes the impressive picture. There was, and still is, a certain bucolic charm to the Clifton area which appealed to its Georgian and Victorian visitors. Nature is very much on the doorstep, and the flat, grassy expanse of the Downs adds to the feeling of openness. There are very few places in Britain that are blessed with such easy access to the countryside (via, of course, Isambard Kingdom Brunel's world-famous Suspension Bridge), while remaining a very short walk from the bustling heart of a major city.

Architects made use of Clifton's natural height advantage over its neighbouring suburbs when designing its grand terraces and crescents at the end of the eighteenth century. Merchants had a vantage point overlooking the docks and warehouses which provided the income for their fine houses. The unsavoury truth that much of that wealth was earned through the transatlantic slave trade was conveniently hidden from both mind and view. With the construction of the Great Western Railway (another of Brunel's achievements) in the mid-nineteenth century, Bristol became a hub of the national transport system, and Clifton benefited accordingly. The journey time to London could now be calculated in hours rather than days, bolstering the emergence of Bristol as one of the most important cities in the country.

Bristol continued to flourish in the twentieth century through the profits of the tobacco and chocolate businesses (largely owned by Wills and Frys respectively) and the fledgling aviation industry (based at Filton). Like the rest of the city, Clifton was a victim of air raids during the Second World War. A sign of the changing times is best illustrated by the redeployment of the funicular railway linking Clifton with Hotwells. Originally constructed to transport visitors from their accommodation in Clifton village to the spa below, it now became a shelter and storage facility.

Clifton life continues to be vibrant (aided by the annual influx of University of Bristol freshers) and trade and commerce is still prospering, although it now predominantly relies on high-tech industry and banking for its income. Today, many of the imposing houses of the nineteenth century have been split into flats and maisonettes, and old churches have been converted into offices and apartments. Traditional tea rooms have been changed into coffee shops and cafés, and butchers, bakers, greengrocers, hardware stores and pharmacists are all much rarer. Travel agents are replacing newsagents. Clifton has become another victim of out-of-town shopping malls; indeed it doesn't even have a local cinema anymore, but despite this there remains a strong sense of community. And like any community, Clifton cannot be seen as a separate entity divorced from its surroundings. Hotwells, Cliftonwood, Brandon Hill and Park Street are integral parts of the story of Clifton, in the same way that Clifton is an essential element in the history of Bristol. I have taken the liberty of including these suburbs where appropriate as they are key to an understanding of Clifton as a whole. Some boundaries are simple: the emphatic scythe of the Avon Gorge and the borders of the Downs are clear-cut, but some are more debatable. For instance, the funicular railway's topmost endpoint is in Clifton, while its bottom is in Hotwells. What is more, Clifton is now viewed both as an area and a village (for simplicity's sake its easiest to view Clifton village as being surrounded by Clifton the area, and it's probably best to leave it up to whoever has the unenviable task of deciding where postcode boundaries lie to split the difference).

Looking backwards tends to have negative connotations today, but it can be an inspirational experience. The majestic achievements of Brunel and others stand testament to the human imagination. Seeing what our predecessors aspired to and achieved can set us thinking about how we too can improve our lives and environment, and makes us consider what type of legacy we will leave for future generations.

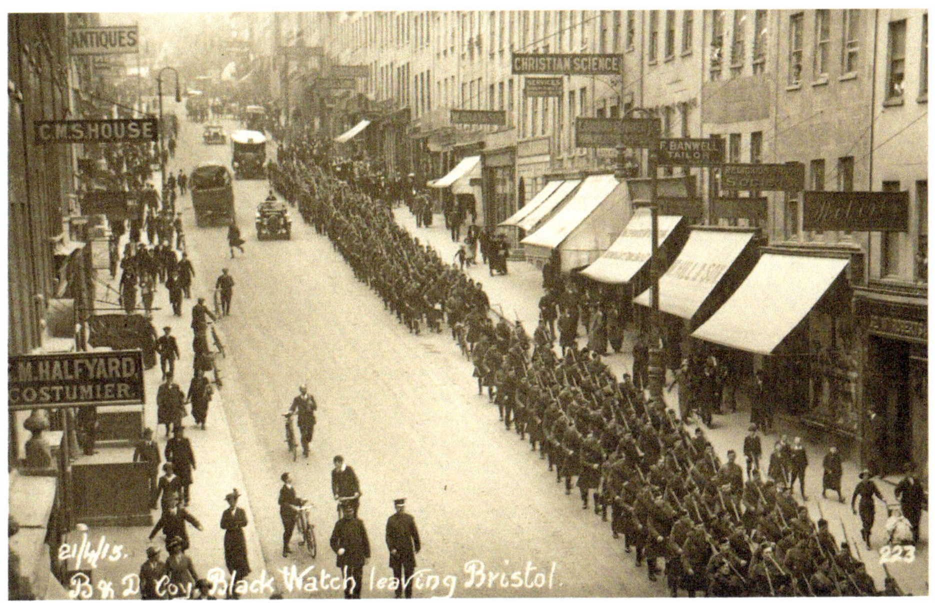

Park Street, 1915

This shows the B and D companies of the Black Watch, which had been billeted at the Victoria Rooms and at the Coliseum Cinema in Park Row, marching to Temple Meads station to go for artillery training. Many would not return. They are going down Park Street, which is the main road from Clifton to the city centre. It was laid out in 1758 by George Tully and mainly built by Thomas and James Paty, and is probably the first stepped hillside terrace in Bristol. To begin with it was a residential street, but it was not long before the rooms on street level became shops and they have remained as such. The only major change is that the Wills Memorial Building now dominates the skyline.

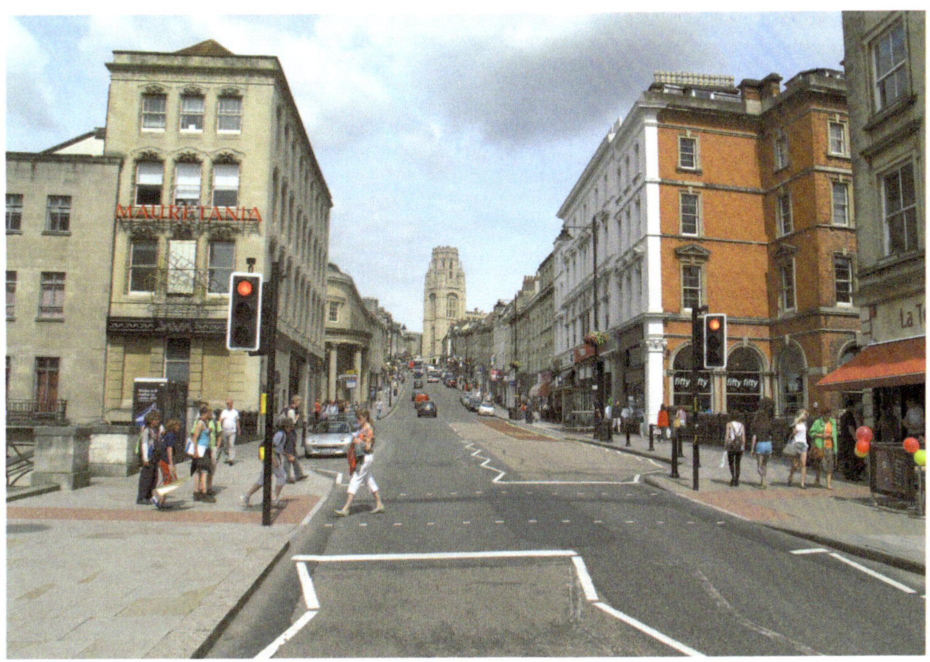

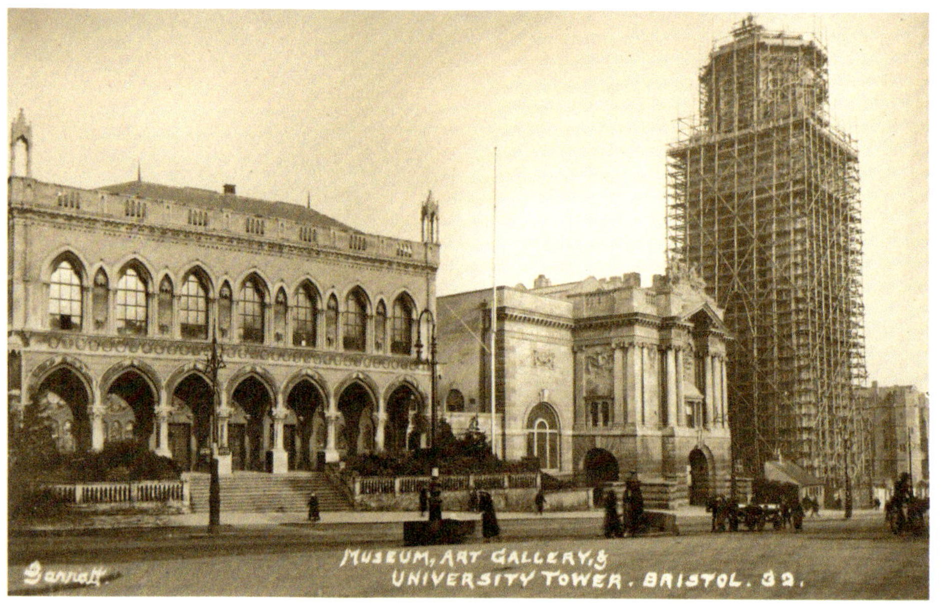

Bristol Museum and Art Gallery and Wills Memorial Tower, Early 1900s

These buildings reflect the beneficence of the Wills family, the cigarette magnates of Bristol. The Wills Tower (surrounded by scaffolding in the old photograph) was built as a memorial to Henry Overton Wills, who donated £100,000 to help found the university. It was designed by Sir George Oatley and opened in 1925. The Museum and Art Gallery (donated by Sir W. H. Wills) next to it has a grand baroque façade, on top of which sit three muses of architecture, painting and sculpture. To the left is the old museum and refectory. These buildings stand on the sites of the Rifle Drill Hall and the Blind Asylum.

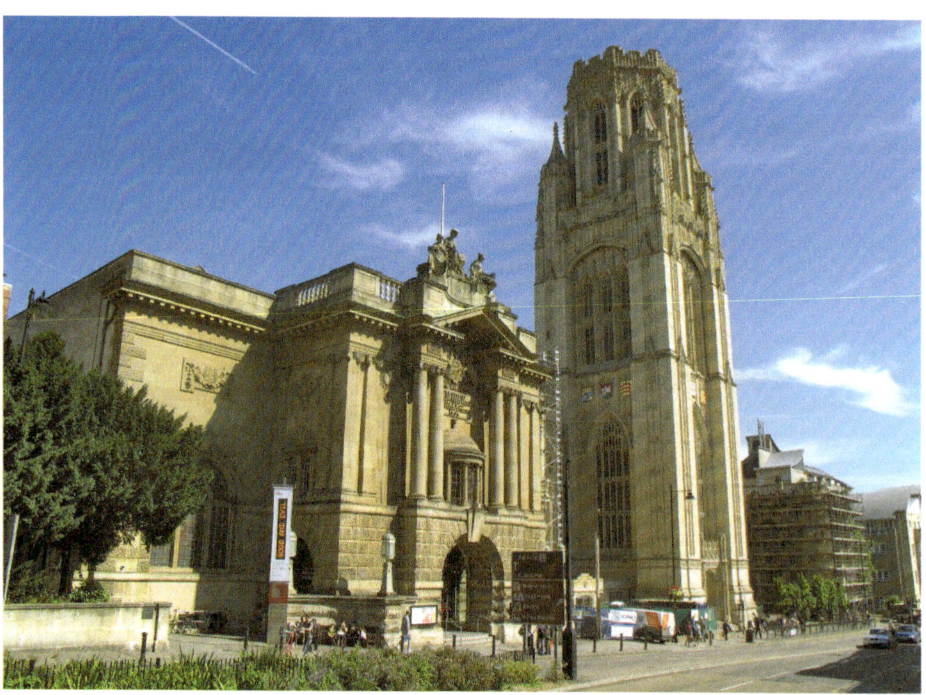

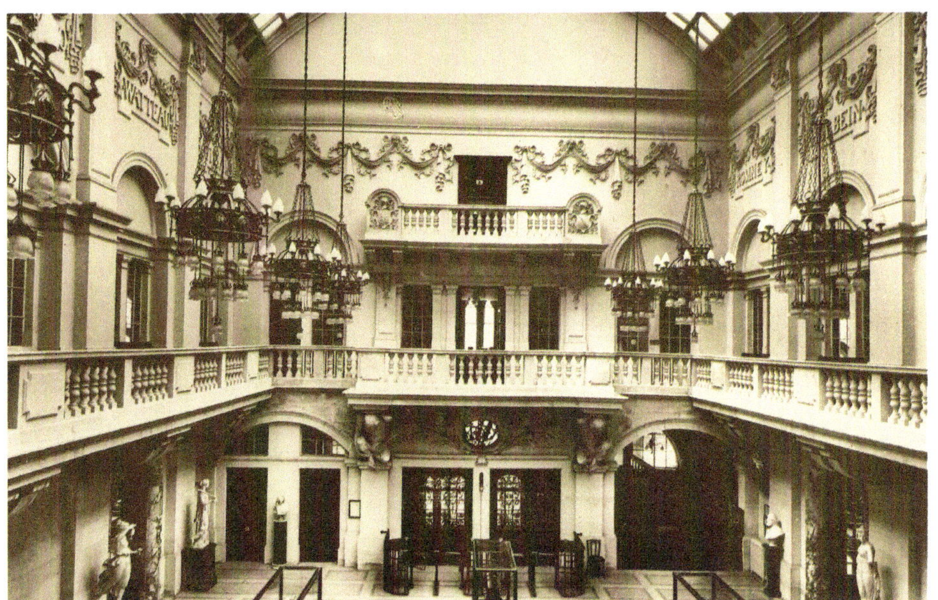

Interior of Bristol Museum, Early 1900s

The Bristol Museum and Art Gallery provides a welcome haven from the hustle and bustle of Queen's Road. It also happens to house a fine selection of art, historical artefacts and natural history displays. Temporary exhibitions (recently several of Leonardo Da Vinci's drawings were shown) augment the museum's collection. Technologically, much has changed since the museum opened its doors in 1904 (the box kite hanging from the ceiling would have been seen as high-tech then) but children still seem to be drawn to the display of stuffed animals from Edwardian times.

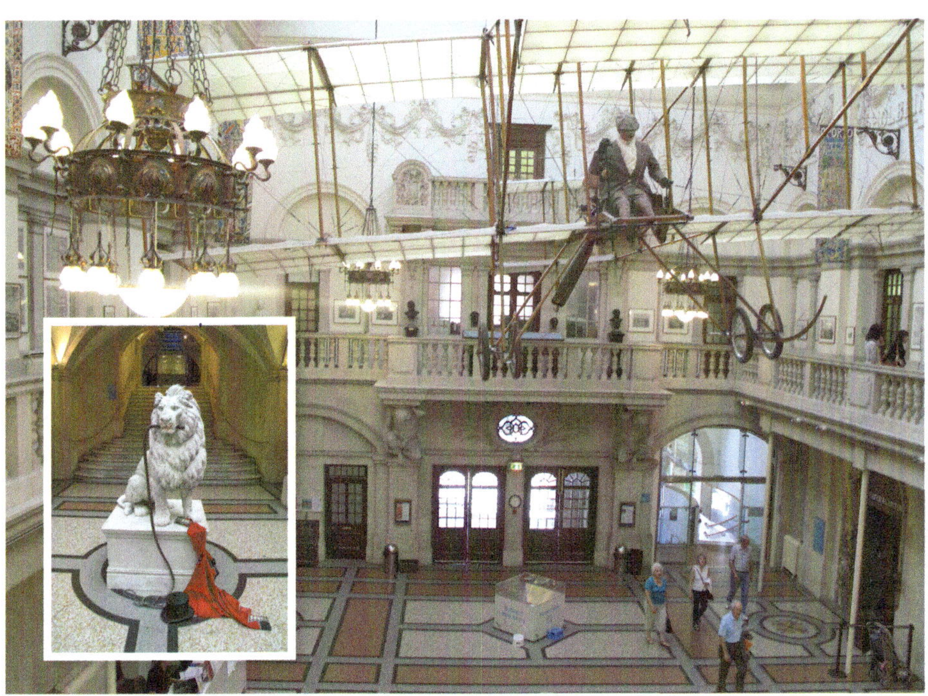

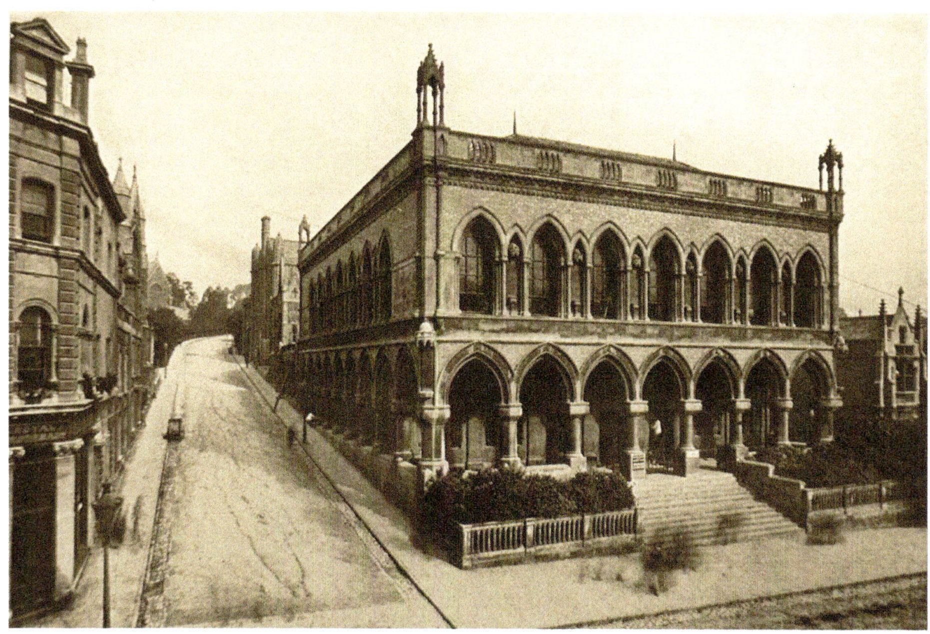

University Road and Banksy Exhibition

Standing at the corner of Queen's Road and University Road is the former City Museum and Library, built in 1867, which became the University Refectory in 1949 and is now a bar and restaurant. Bristol Grammar School can just be seen at the top of the road but access is blocked by a crowd of people queuing to see local artist Banksy's exhibition at the Museum and Art Gallery in 2009 (one of his works displayed at the museum is shown in the inset on the previous page).

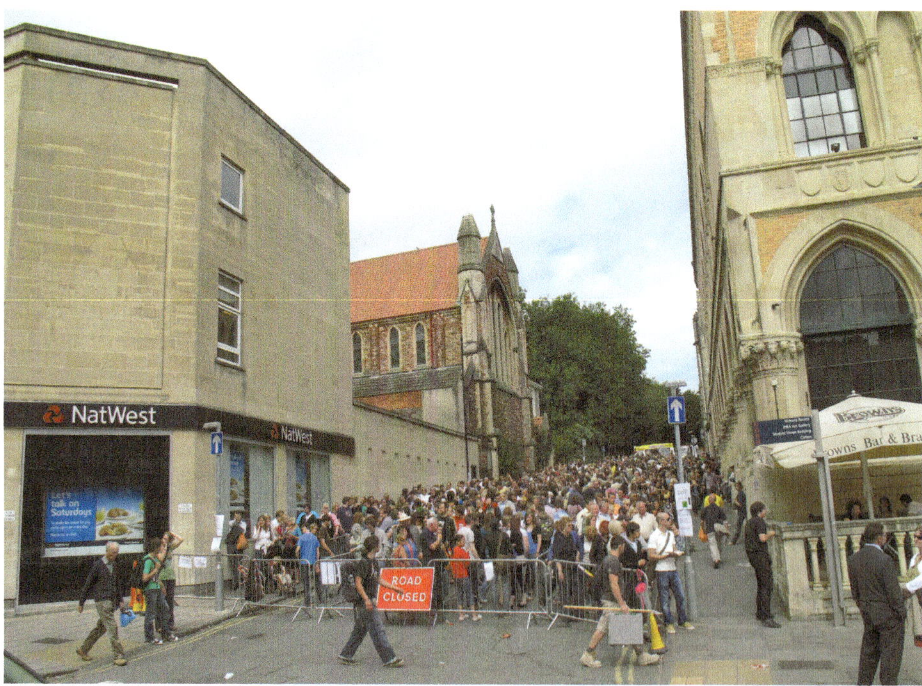

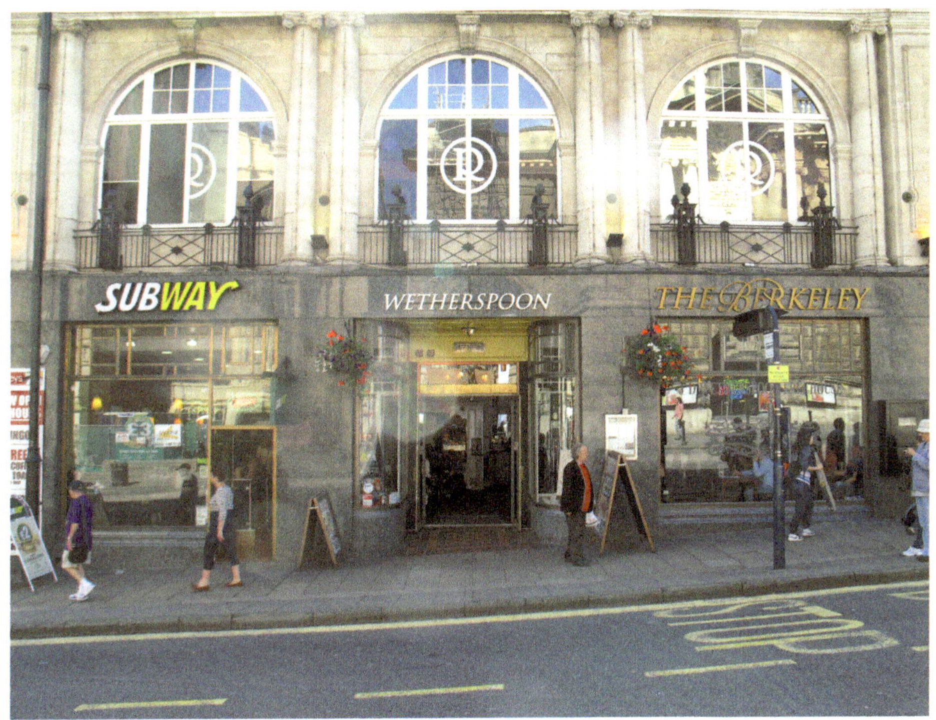

The Berkeley, Queen's Road, 1900s

Now part of a pub chain, the Berkeley stands between the top of Park Street and The Triangle, opposite the Bristol Museum and Art Gallery (the reflection of the latter can be seen in the windows). A popular destination for those seeking refreshment, the Berkeley formerly housed Carwardine's and Cadena tea and coffee shops. Fortunately, the interior of the bar still retains some of the grandeur of past days.

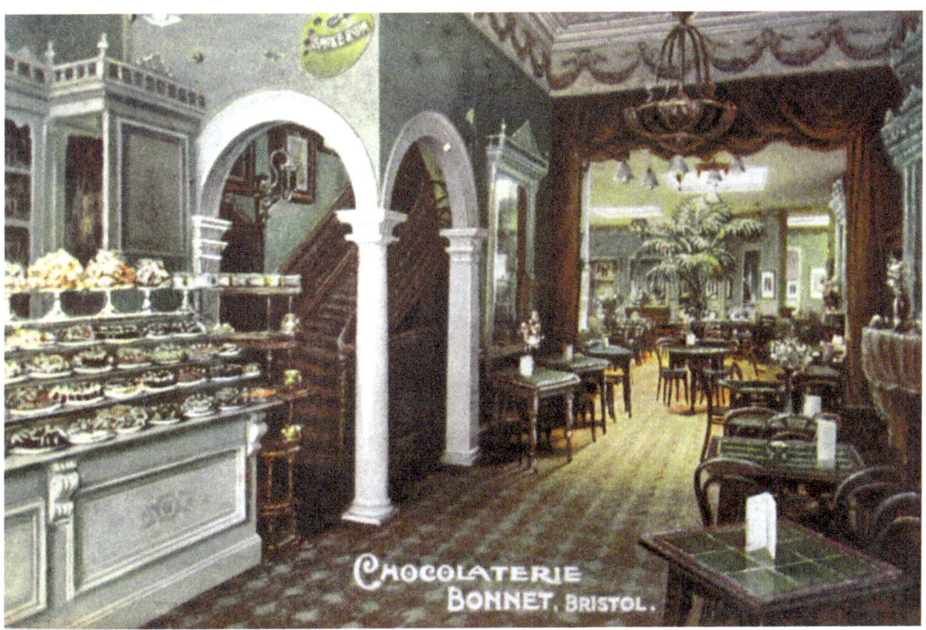

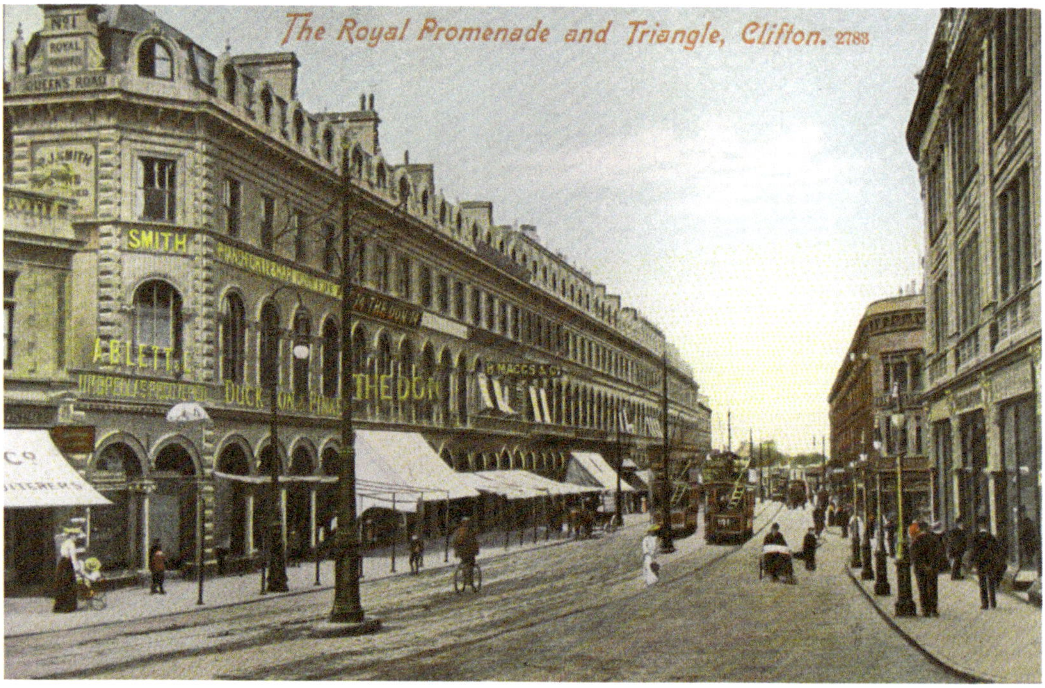

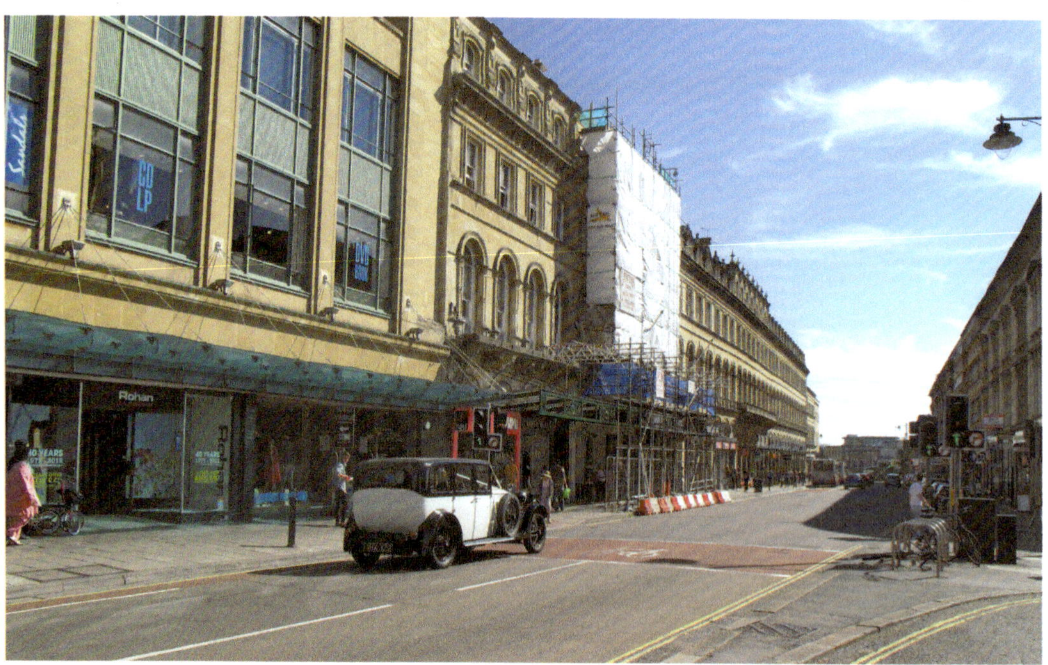

The Triangle, Early 1900s

Designed by Foster and Wood in the 1850s, this commercial terrace with fashionable shops aimed to give architectural character and unity to both the ground and upper storeys. This has been largely retained in the upper storeys. Out-of-town stores forced the closure of multi stores such as Maggs and Dingles, and smaller units and supermarkets have taken their place. The modern picture has an unintended juxtaposition of an old Rolls-Royce in front of a post-war rebuilding.

West Triangle, Early 1960s

A newspaper cutting from the early 1960s trumpeted how this tower block called Clifton Heights would bring 'the luxuries of Mayfair living with luxury services'. Sadly, this over-optimistic period of urban architecture still blights the landscape of Clifton and many other parts of Bristol. Today, like the University of Bristol's Students' Union building, Clifton Heights sits incongruously amid its more inspiring surroundings.

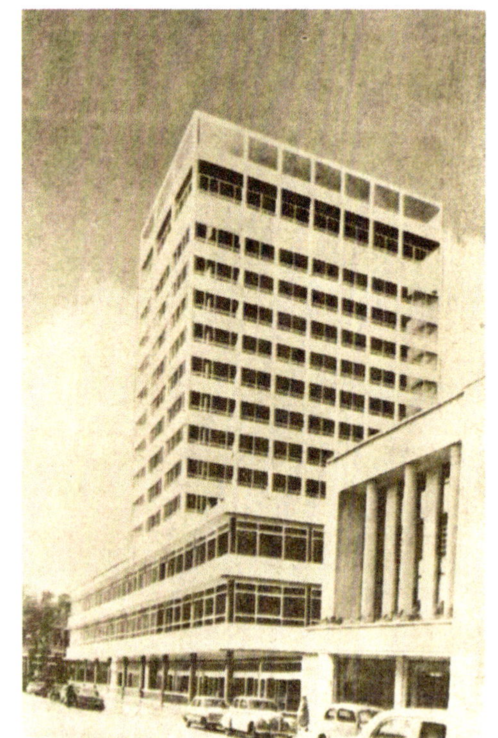

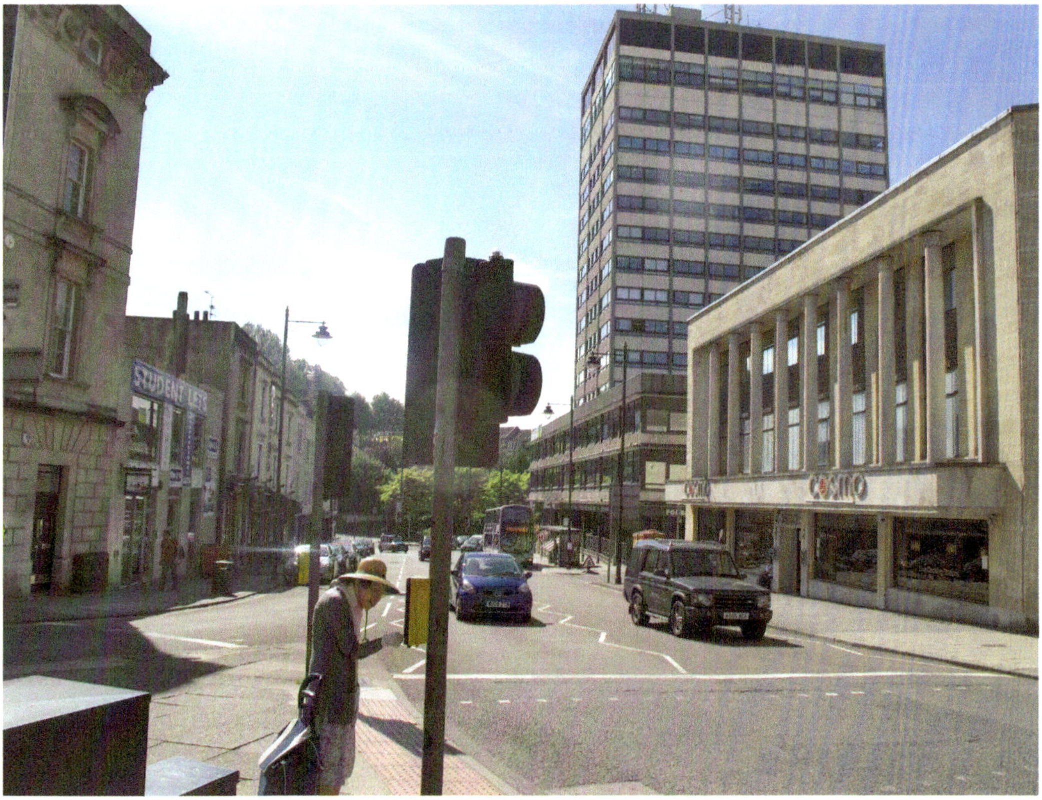

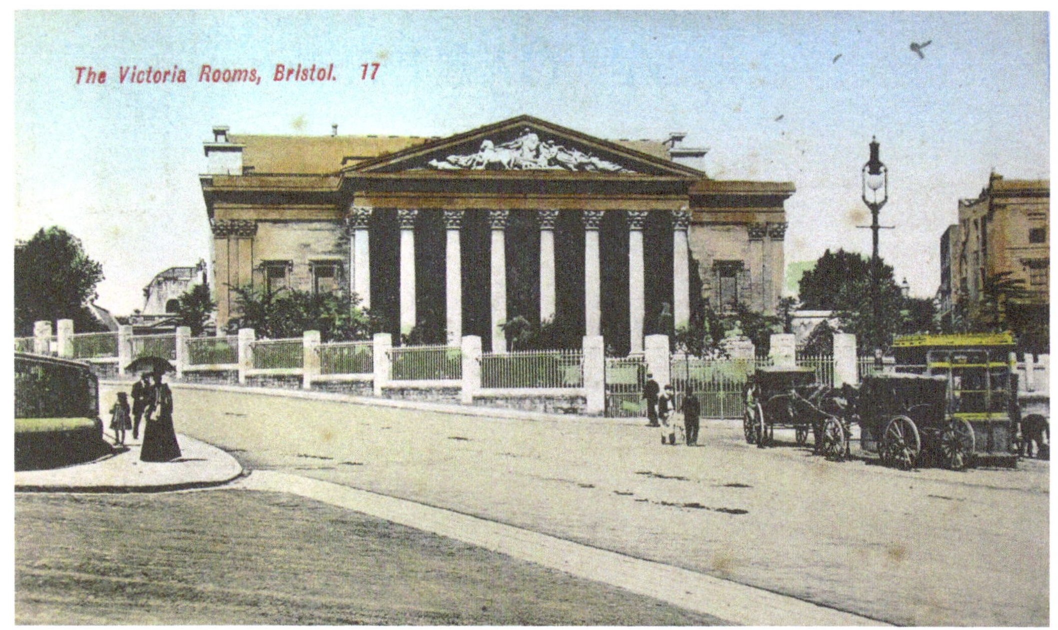

The Victoria Rooms, Early 1900s

Sitting in an imposing position between Queen's Road and the bottom of Whiteladies Road, the Vic Rooms (as it is locally known) started life as a rather aristocratic entertainment venue. The residents of Clifton in the first part of the nineteenth century clearly felt the area required a touch of class, and the architect Charles Dyer was duly commissioned to design a suitably grand neoclassical assembly room. Finance for the project (an impressive £23,000) was raised by local Conservative citizens and construction began in 1838.

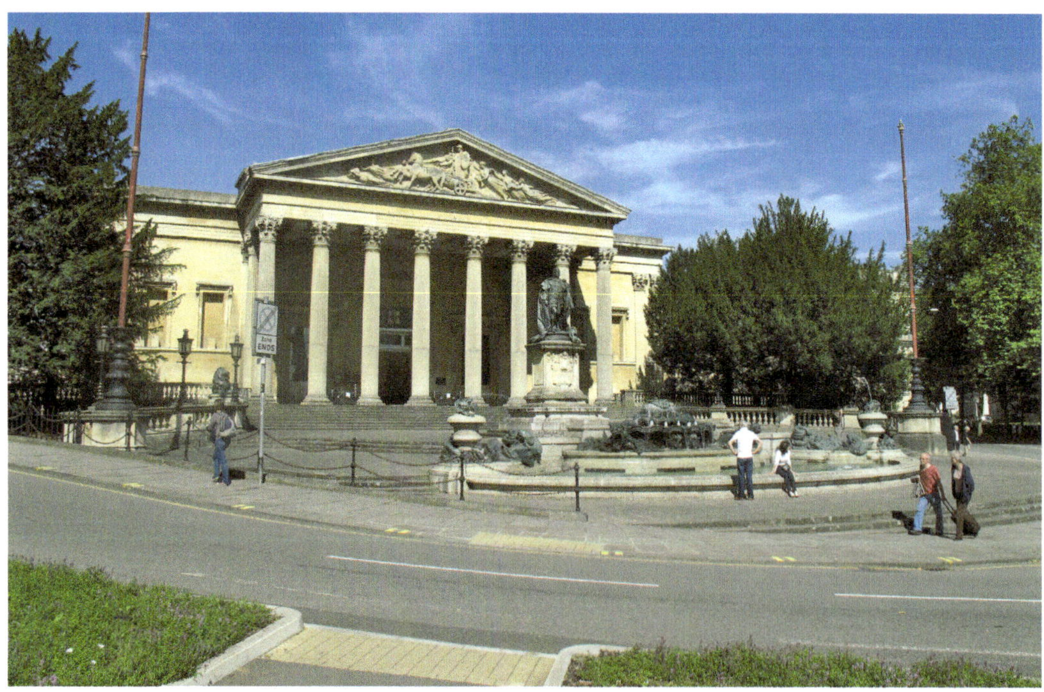

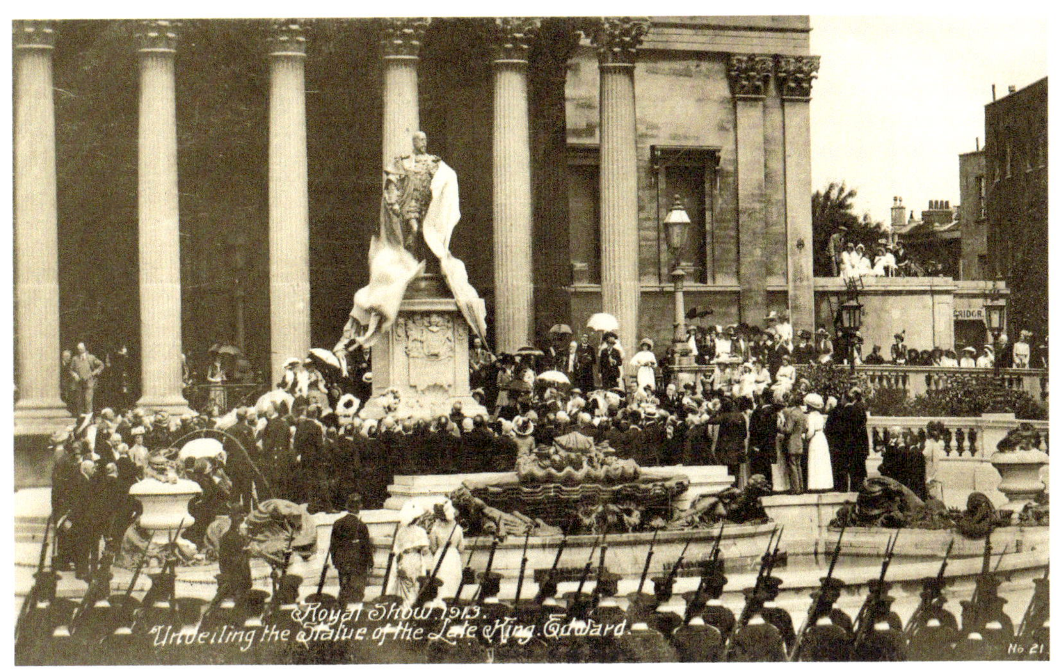

Unveiling the Statue of Edward VII, 4 July 1913

The exterior of the Victoria Rooms has changed somewhat over time: a bronze memorial statue of Edward VII, sculpted by Henry Poole, was erected outside the entrance in 1912, along with baroque fountains and figures. The railings surrounding the building were removed as part of architect Edwin Rickards' design for the monument. The view from behind Edward VII looks down Queen's Road to The Triangle; on the left is the Royal West of England Academy with one of its exterior installations cheering up a gloomy day.

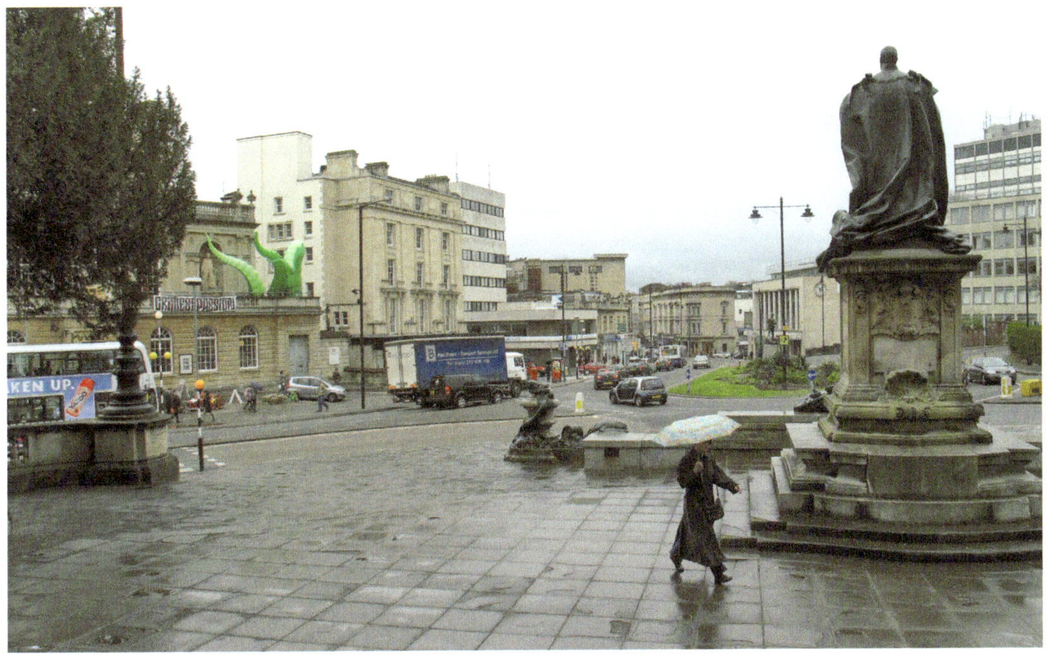

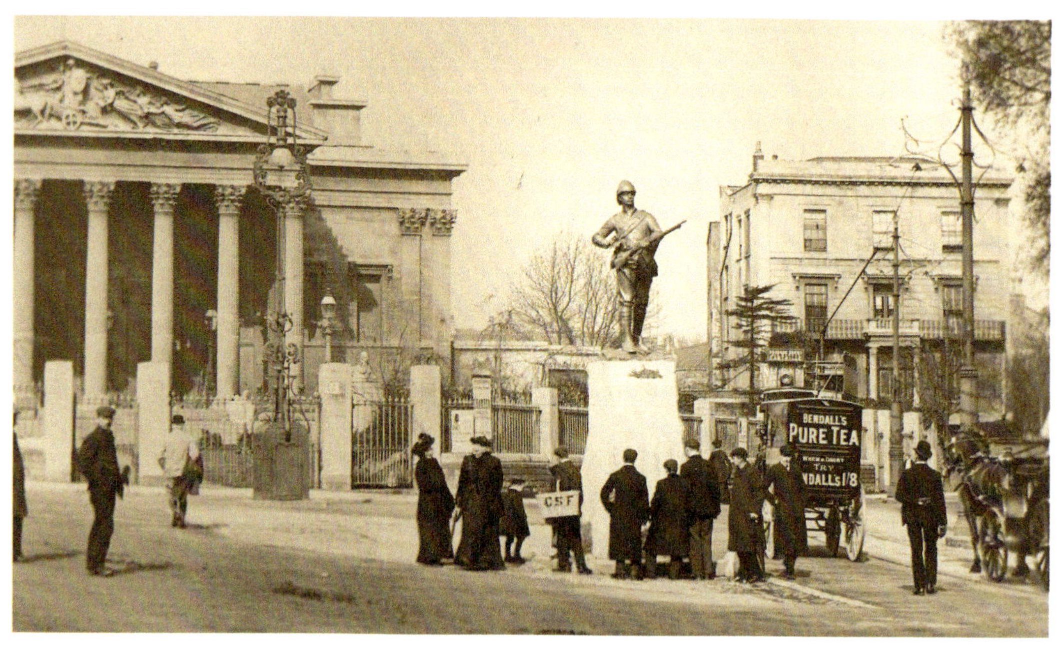

War Memorial and Victoria Rooms, 27 March 1905

In the foreground stands the elegant bronze statue of a soldier commemorating the Boer War. Designed by Mr Onslow Whiting of London and unveiled by Lord Roberts on 4 March 1905, it is dedicated to the soldiers of the Gloucester Regiment. The Gloucesters suffered heavy casualties at Nicholson's Nek during the Siege of Ladysmith; later, under the overall command of Lord Roberts, they assisted at the relief of Kimberley.

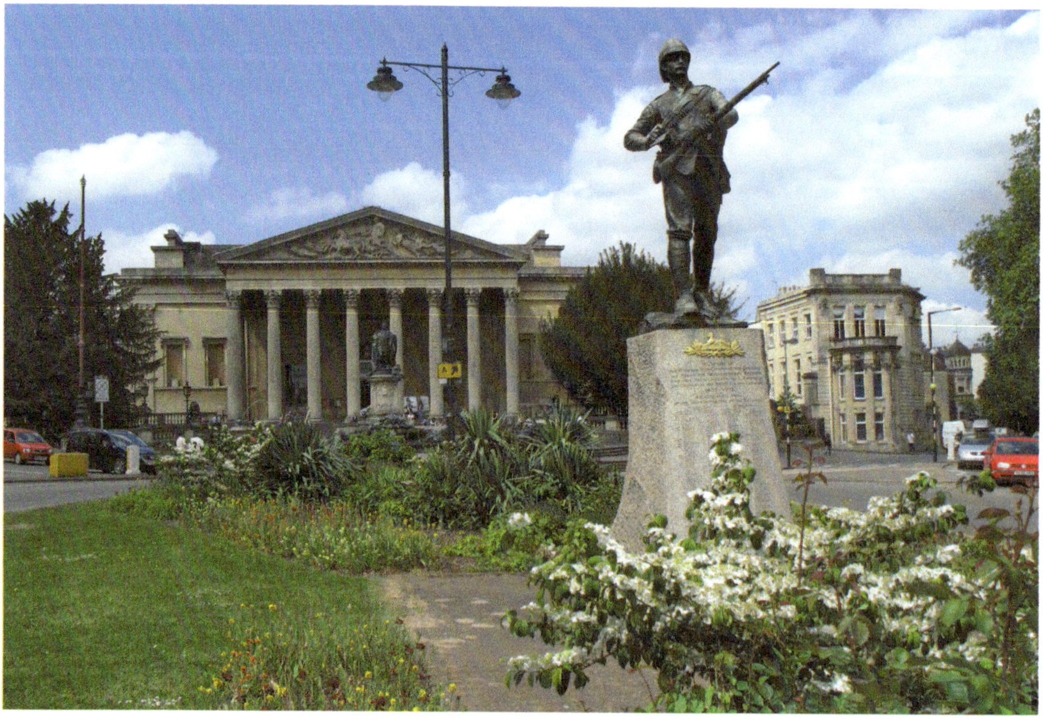

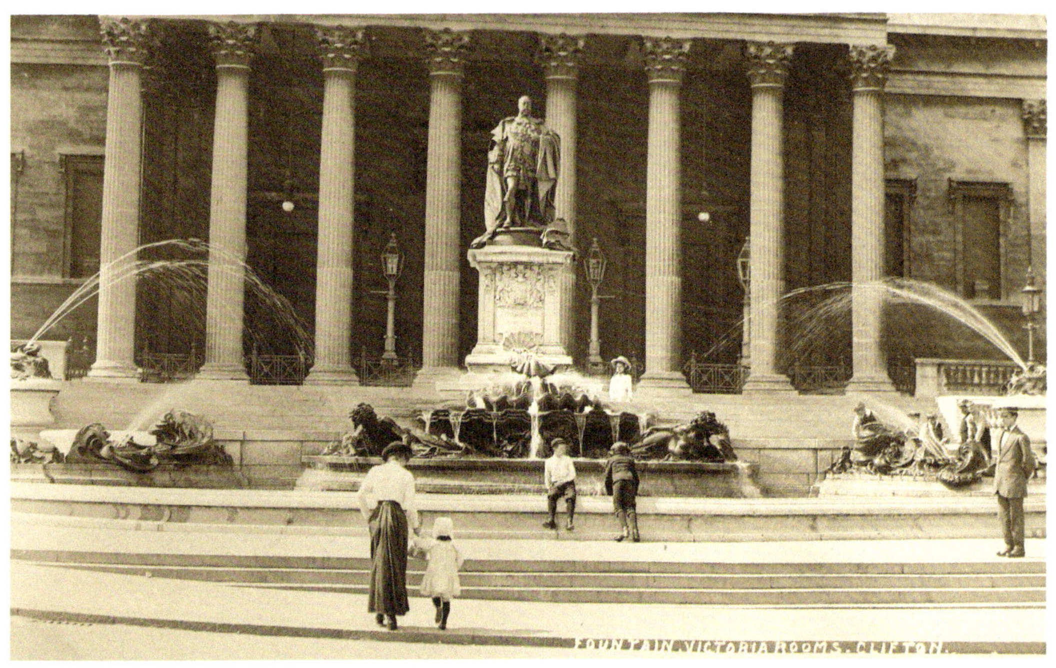

Victoria Rooms, 1910s

The Victoria Rooms (seen here being admired by an Edwardian mother and child) first opened its doors to the public in May 1842 and for the next eight decades was the site of numerous balls, banquets, public meetings, lectures, concerts and recitals. Charles Dickens visited twice; on the second occasion he read extracts from various novels, including *The Pickwick Papers* and *David Copperfield.*

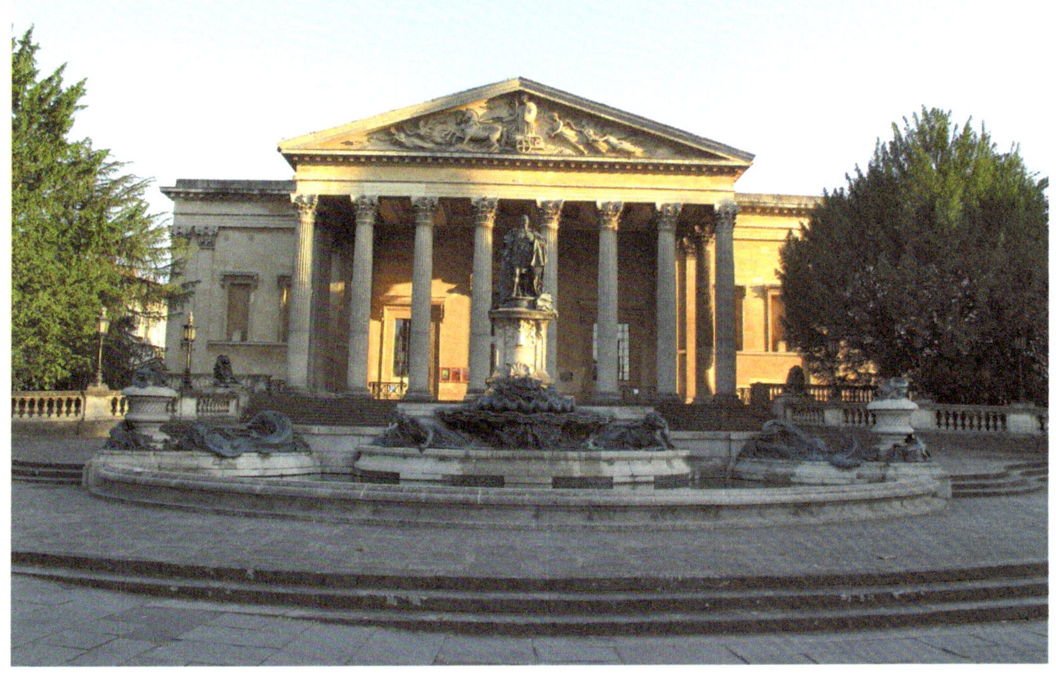

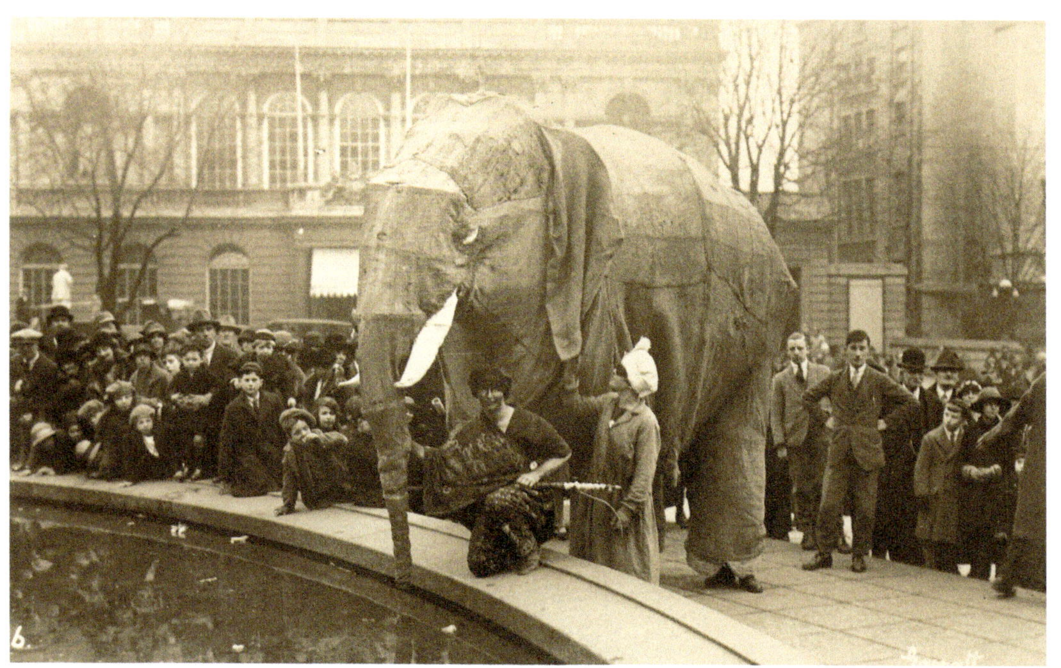

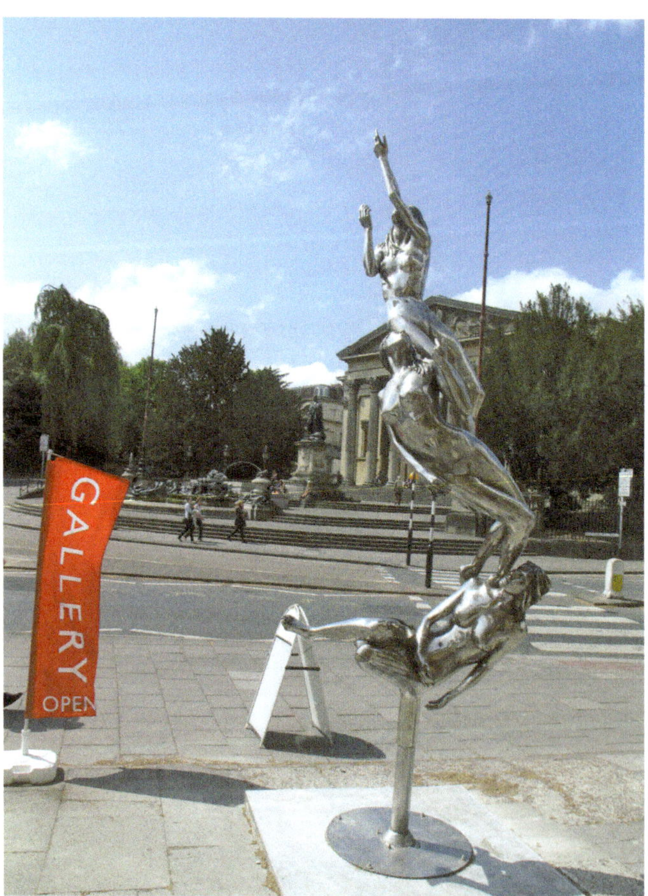

Pretend Elephant at Victoria Rooms

The area around the Vic Rooms seems to inspire people: here a fake elephant from the 1920s (complete with two human feet poking out of its hind leg) 'drinks' from the fountain pool, while David Backhouse's temporary sculpture outside the Royal West of England Academy drew great praise. (Sadly, it was destroyed by a drunken student.)

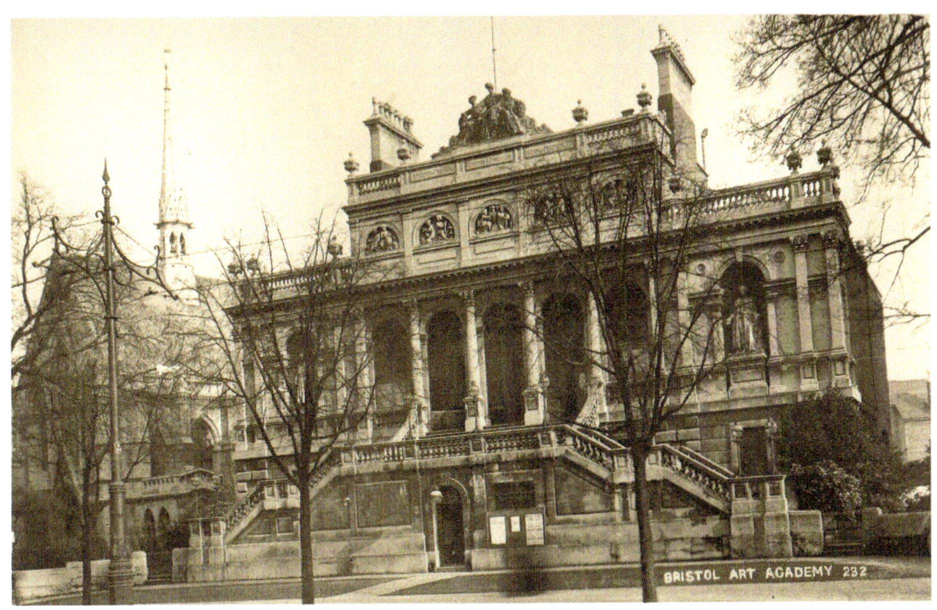

Royal West of England Art Academy, 4 August 1911

Founded in 1845, the academy was the first art gallery in Bristol. It was designed by Hirst and Underwood, and the sculpture is by John Evans Thomas around 1857. The external double-staircase was demolished for an entrance extension in 1911. During the Second World War, the academy building was taken over by various organisations, including the Bristol Aeroplane Company and the US Army. After the war it was used by the Inland Revenue until 1950. In recent years, the façade has been used in a number of imaginative ways to advertise exhibitions.

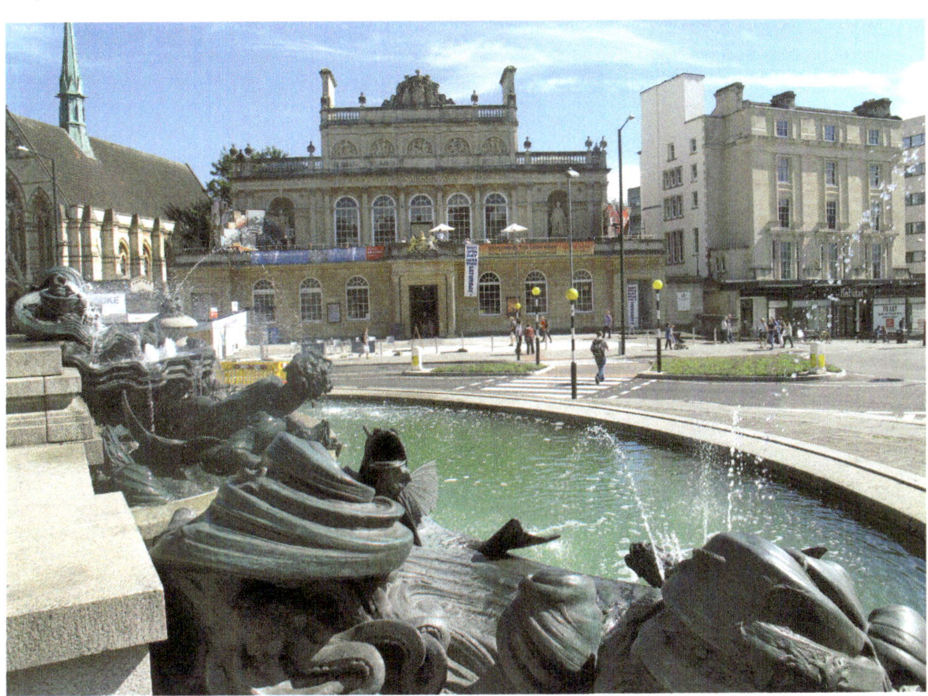

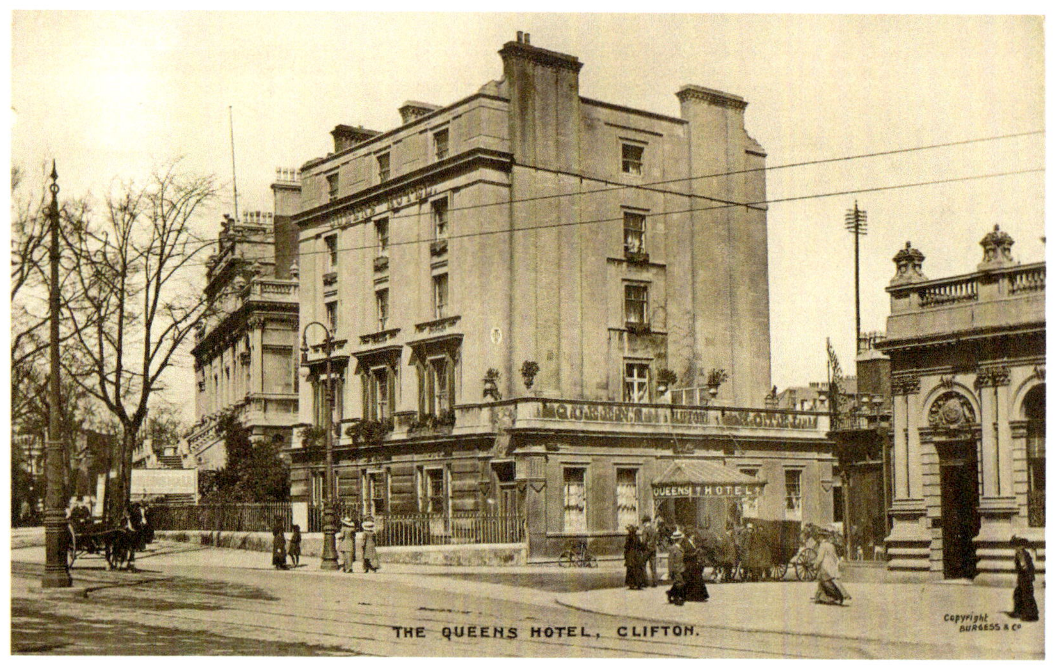

Queen's Hotel (Later Beacon House), Early 1900s

The hotel was opened in 1854 and remained as such until 1914, when it was requisitioned by the Army. Subsequently it was taken over by Gardiners as a household ironmonger. From the 1950s, the property was used by a succession of retail stores – Taylors, Debenhams and finally Habitat, which sold up several years ago. Currently the Habitat site is for sale, while the other floors are occupied by the Policy Press and JISC, both University of Bristol departments. The exterior has not changed significantly, though the main entrance has moved from the south side to the west.

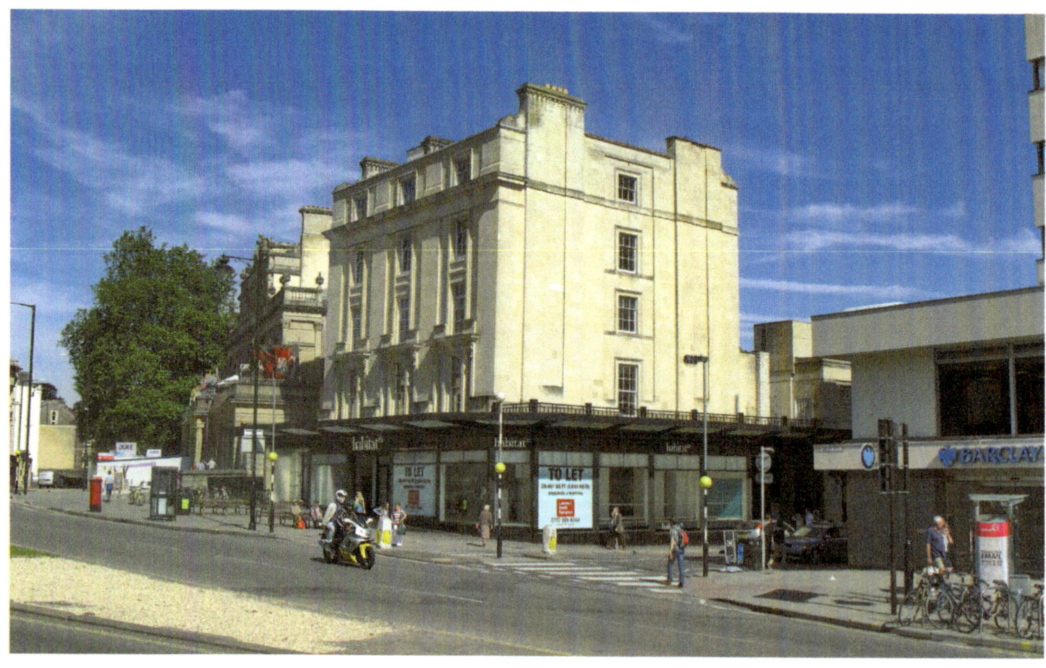

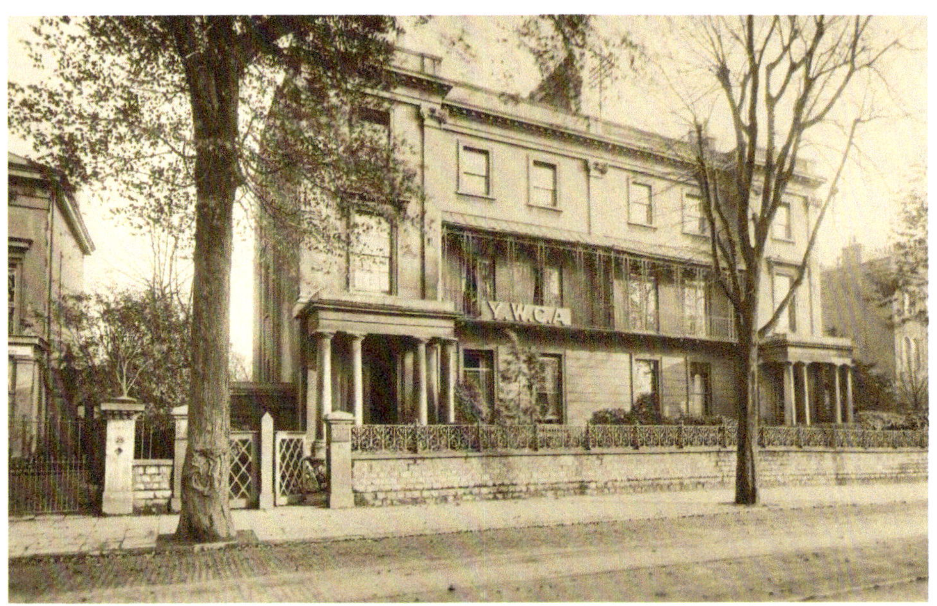

British Broadcasting Corporation, Whiteladies Road

Formally opened by the Lord Mayor of Bristol on 18 September 1934, the British Broadcasting House, Bristol, is located at the bottom of Whiteladies Road close to the Victoria Rooms. It houses offices and technical facilities over four buildings (including the former YWCA) for the production of regional television and radio programmes, including *Points West* and Radio Bristol, and the world famous Natural History Unit (where it has been based since its formation in 1957).

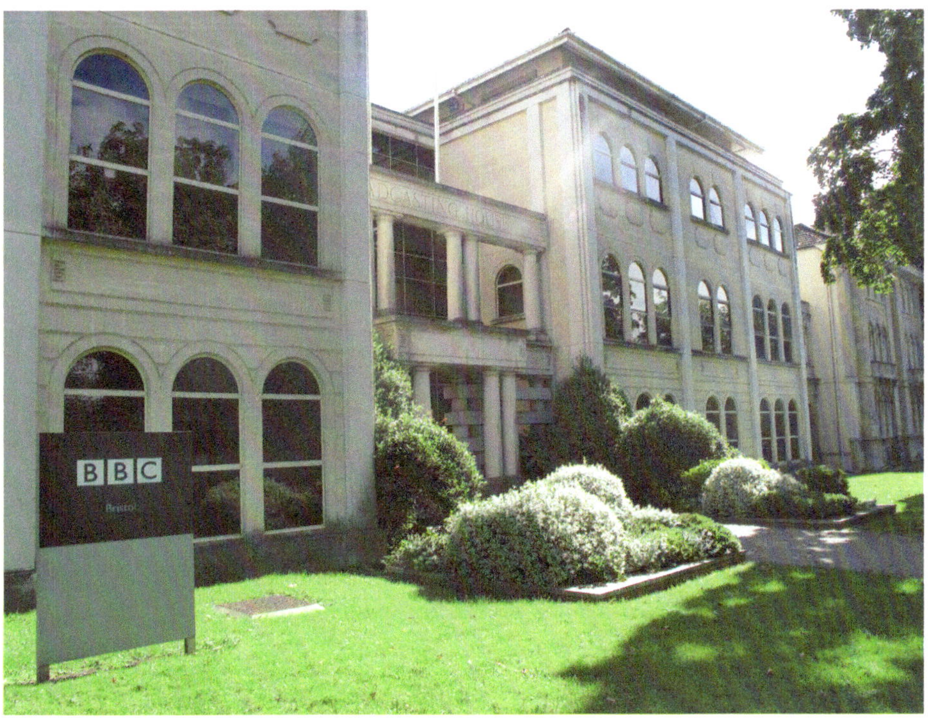

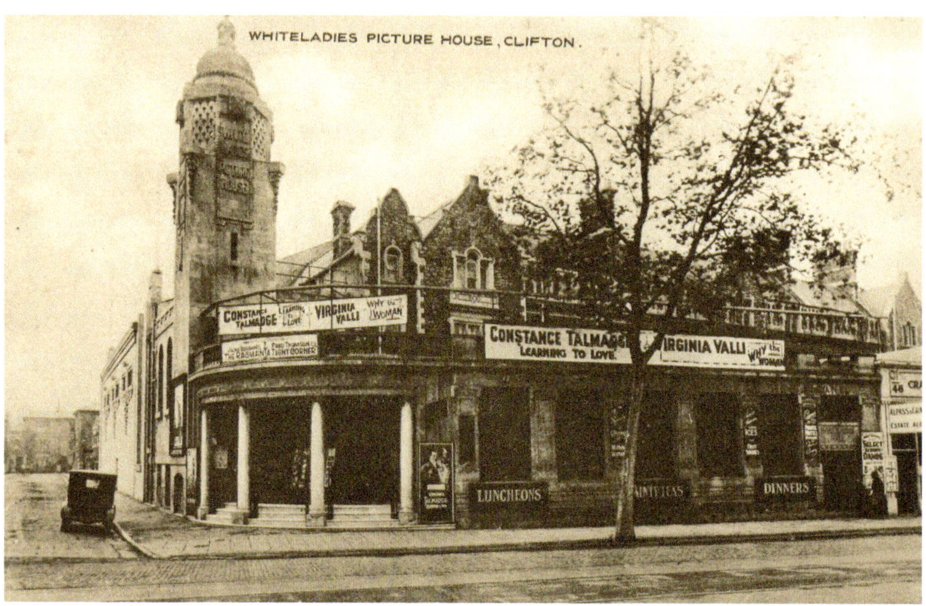

Whiteladies Picture House, Early 1920s

The Picture House was designed by the architects James LaTrobe and Henry Weston and was opened in 1921. It is an early Art Deco-style cinema and was originally conceived as an entertainment complex with a restaurant to the right of the foyer and an upstairs dance hall. In 1978 it was divided into a triple cinema, but as part of the ABC chain it was absorbed by Odeon and sold in 1999. As of 2012, the future of the building is uncertain.

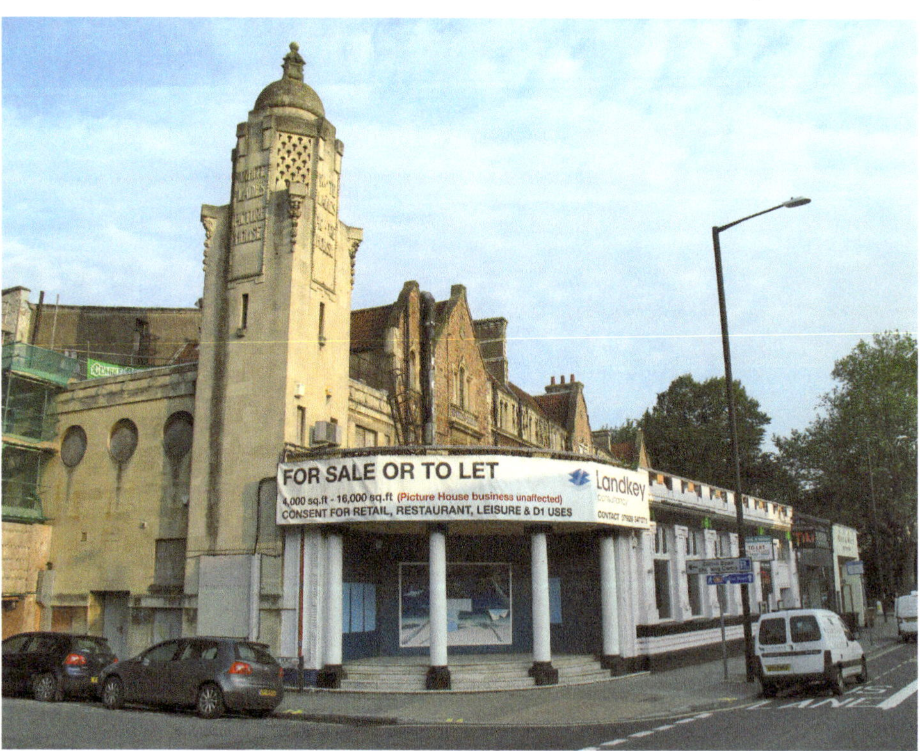

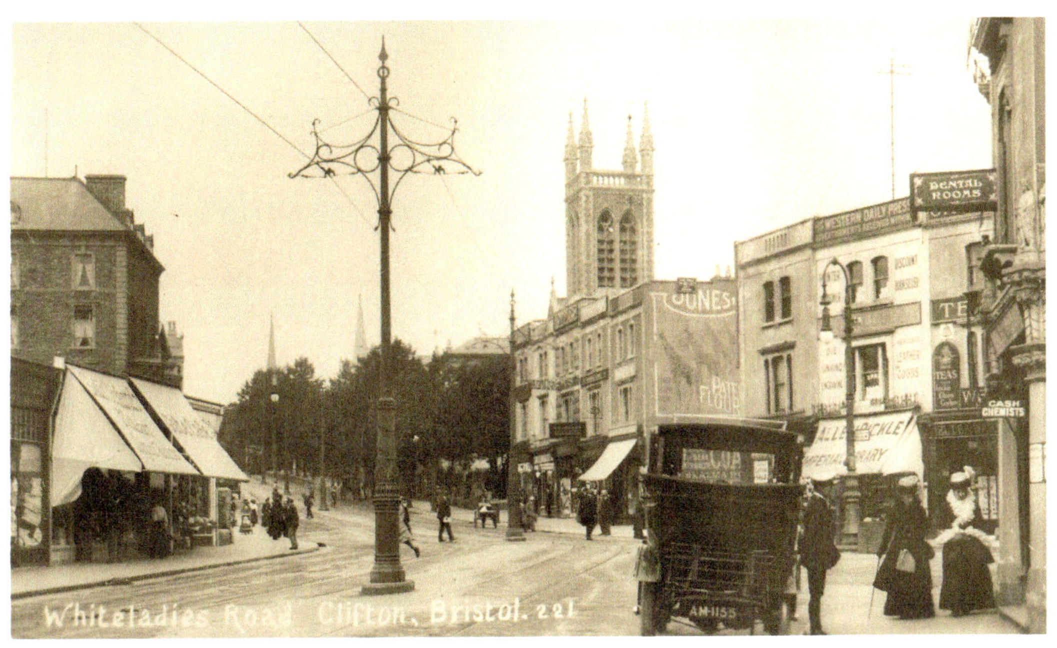

Whiteladies Road, Early 1900s

Whiteladies Road appears to have been named after a pub known as the White Ladies Inn, shown on maps in 1746 and 1804. The popular belief that both it and Blackboy Hill had connections with the slave trade is untrue. In the nineteenth century the road was sometimes referred to as Via Sacramenta, because of the number of religious establishments within a mile of it (three chapels and one church), though by the 1980s nightclubs started coming in and it became known as 'The Strip', drawing in people from the West Country and Wales to enjoy themselves.

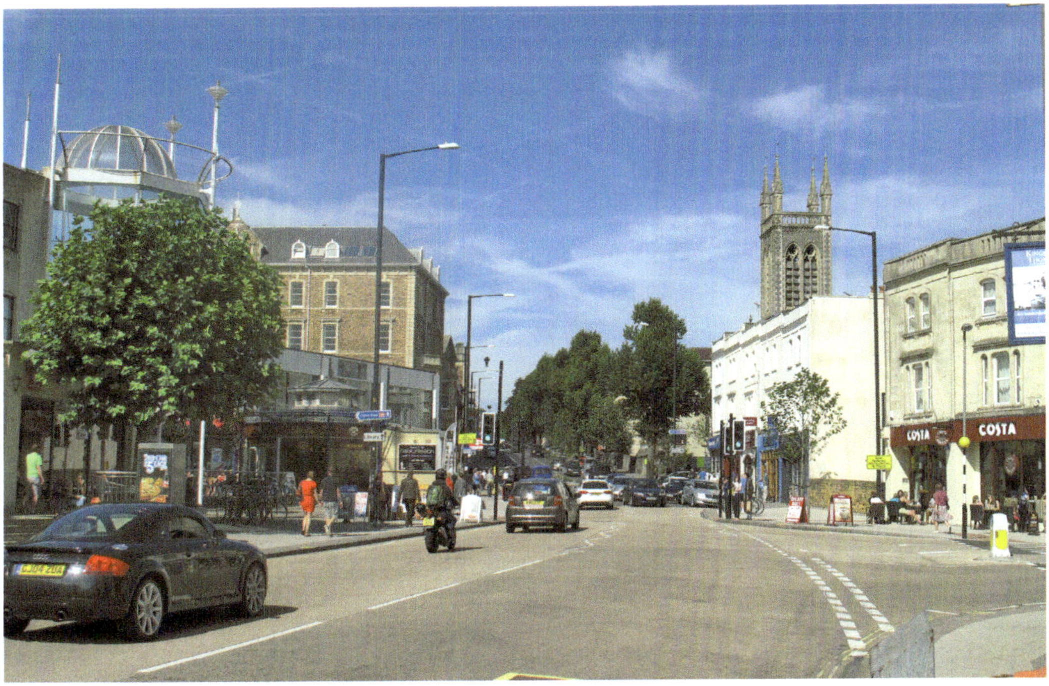

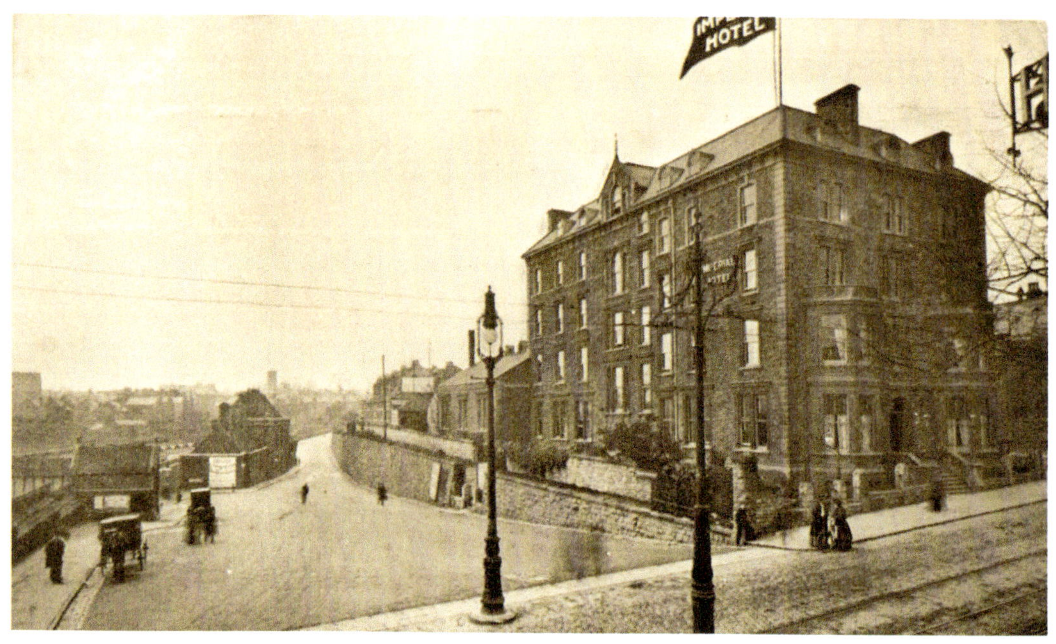

Imperial Hotel, 17 September 1910

Built in 1878 on part of the nursery gardens of Messrs Garroway & Co., the hotel provided refreshment rooms for passengers using Clifton Down railway station (which can be seen at the bottom of the hill). The university acquired the property in 1915 and after the war it became a hall of residence for seventy-eight men until 1929, when Wills Hall was completed. It is reported that both hotel visitors and undergraduates complained about the early morning noise from the railway and nearby dairy. It is now the Department of Social Medicine.

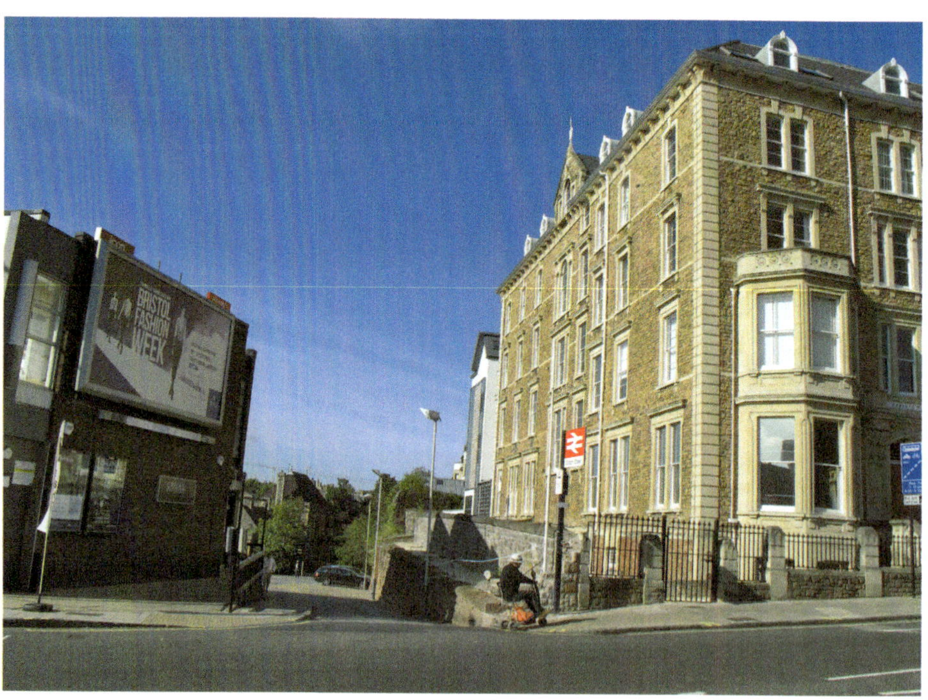

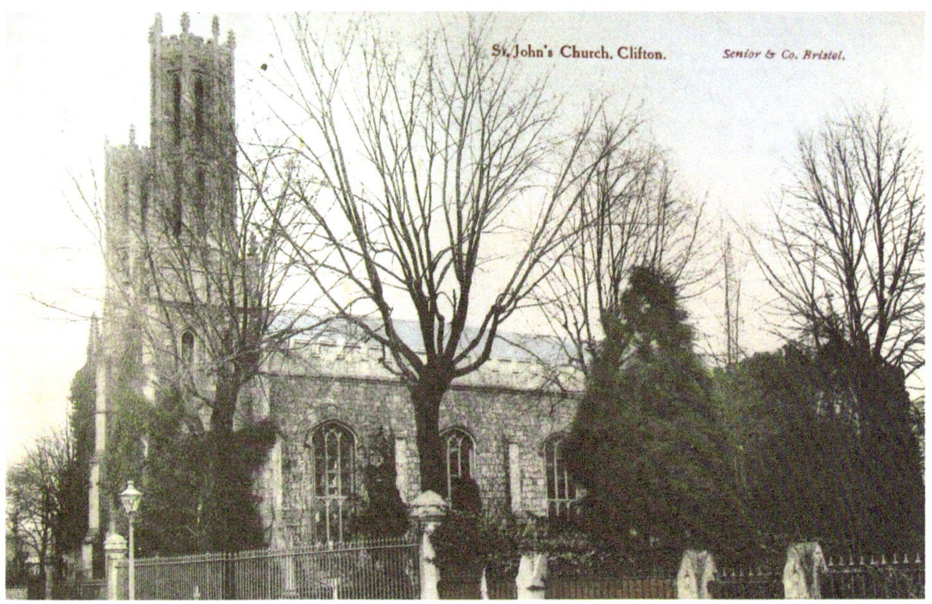

St John's Church, 25 January 1909

Halfway up Whiteladies Road on the left-hand side is St John's church. Designed by S. J. Hicks and built in 1841, the church was enlarged by S. B. Gabriel in 1864 when the chancel was added. By 1984 it had ceased functioning as a place of worship and, after being used for a while by a local theatre group, the interior was subdivided in 1990 to create the Bristol Auction Rooms on the ground floor and a media production company upstairs. A popular, twice-monthly farmers' market is held on the forecourt, around the war memorial.

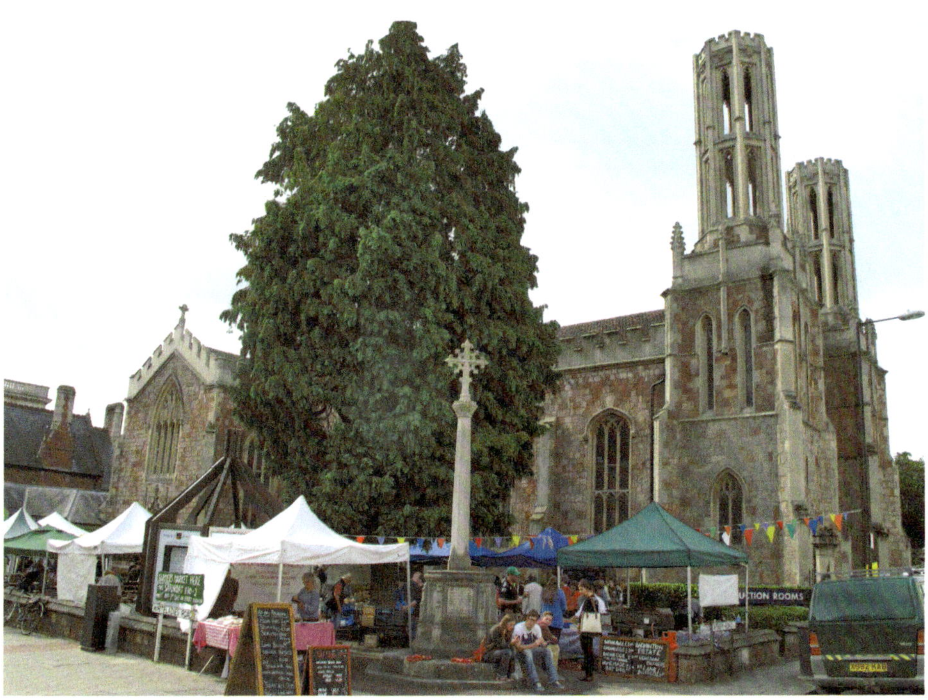

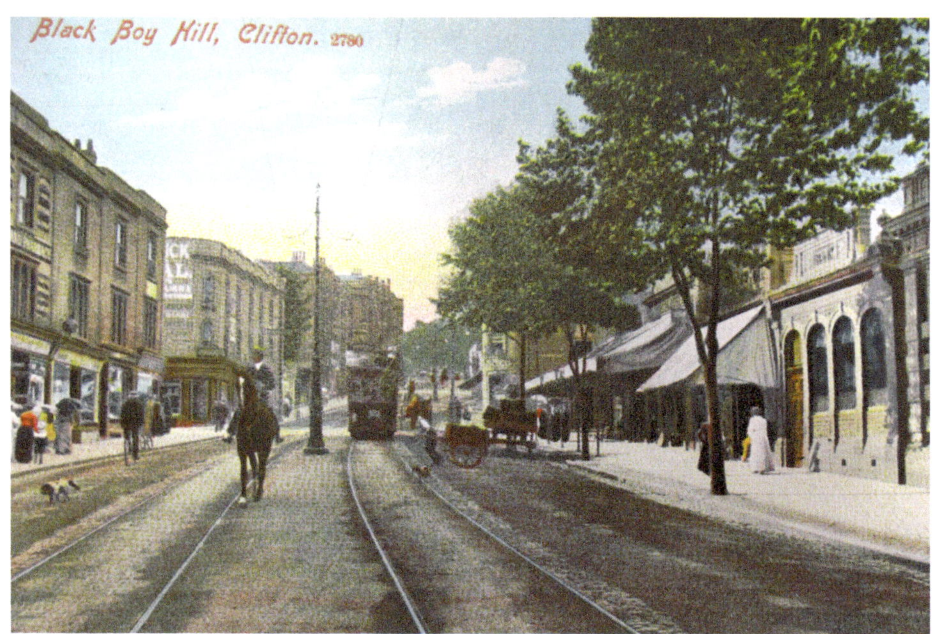

Blackboy Hill, Early 1900s

Differences in transport are well illustrated here: nowadays trams are no longer an option, it's probably not be a good idea to ride a horse down the centre of Blackboy Hill and crossing the road with a handcart would be an interesting challenge. On the right of the modern photograph is the 'new' Blackboy Inn at the corner of Lower Redland Road – the original was demolished in 1874.

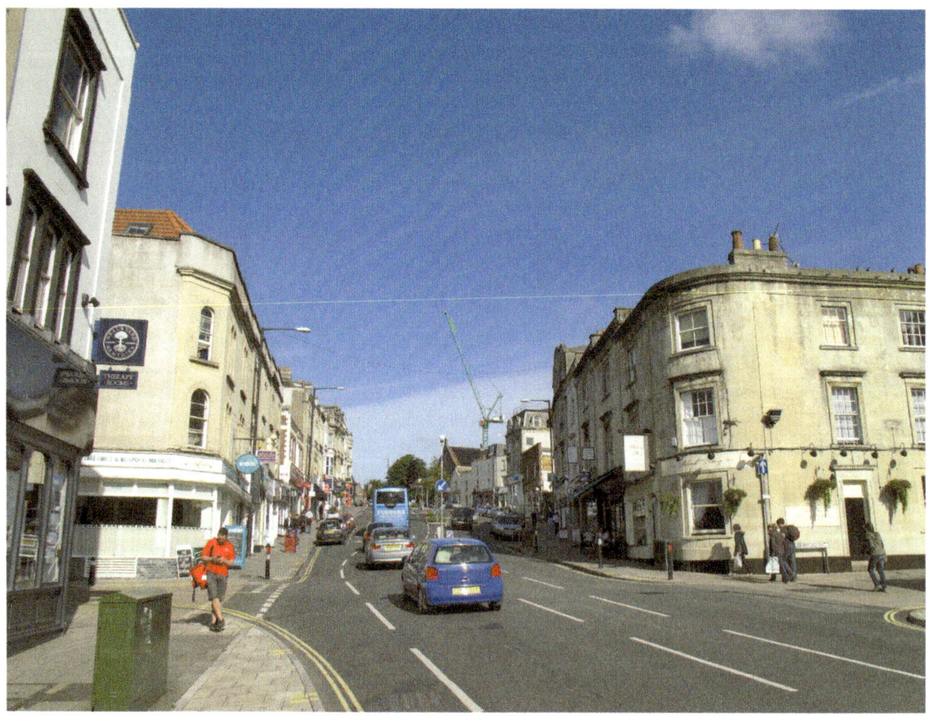

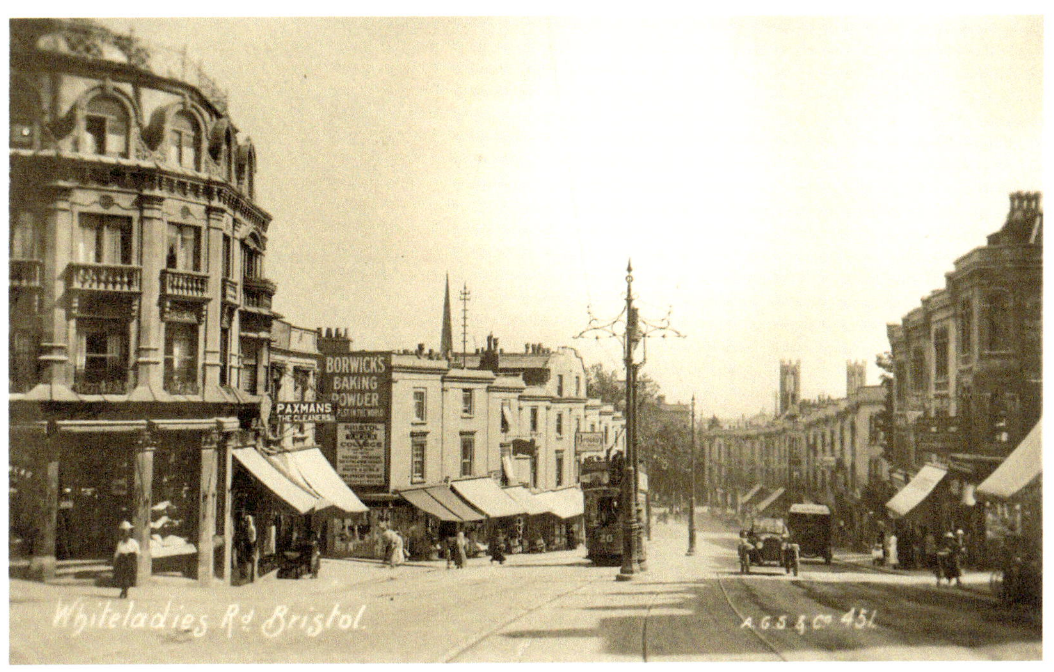

Blackboy Hill, Early 1900s

Tramlines were laid down in 1874 and opened as far as Blackboy Hill on 9 August 1875. Trams brought in an era of mass public transport which, some would argue, has not been improved on since. The age of the tram in Bristol came to an end after the Second World War, when the infrastructure damaged during the Bristol Blitz was not repaired or replaced. The other major difference in this view down Blackboy Hill is the appearance of the Wills Memorial Tower in the central skyline.

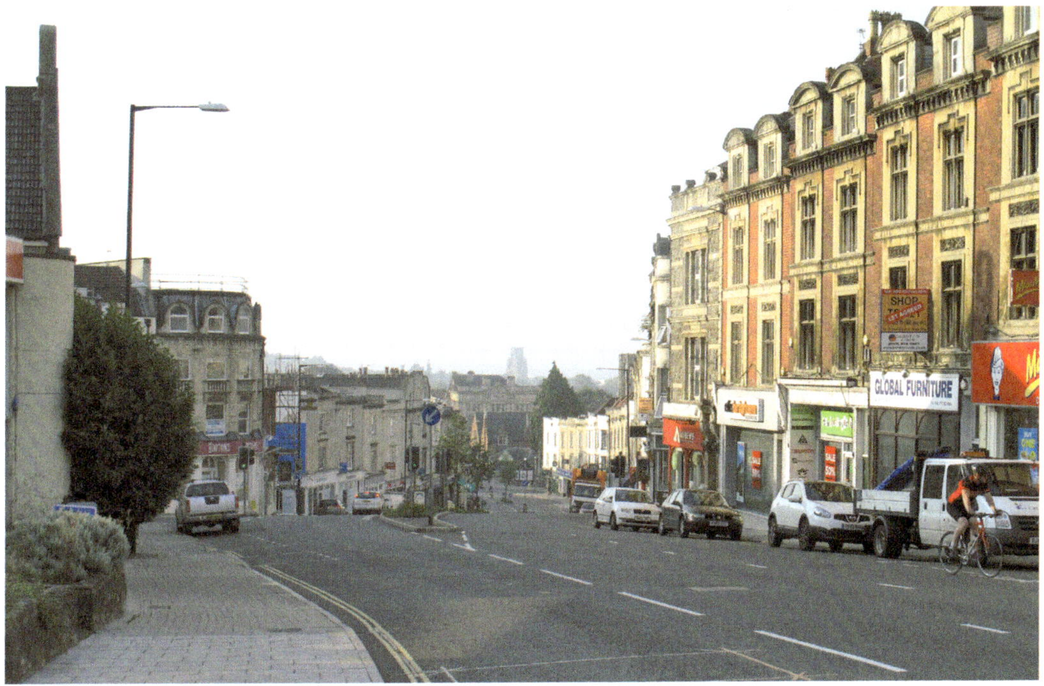

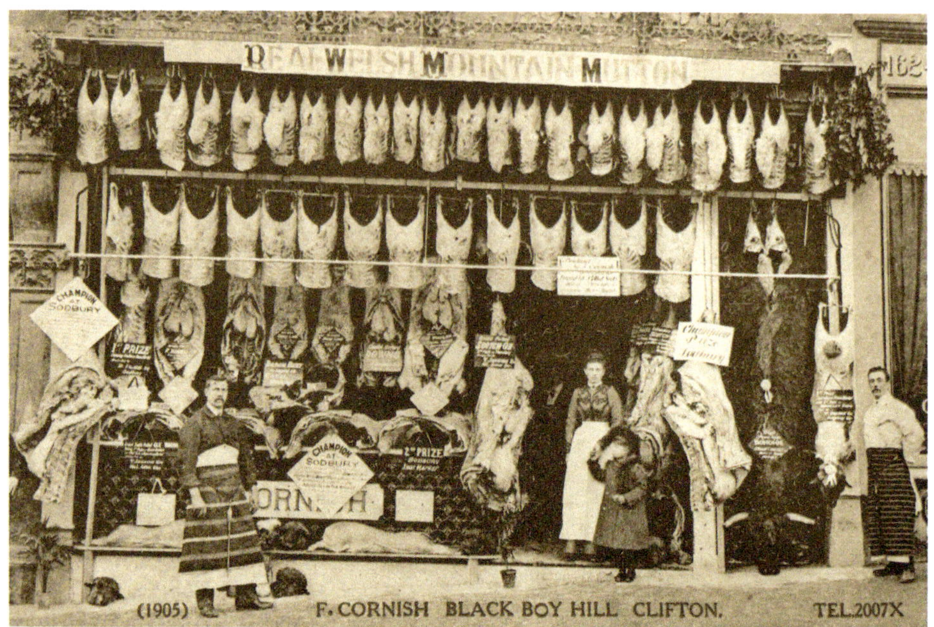

F. Cornish, Butcher's, 1905

This is a splendid picture of a family butcher with the carcasses of sheep hanging up and an advertisement for Real Welsh Mountain Mutton (a nice, if somewhat tenuous, link with the modern shop, which specialises in mountain sports). Almost in front of this shop, in what is now the main road going up Blackboy Hill, stood the original Blackboy Inn (hence the name of the road), which was demolished to allow road improvements.

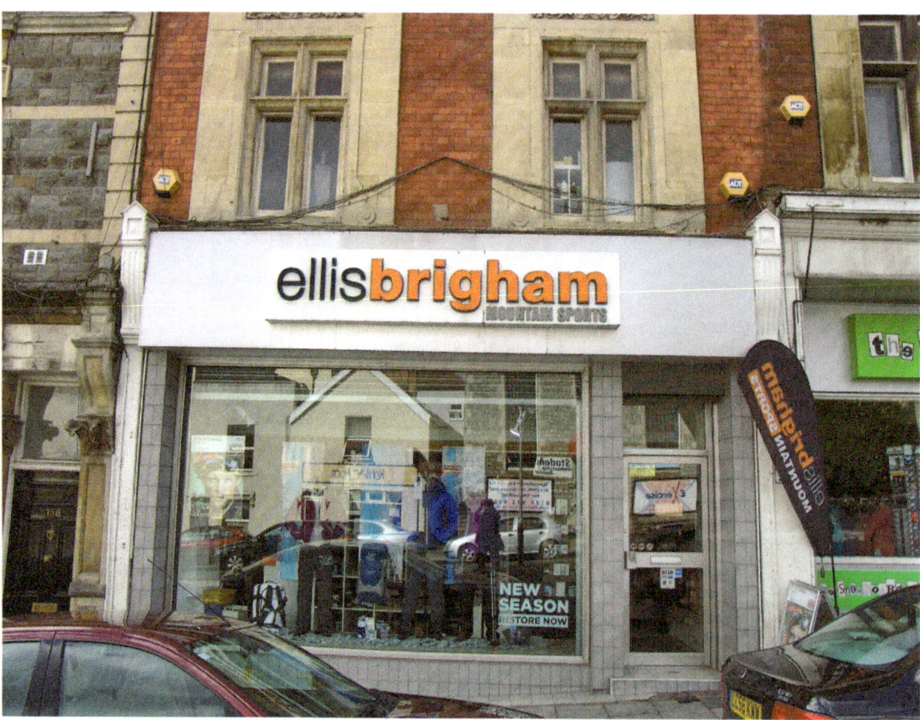

Durdham Down Café, Early 1900s

The edifice of what was Durdham Down Café remains virtually unchanged but the internal usage reflects the different periods. The Private Hotel, which spread over two buildings and catered mainly for long-stay residents, is now an estate agents and private residences, while the café itself, photographed around 1900, is empty. It was only 100 yards from the tram terminus at the top of Blackboy Hill, to which many people travelled to enjoy the fresh air, freedom and amusements offered by the Downs.

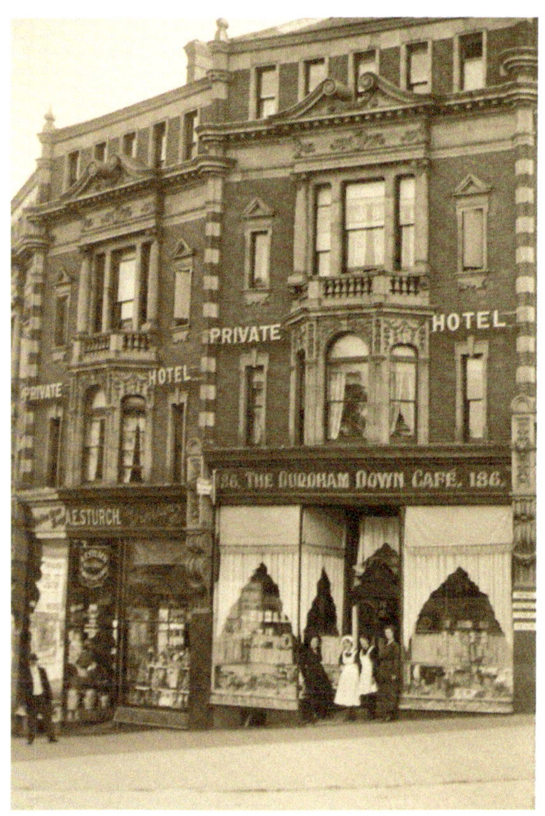

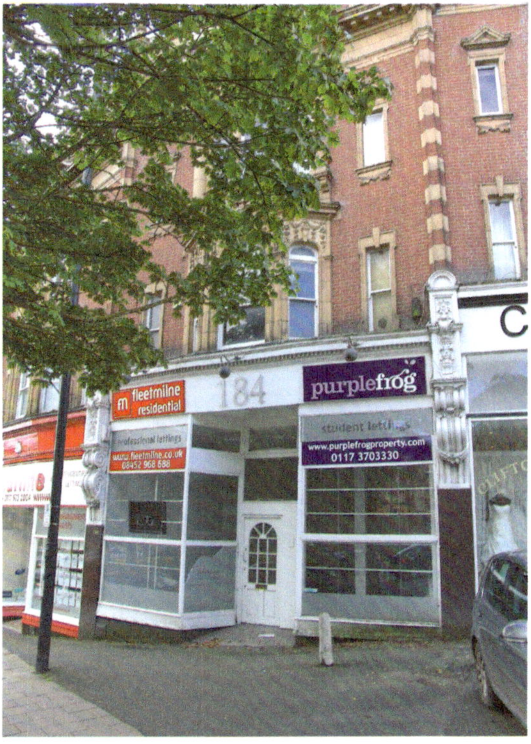

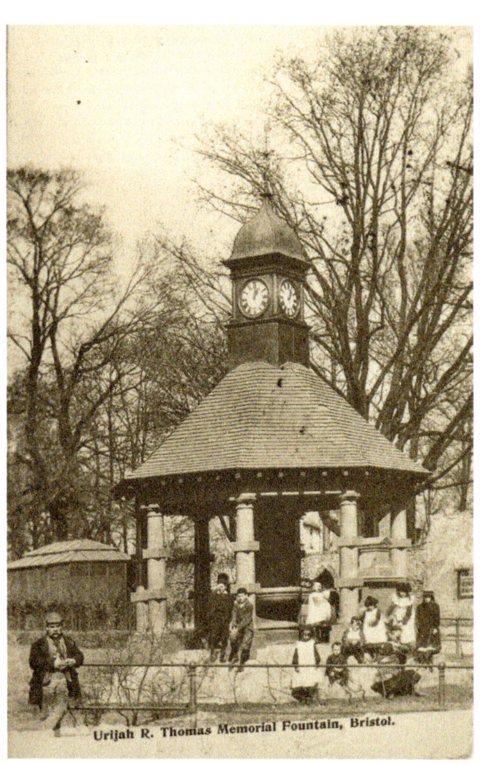

Urijah R. Thomas Memorial Fountain, 28 July 1904

Erected in 1904 to the Reverend Urijah Thomas, who was the first minister of Redland Park Chapel, a position he held for forty years until his death in 1901. The chapel stands opposite the fountain and is now a fitness centre, which is quite appropriate as Thomas initiated many public services, including health and fitness schemes for children and young people.

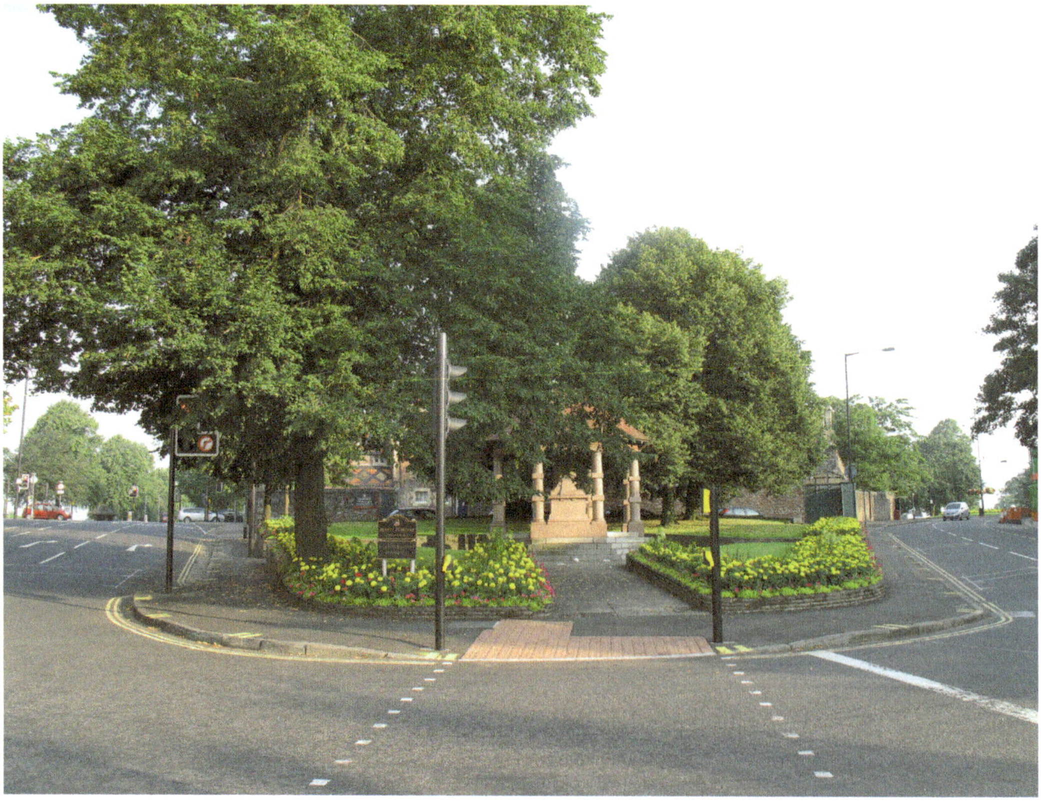

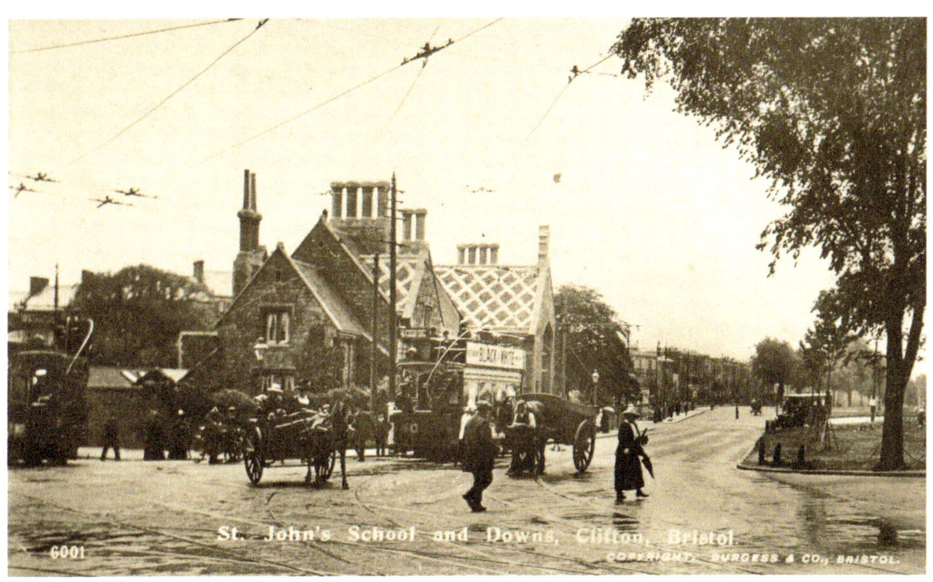

St John's School and Downs, Early 1900s

Straddling the top of Blackboy Hill is the St John's School building, with its distinctive cross-pattern roofing (it's hidden by trees in the modern photograph). Built in 1851 and used as a school until 1979, it then became local government offices. As of 2012, it is up for sale. The green building in the front of the modern photograph is an Edwardian public shelter, and just visible further down is a urinal in the same style. On the right in both pictures one can see the edge of the Downs. The tram terminal was about 100 yards further to the right.

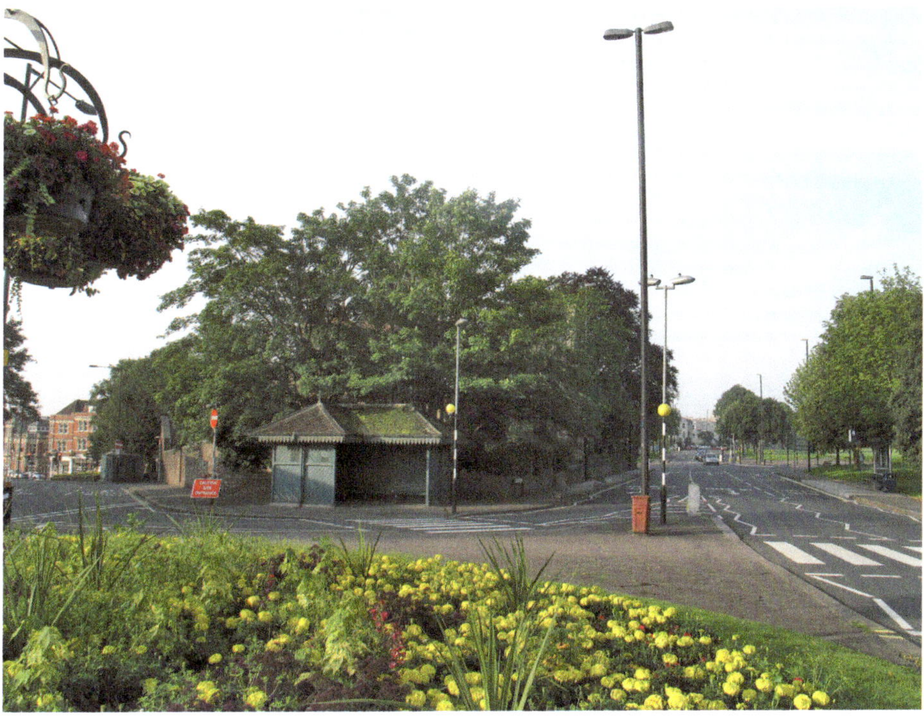

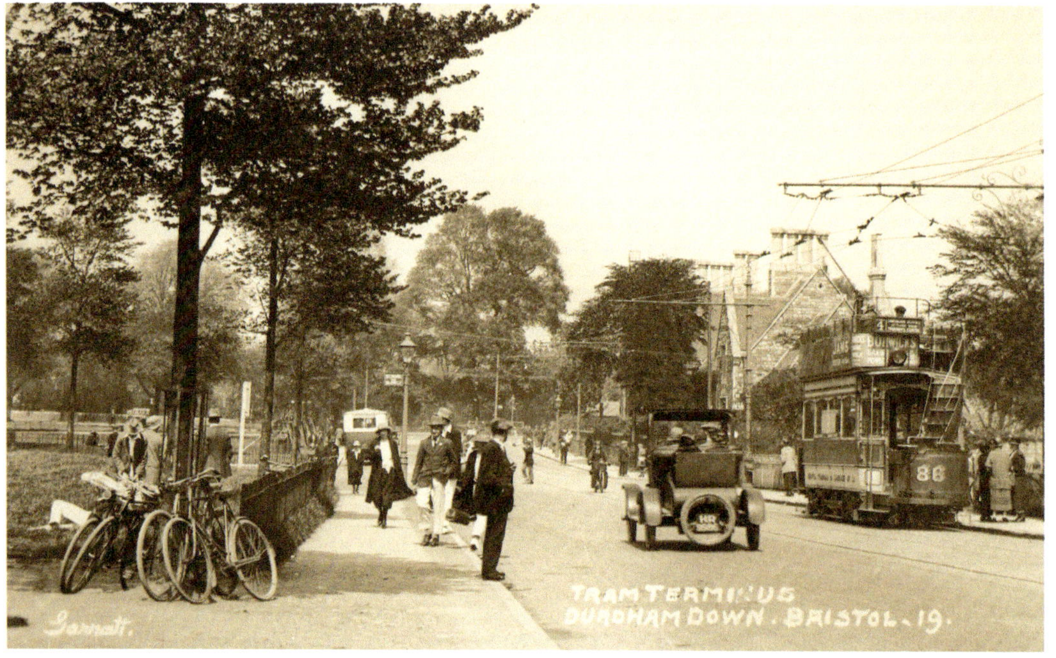

Tram Terminus, Durdham Downs, 1920s

St John's school on the right marks the end of the spread of Clifton to the north. On the left-hand side, the Downs stretches out to be met on the other side by Sneyd Park, Westbury and Henleaze. Covering a total of 441 acres, the Downs is actually split into two: Durdham Down, which lies from the northern corner to the Sea Walls in the west, and Clifton Down, which is south-west of the dividing line – Ladies Mile.

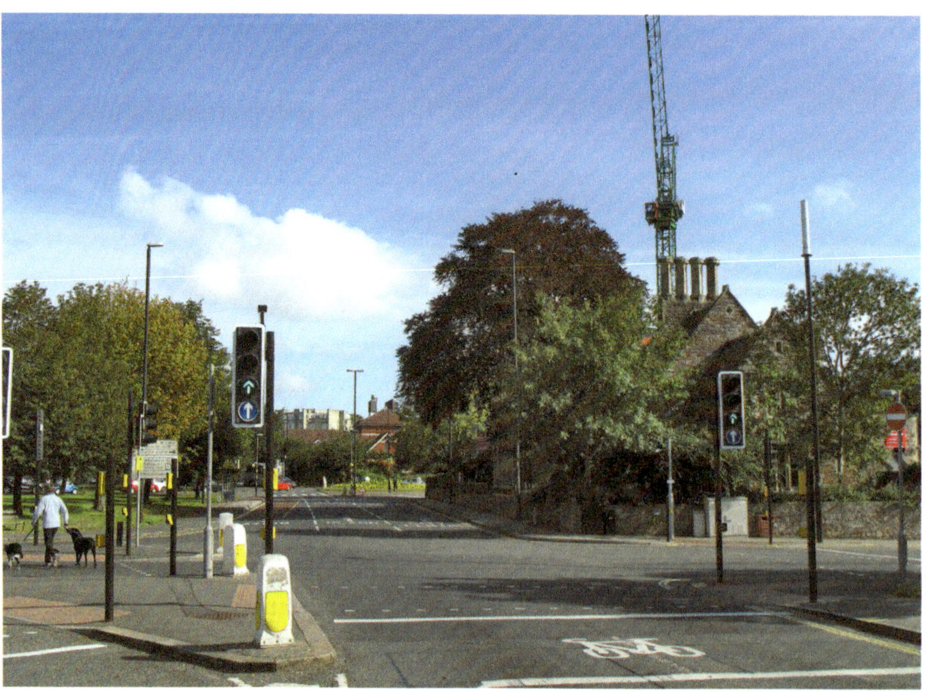

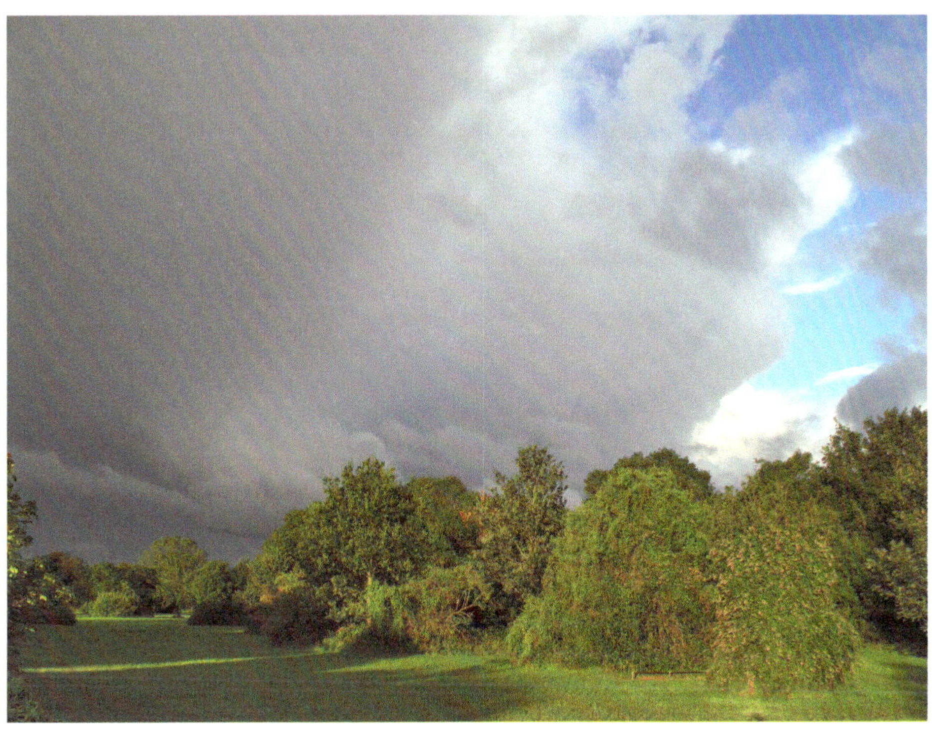

On the Downs, Early 1900s

For centuries, commoners of Bristol had the right to graze their animals on Clifton and Durdham Downs, but by the nineteenth century the expansion of the city threatened this large swathe of open land. The Merchant Venturers (a society set up by Bristol merchants) and Bristol City Council combined forces in 1861 to purchase the Downs to preserve this 'green lung'. The passing of the Clifton and Durdham Downs Act in that year ensured the management and maintenance of the land to this day. Grazing may be a thing of the past but the Downs remain, and have become a vital recreational area for the whole of the city.

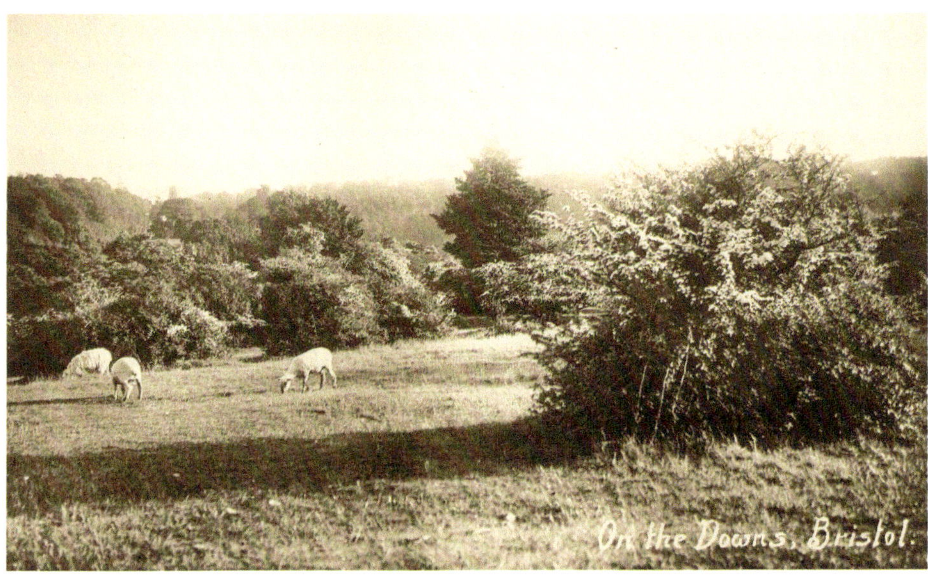

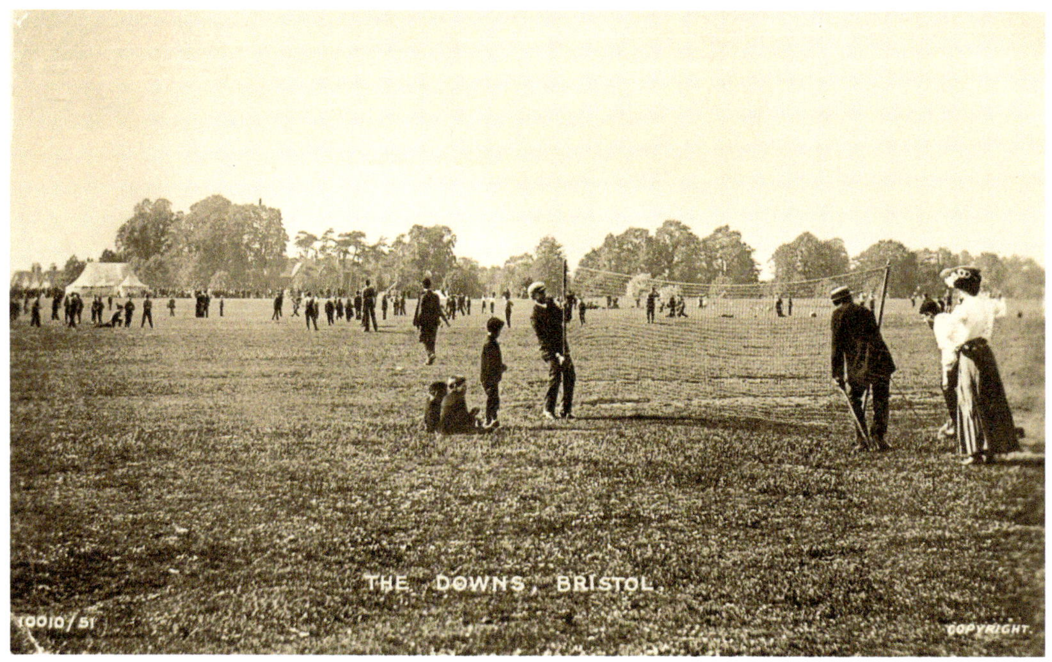

Sport on the Downs

Besides being a natural beauty spot, the Downs is ideal for recreation. All manner of sports, fairs, horse racing, flying displays, exhibitions and agricultural shows have taken place on the flat grasslands over the years. Football became popular in the 1880s and the Downs League was set up in 1905 and has expanded to include four divisions. Today the Downs is primarily used by joggers, cyclists, dog-owners, and people who enjoy a bracing walk in the fresh air.

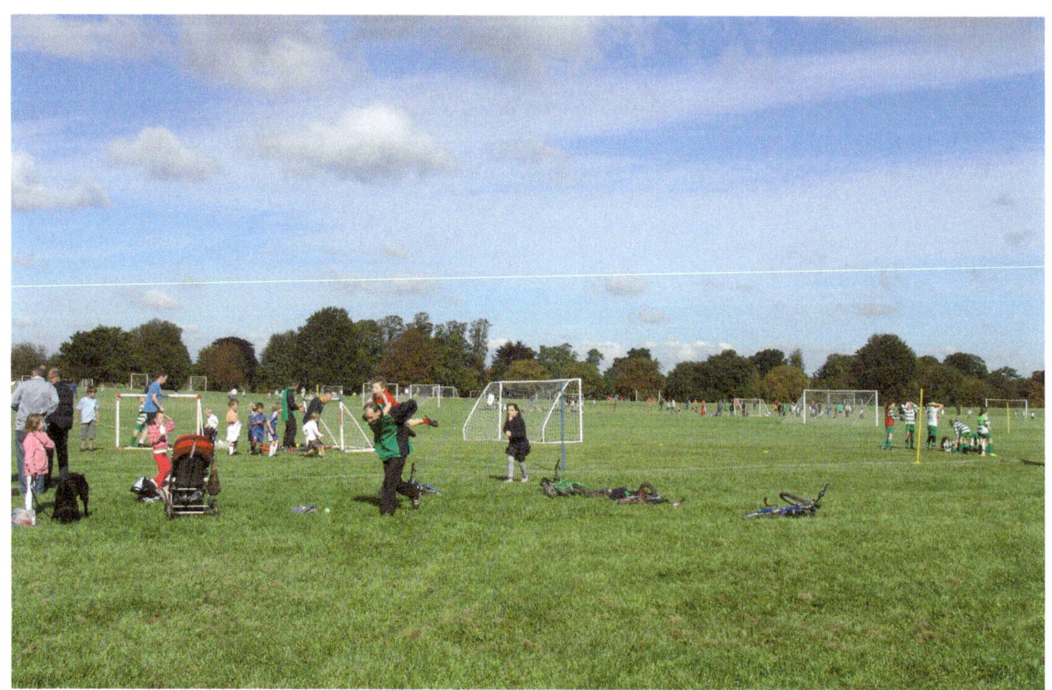

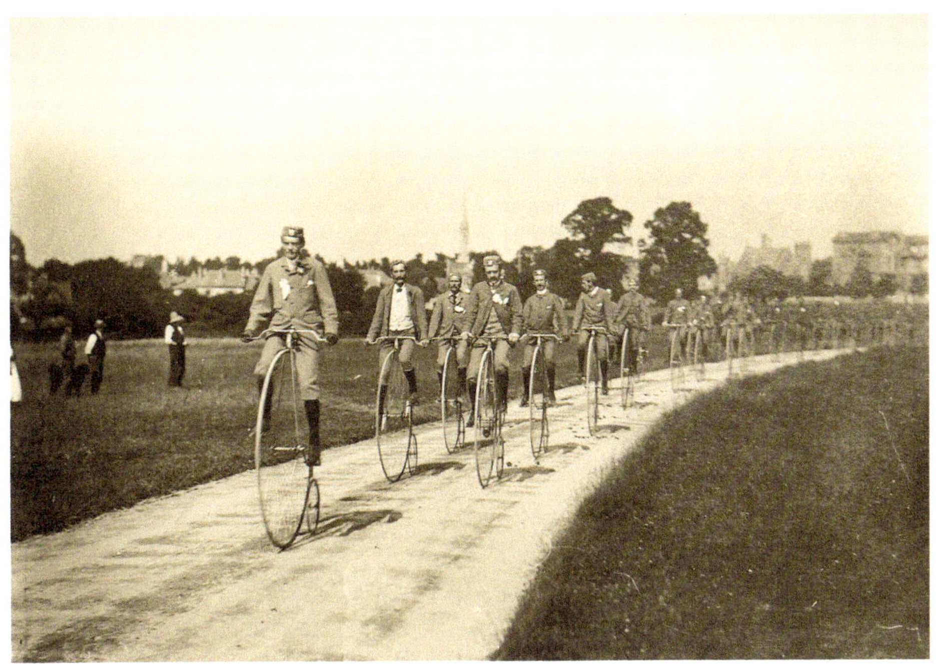

Cycling on the Downs

Cycling fashions have certainly changed in the last 130 years. Here the dapper members of the Clifton Cycling Club, photographed atop of their penny farthings in 1886, are following the circuitous road around Sea Walls at the western end of Durdham Downs. The 'No Cycling' sign in the picture below is admittedly rather disingenuous – it refers only to the path beside the road.

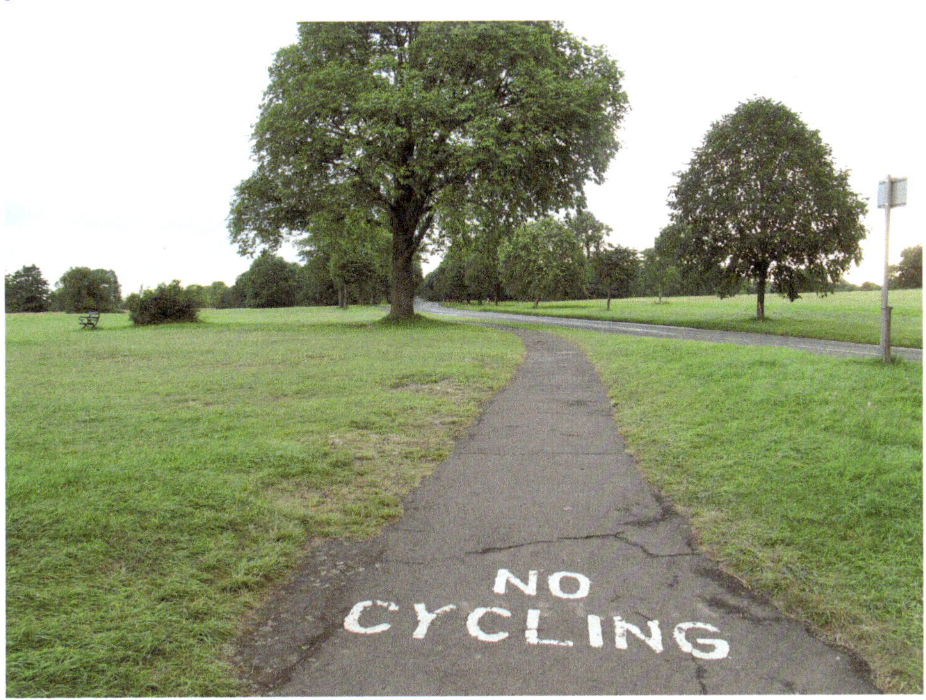

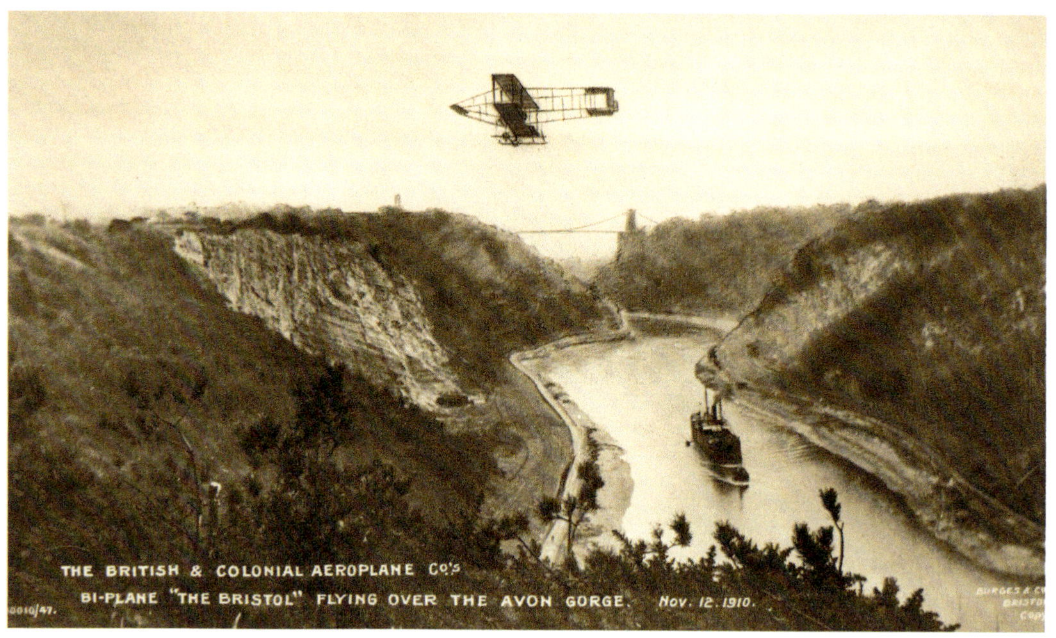

Biplane Flying over the Avon Gorge

In its time the Downs has witnessed some rather unusual sights: in 1826 an American called Mr Courtney entertained people by flinging himself off the edge of the Avon Gorge attached to a rope – he sustained head injuries and was barred from repeating the leap due to his intoxication. In November 1910, a flying display was organised to promote the Bristol and Colonial Aeroplane Company's new box kite (a full-size replica of which now hangs in the main hall of the Museum and Art Gallery).

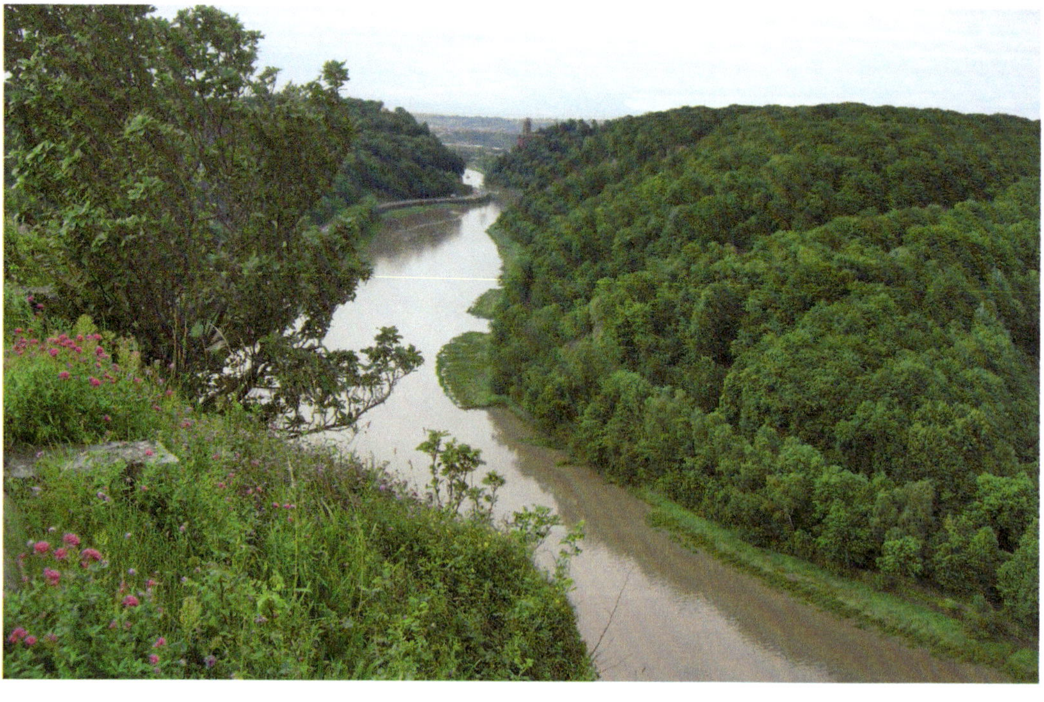

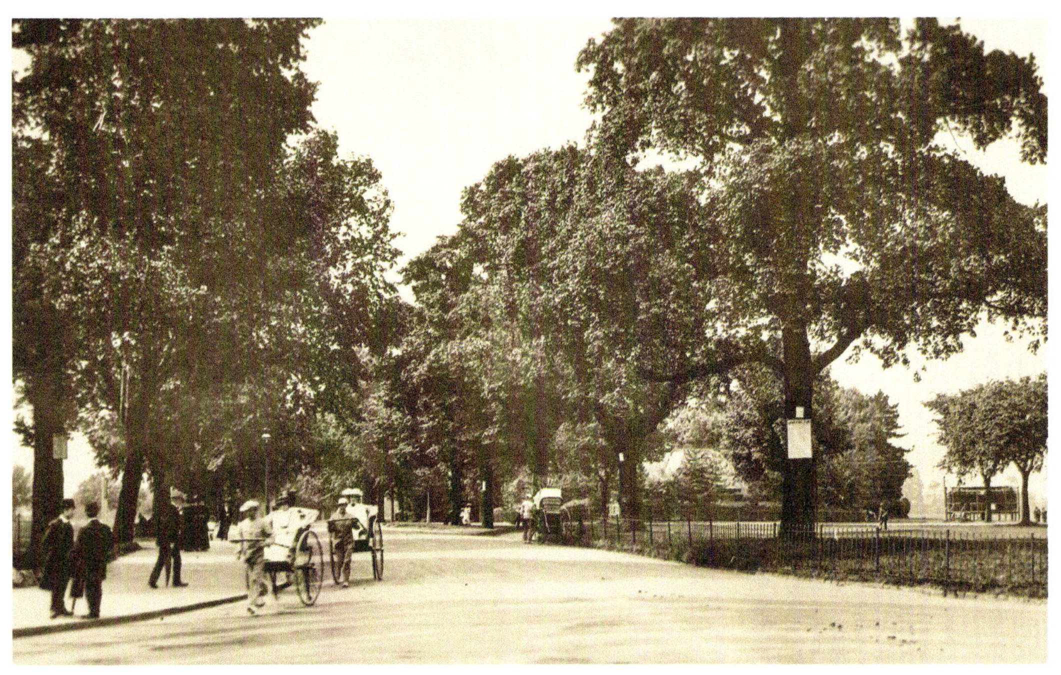

Rickshaws on the Downs, Early 1990s

Rickshaws are seen here plying their trade along Stoke Road. They would have been hired for entertainment rather than any practical reasons (likewise the donkeys that gave rides on the same road until complaints to the RSPCA about their handlers and the noise of their braying stopped them in 1927).

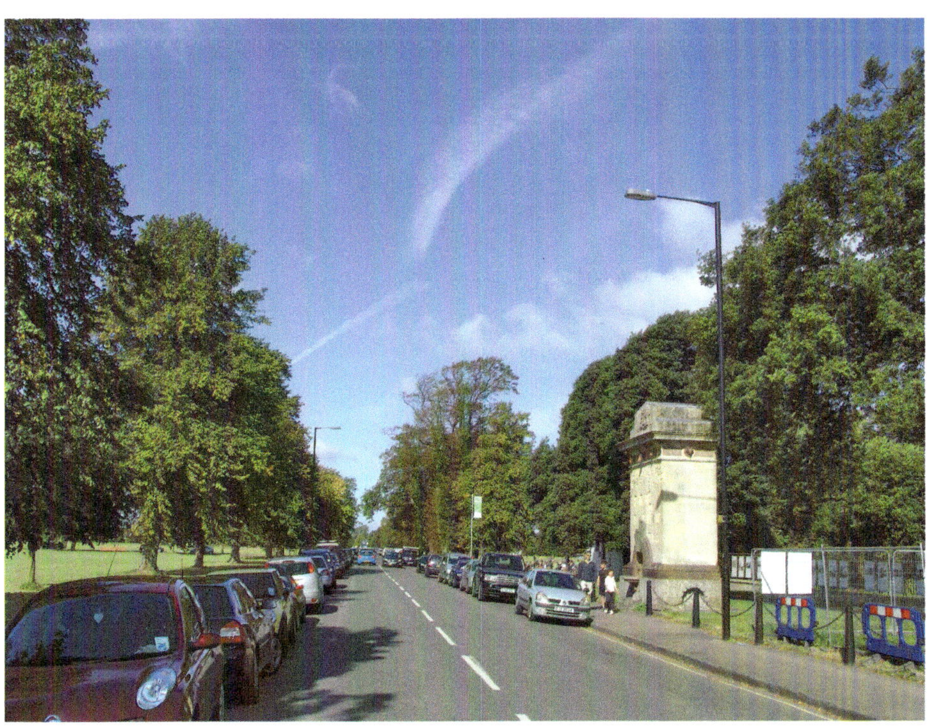

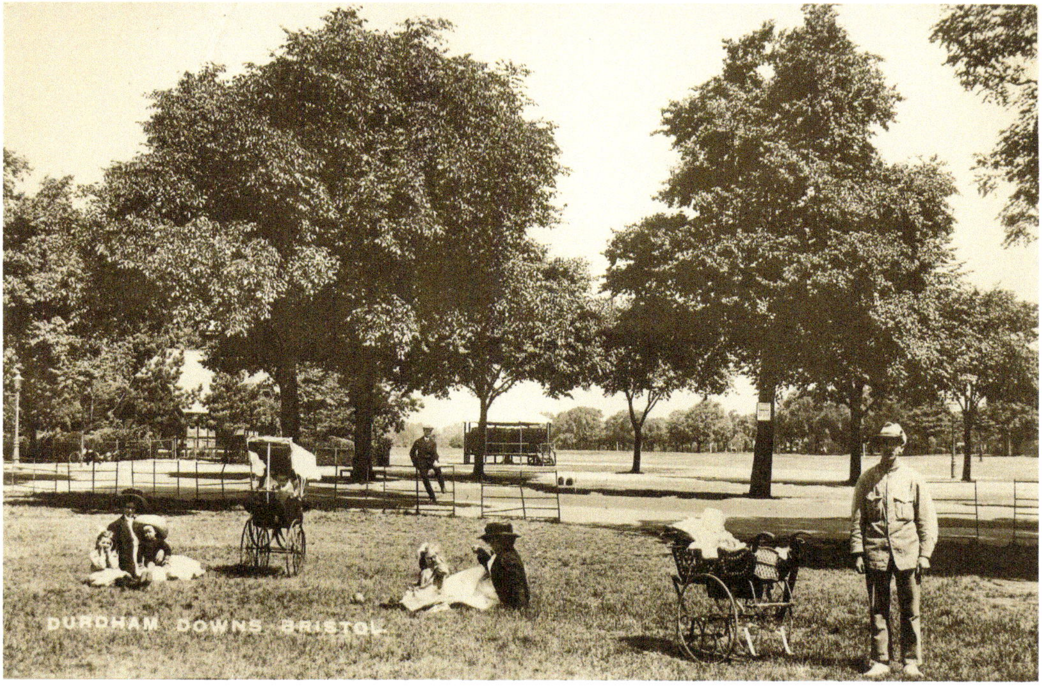

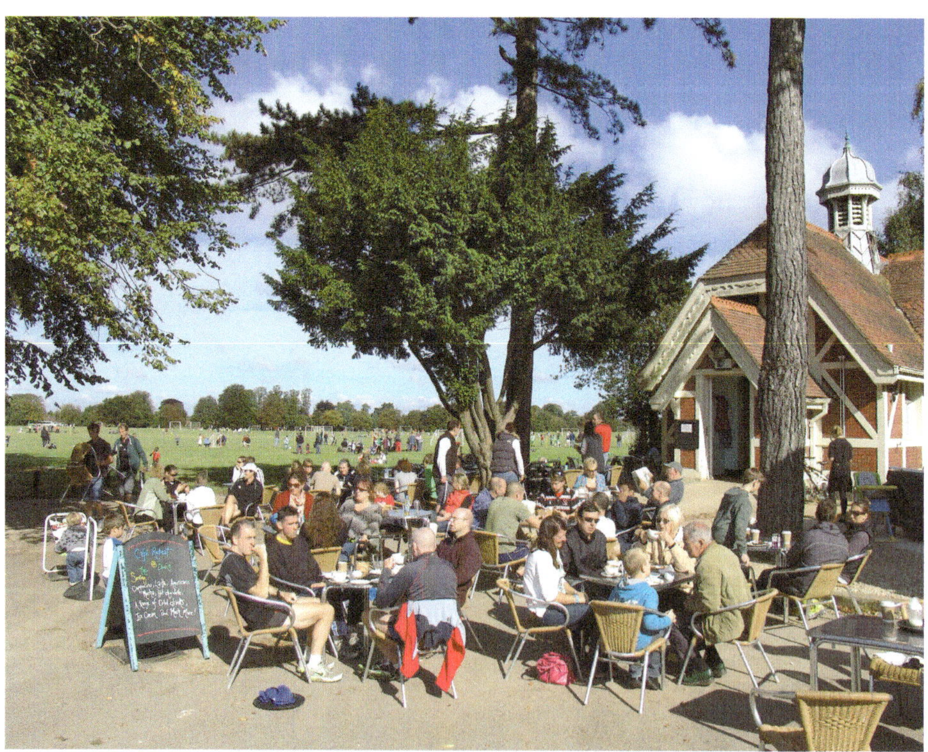

Families on the Downs, Early 1900s

The poses may have been a little bit more rigid and formal in days gone past, but the Downs remain a great place for families to relax and enjoy some British summer sunshine.

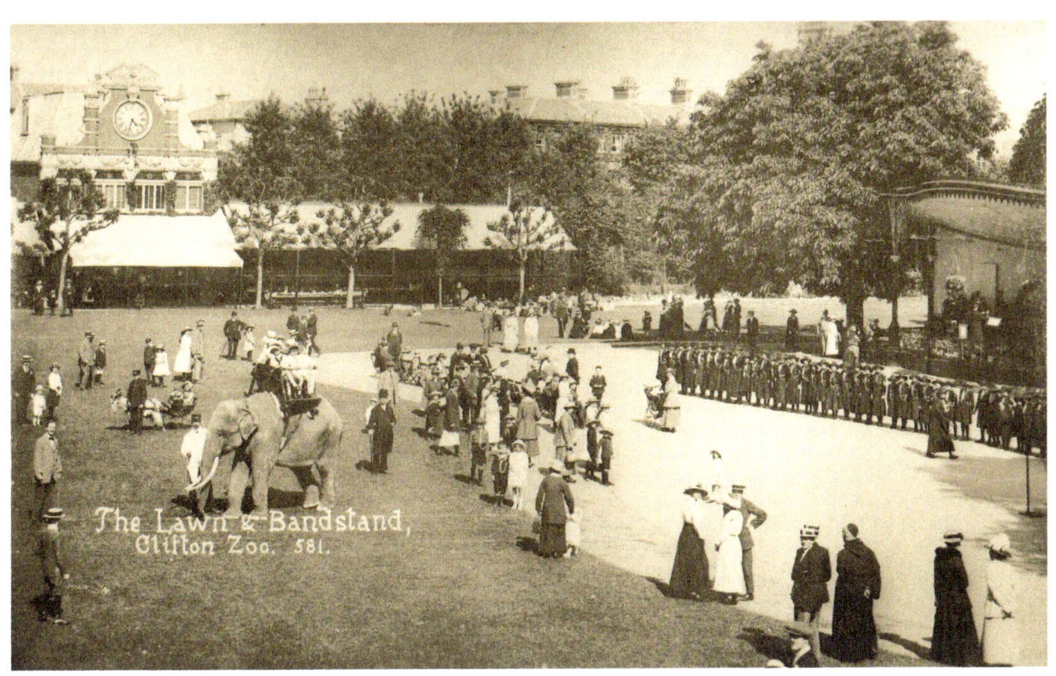

Bristol Zoo, Early 1900s

The Bristol and Clifton Zoological Gardens (better known as Bristol Zoo) first opened its gates in 1836 on a 12-acre plot of farmland just south of the Clifton Downs. Originally, entrance was limited to annual members and the 220 subscribers (including one I. K. Brunel) who financed the project through the purchase of £25 shares; however, it gradually became a popular attraction and by 1904 over a 178,000 visitors came to see exotic animals such as Rajah the Asian elephant, seen here giving rides on the Clock Tower Lawn, and to enjoy the manicured gardens.

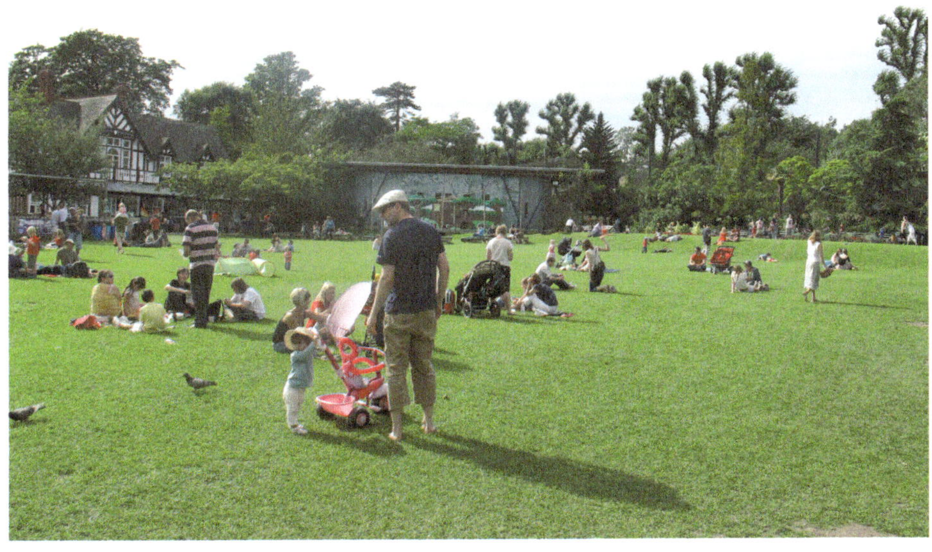

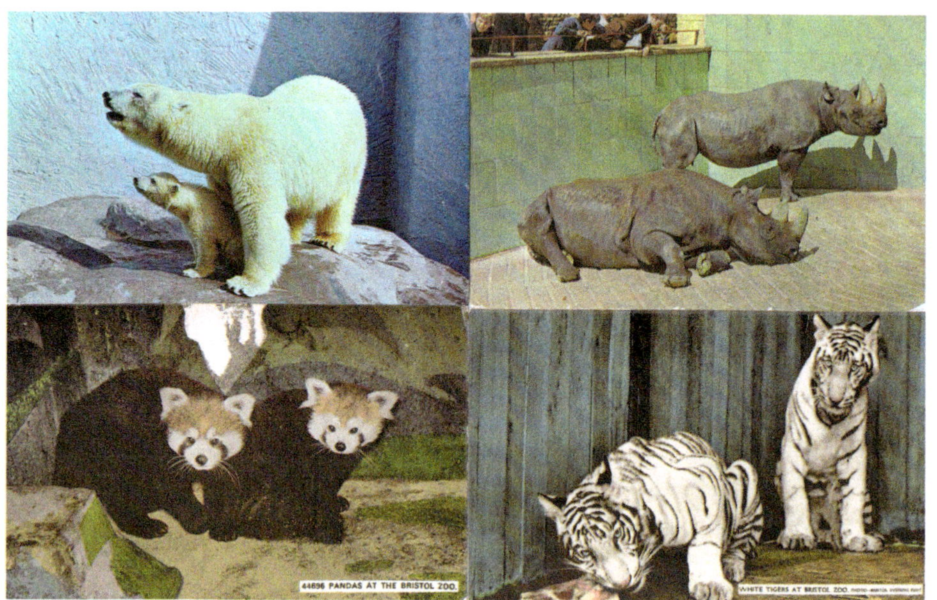

Bristol Zoo Postcards, 1960s

Bristol Zoo's early development was dictated as much by finance as any other nobler aim. The zoo often put on fêtes, carnivals, displays (including tight-rope walking, lion taming and even fireworks!) and other fundraising events. However, the main attractions were the animals such as polar bears, white tigers, rhinoceroses and red pandas seen here on 1960s postcards, and the magnificent floral displays, including its famous herbaceous border. Today, the zoo focuses on conservation and education (the latter was initially helped by Johnny Morris and the BBC's *Animal Magic*, which was filmed here).

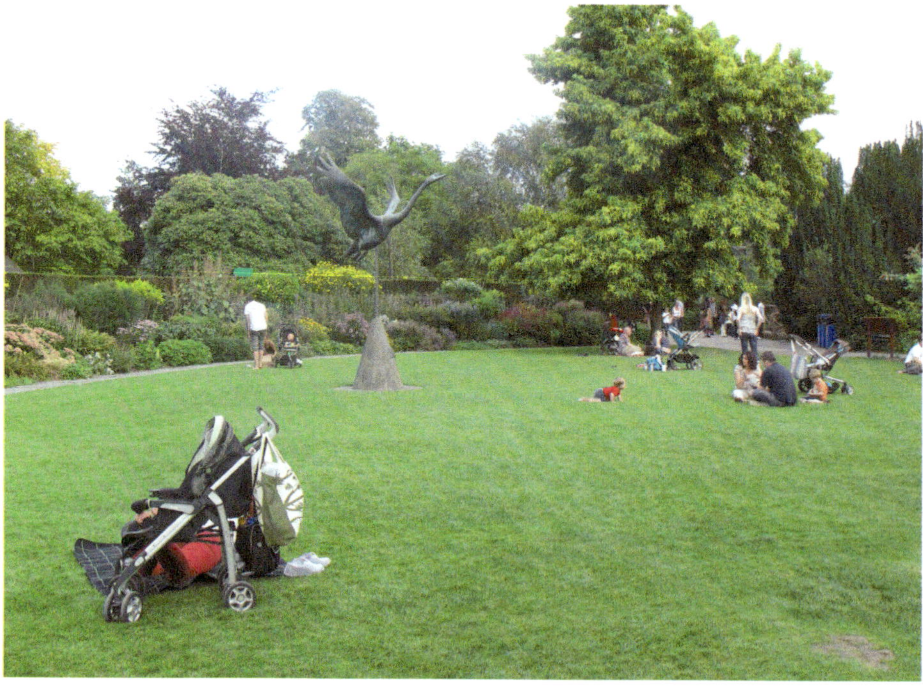

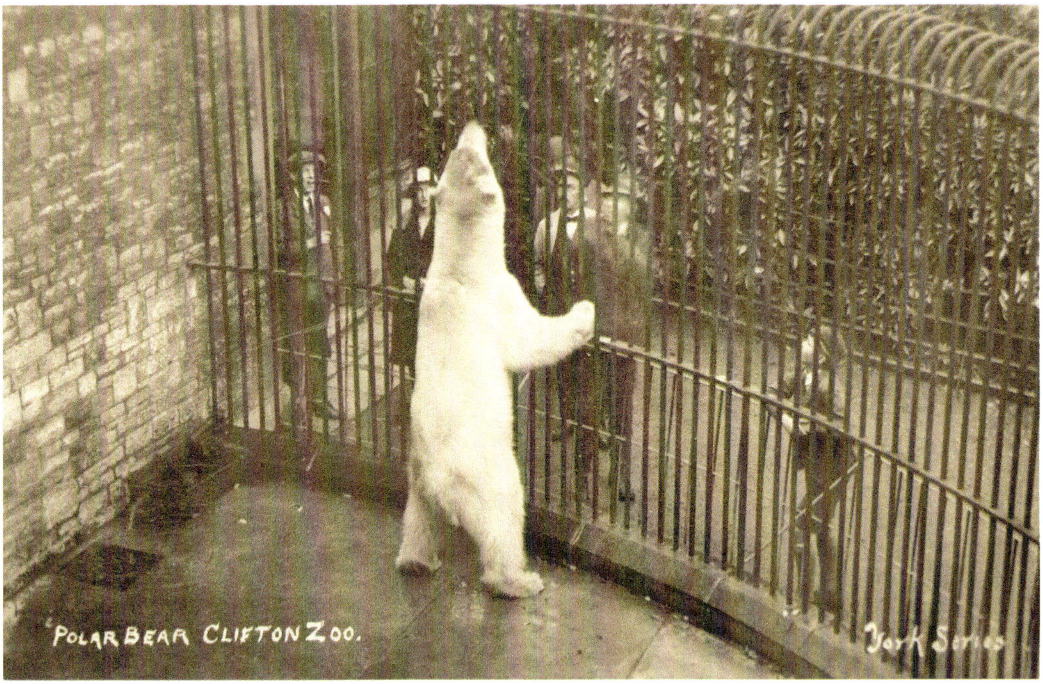

Polar Bear at Bristol Zoo, 1925

Polar bears first arrived at the zoo in 1856 and were a mainstay of the large mammals collection until the 1990s, when issues of keeping them in relatively cramped and unnatural conditions led the zoo to decide not to replace the final pair. Instead, the public can now enjoy being in close proximity to the equally beautiful but far less dangerous butterflies, now on display in their new house.

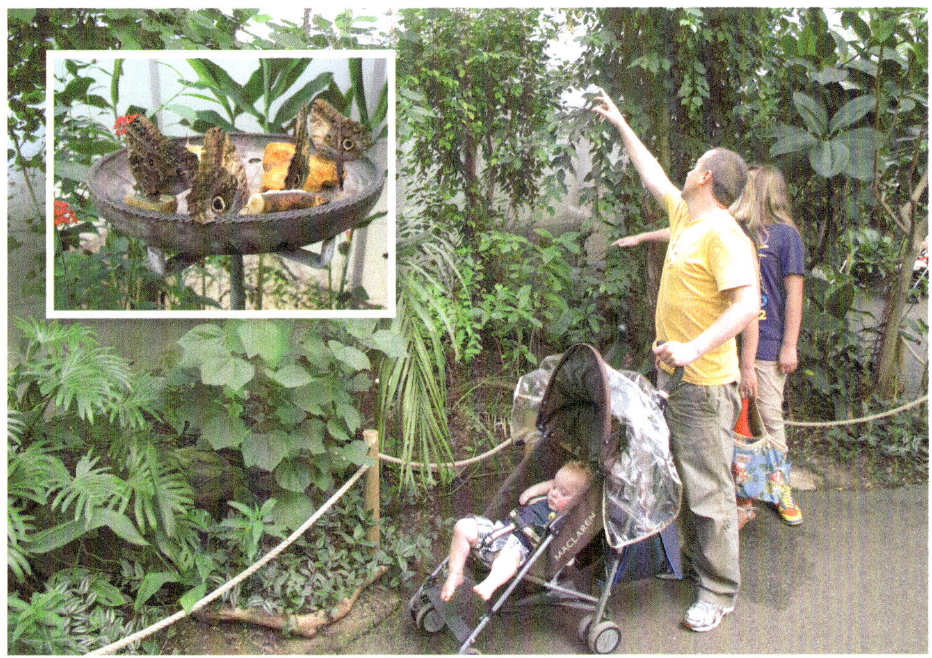

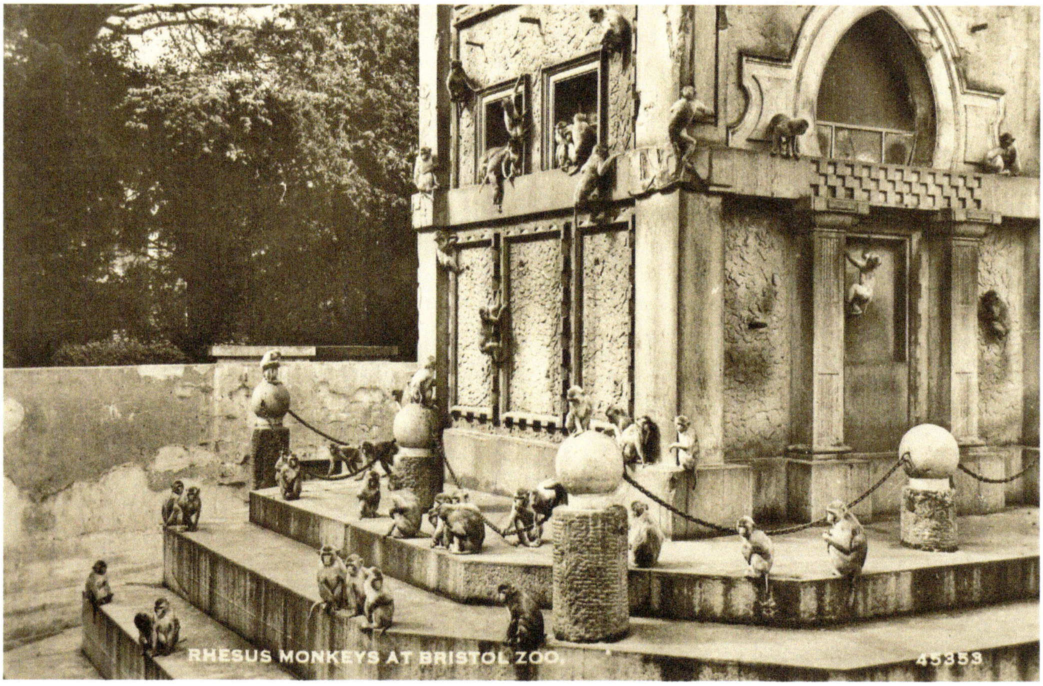

Monkey Temple, Bristol Zoo, Early 1900s

Although the zoo is the fifth oldest in the world, it has adapted to changing public opinion on how best to keep captive animals, while simultaneously adopting the best conditions for breeding endangered species. The small, inadequate enclosures of the past have been replaced. At the time of its construction in 1928 the monkey temple was thought to replicate a natural habitat; it has now been filled in and replaced by fountains.

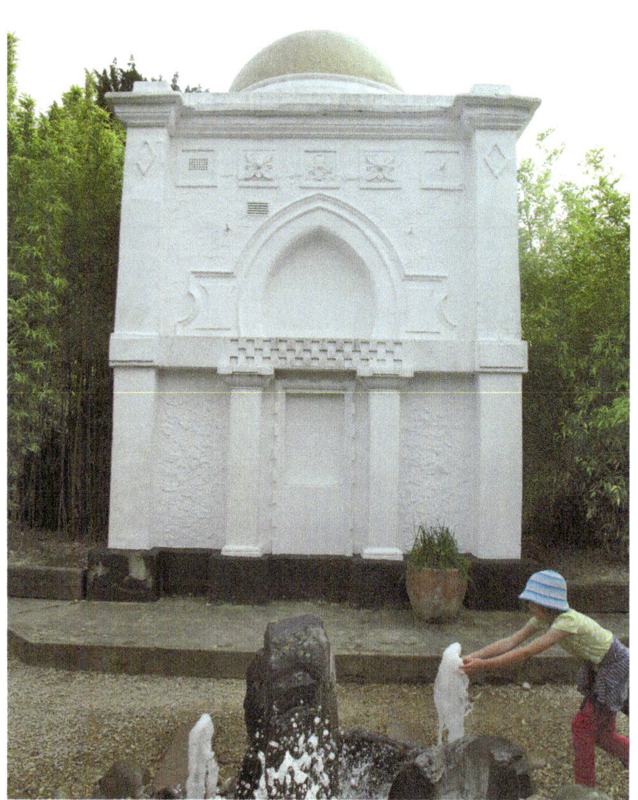

40

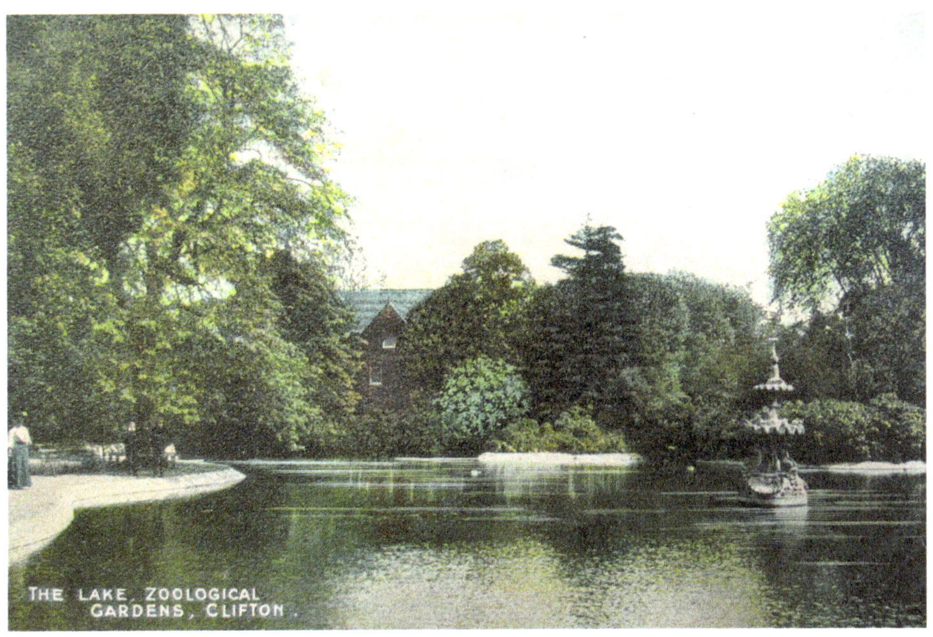

Bristol Zoo Lake, 1920s

Lying at the centre of the zoo, the ornamental lake offered the public the opportunity to take a short boat ride. It was also used as a fundraising pad for lifeboats, a training area for Clifton College sea cadets and as a haven for wild fowl. Today, with space in the zoo at a premium, the lake has been developed and a number of islands now provide homes for gibbons and pelicans among others.

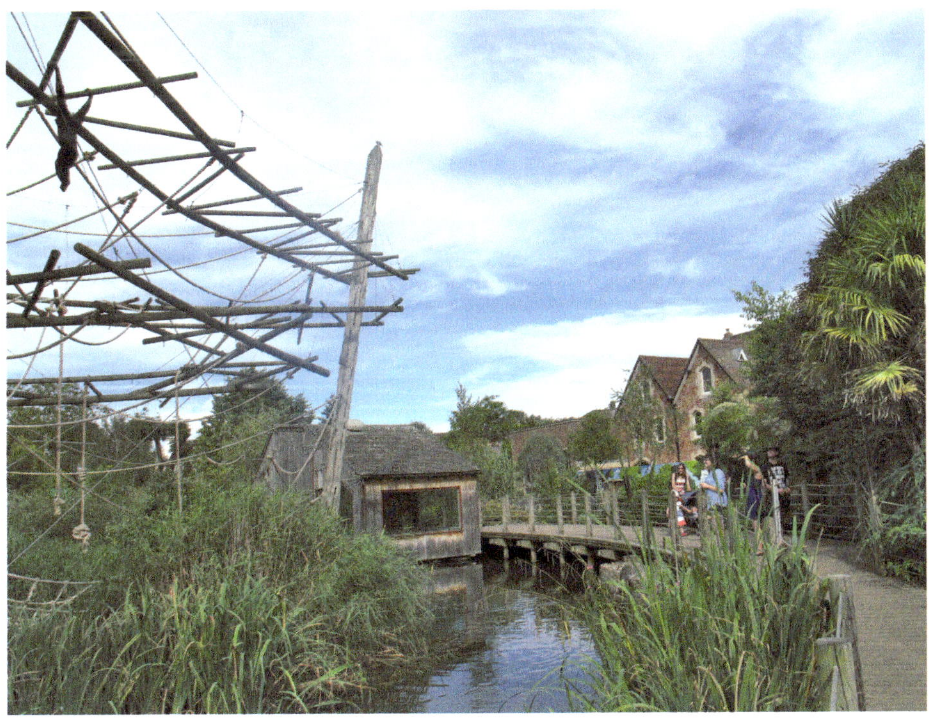

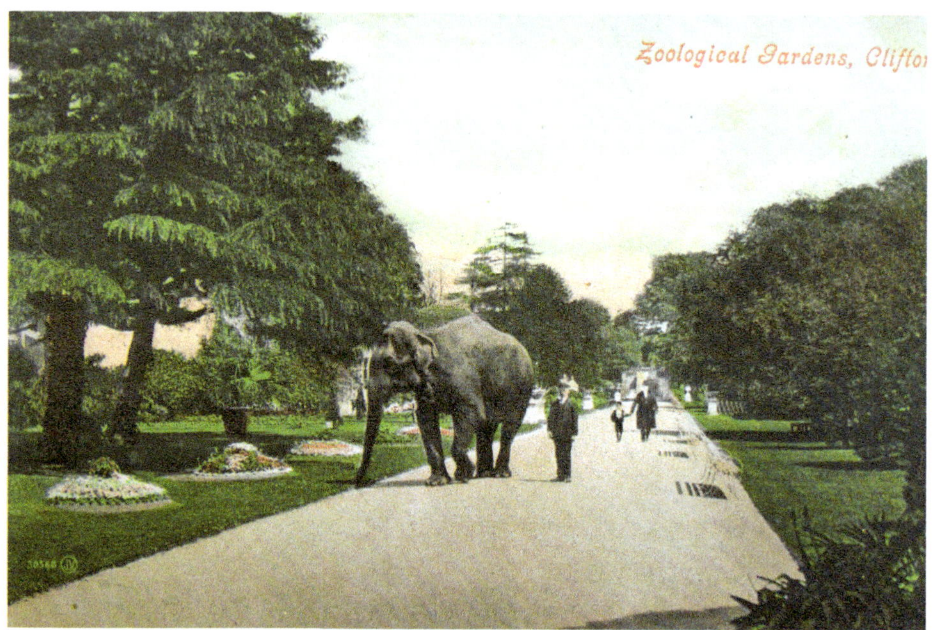

Elephant Walk at Bristol Zoo, Early 1900s

The sight of a fully grown Asian elephant walking past on the top terrace of the zoo must have been truly awe-inspiring to a Victorian child, whose only knowledge of the animal would have come from a book. Pictured here is Zebi, who was presented to the zoo in 1868 by the Maharaj of Mysore. The tradition of taking the elephants for walks continued until the death of Wendy in 2002.

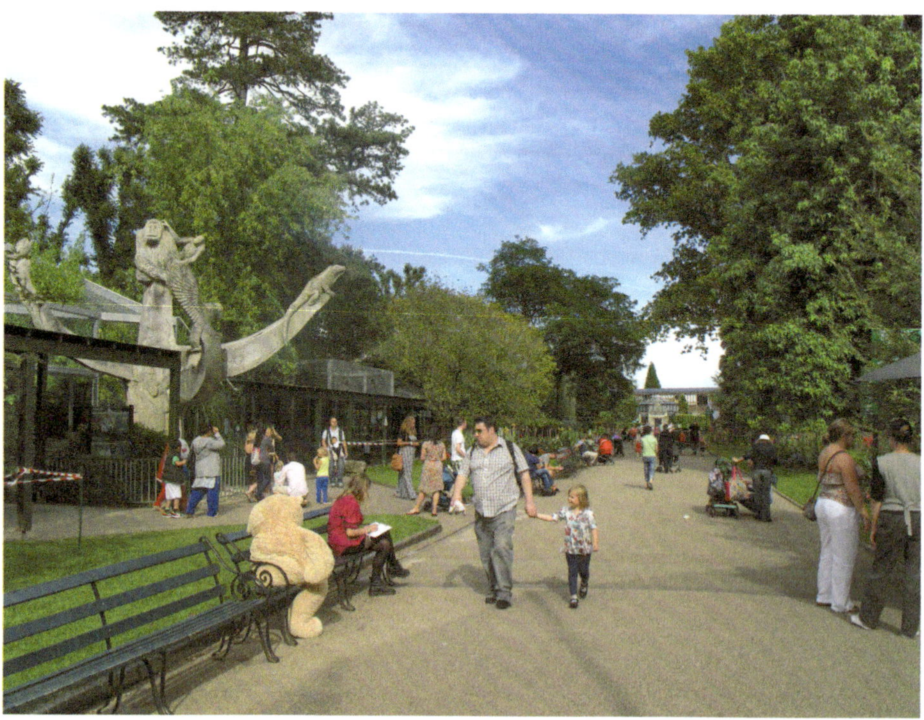

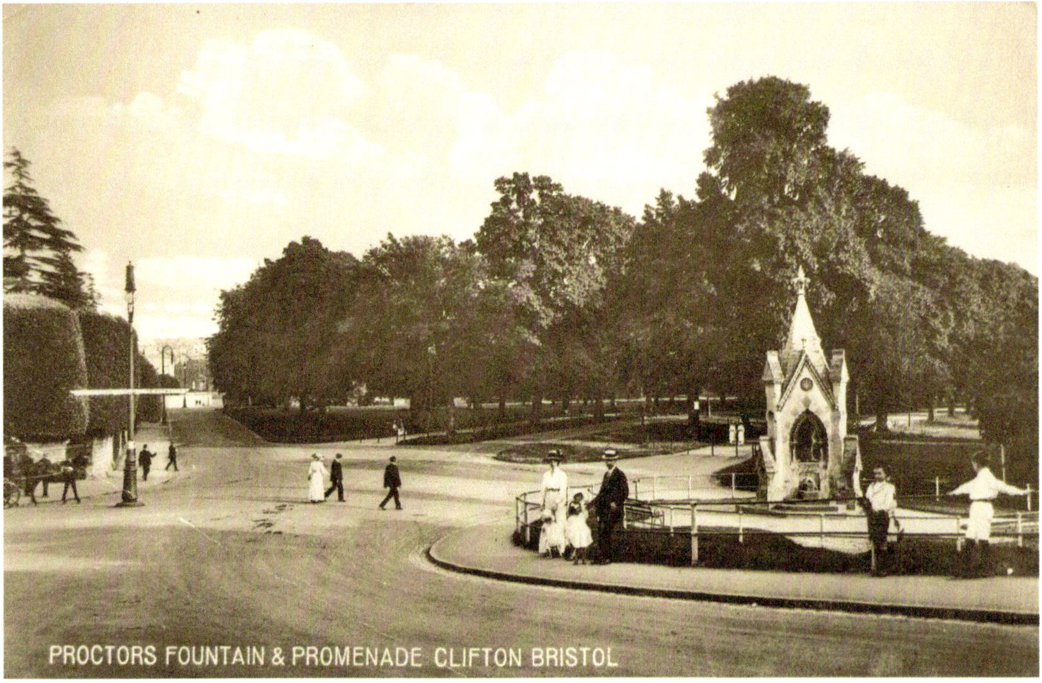

Proctor's Fountain and Promenade, Early 1900s

Originally placed at the junction of Bridge Valley Road and the Bristol Zoo end of The Promenade, Proctor's Fountain was erected in 1872 to commemorate Alderman Thomas Proctor's generosity to the city. It was moved to its present location in the 1980s as it had become a traffic hazard, and is now across the road near the Mansion House (which Proctor had donated to the Lord Major's office).

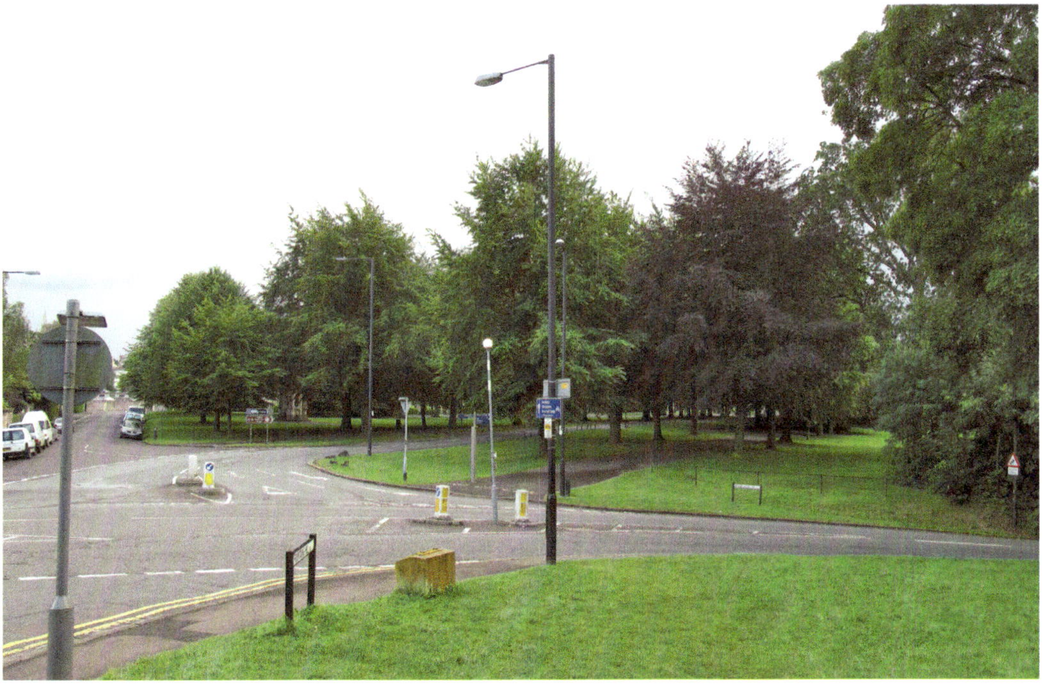

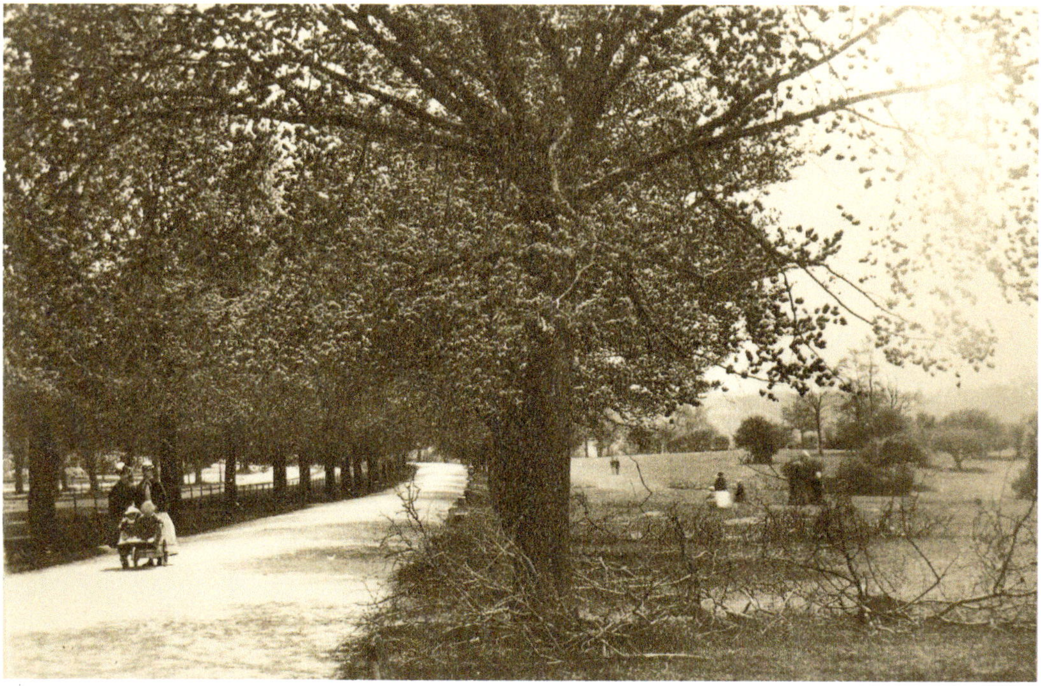

The Promenade, Clifton Down, Early 1900s

Running from the edge of the Downs up to Clifton village, The Promenade is captivating whatever the weather. The beech tree avenues provide a spectacular display of autumnal colours, and a misty morning can add to the magical atmosphere.

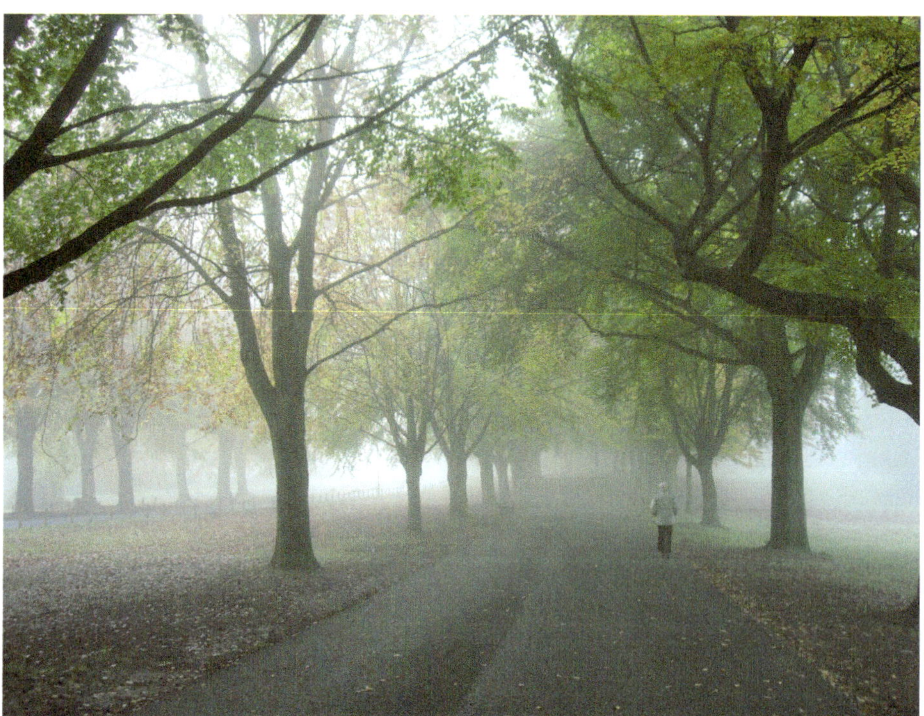

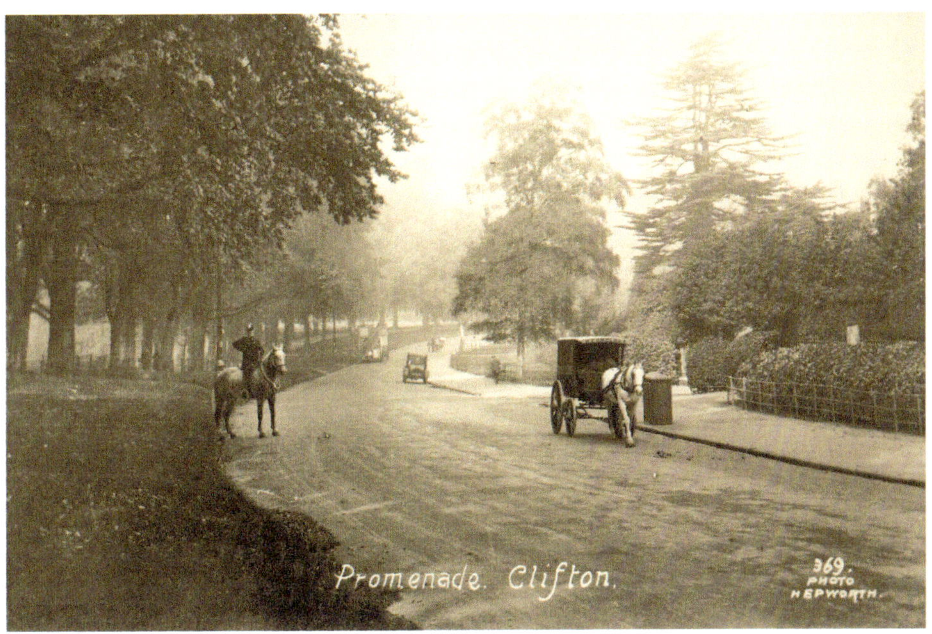

The Promenade, Early 1900s

A policeman is seen here exercising his horse on The Promenade (to this day the police continue to do this). On the right, behind the hedges, are the houses which belonged to the richest merchants, the Lord Mayor and the Merchant Venturers. In its day it was the Bel Air of Bristol. The autumnal shot was taken on the left-hand side.

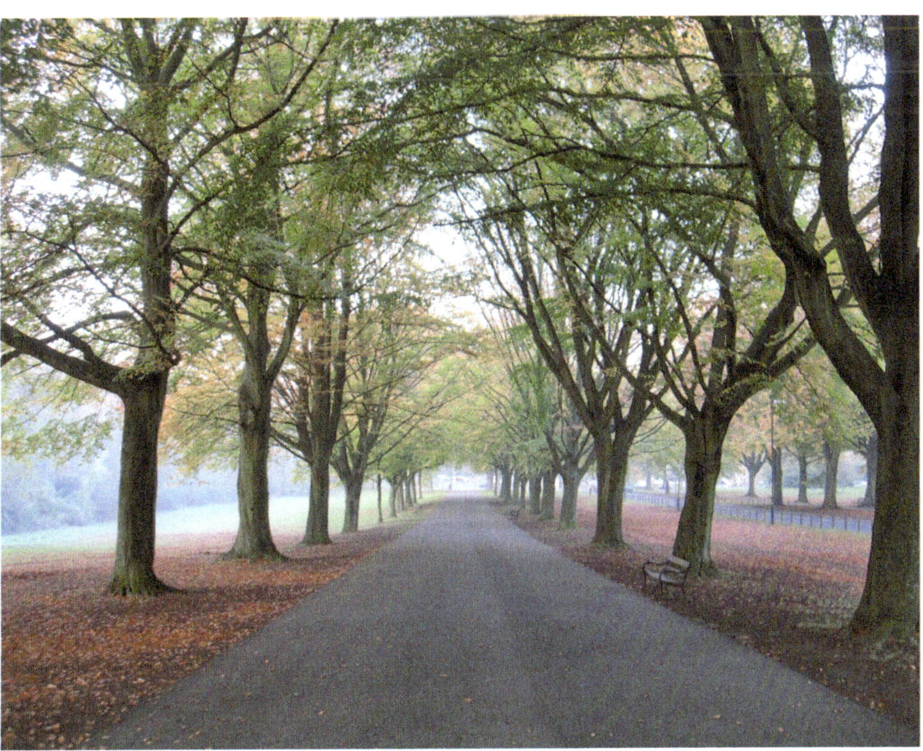

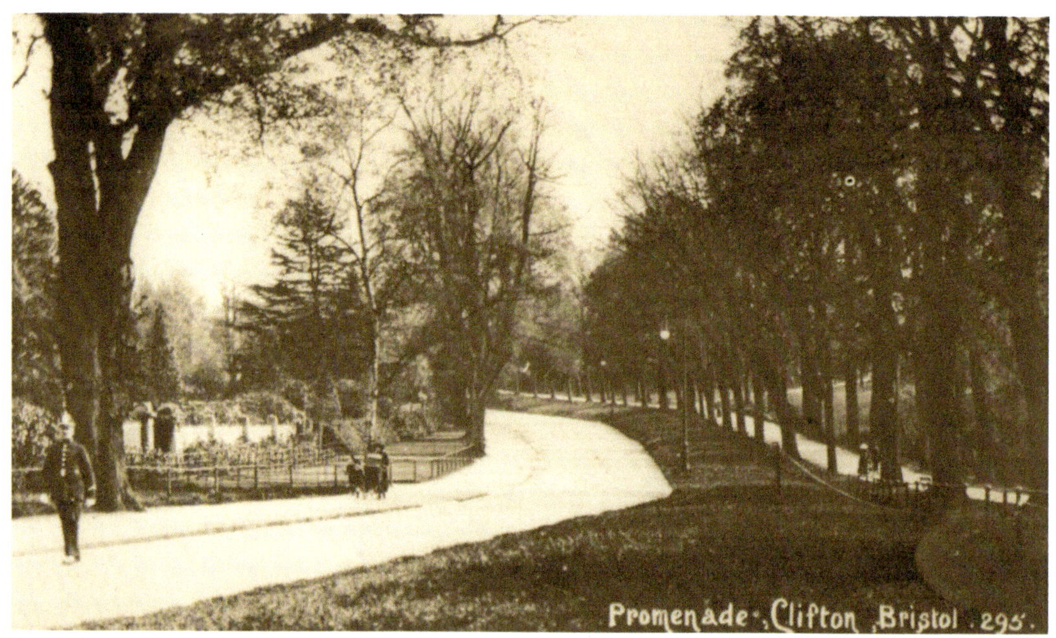

The Promenade, Early 1900s

Looking up The Promenade, the path on the right divides at the top, with the right-hand side going through the remains of the ramparts of the Iron Age fort and onto the Observatory, while the left-hand fork skirts its base and leads on to Clifton village. A policeman can be seen confidently striding down the road. In the modern picture, a monkey puzzle tree looms out of the gloom.

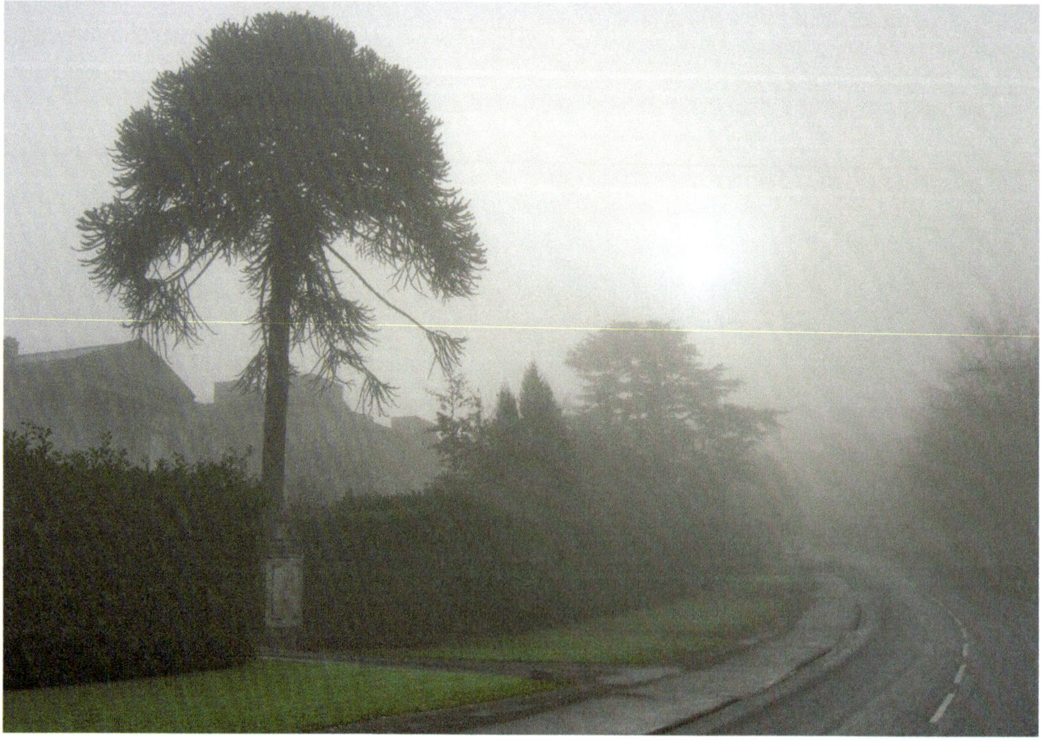

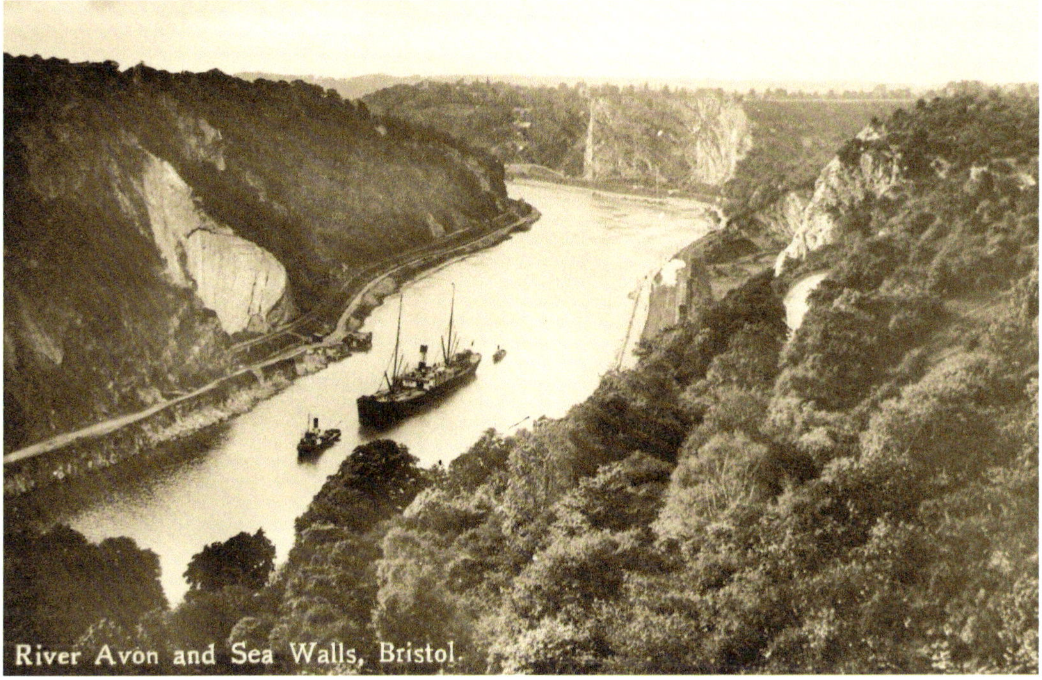

River Avon and Sea Walls, Early 1900s

Taken at the top of the northern edge of the Iron Age fort, the vista looks down the Avon towards Portbury and Avonmouth, and Wales can just be seen in the distance. The steamer in the older photograph is being pulled upriver by a tug boat, while a steam train winds along the foot of the gorge below the Sea Walls (beside what is the Portway today). The newer image looks more verdant, but it was actually cleared recently to improve the view.

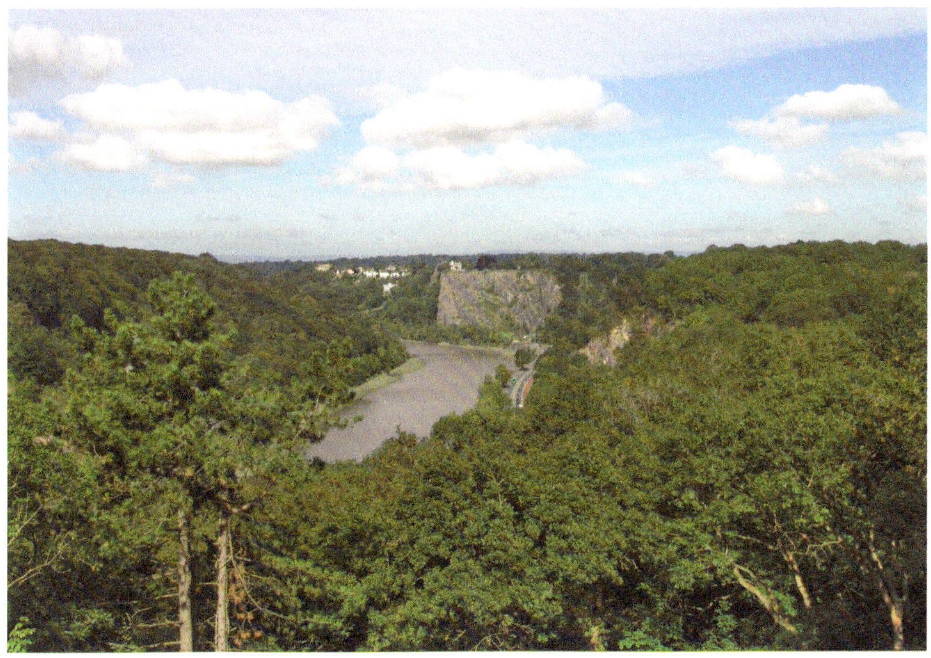

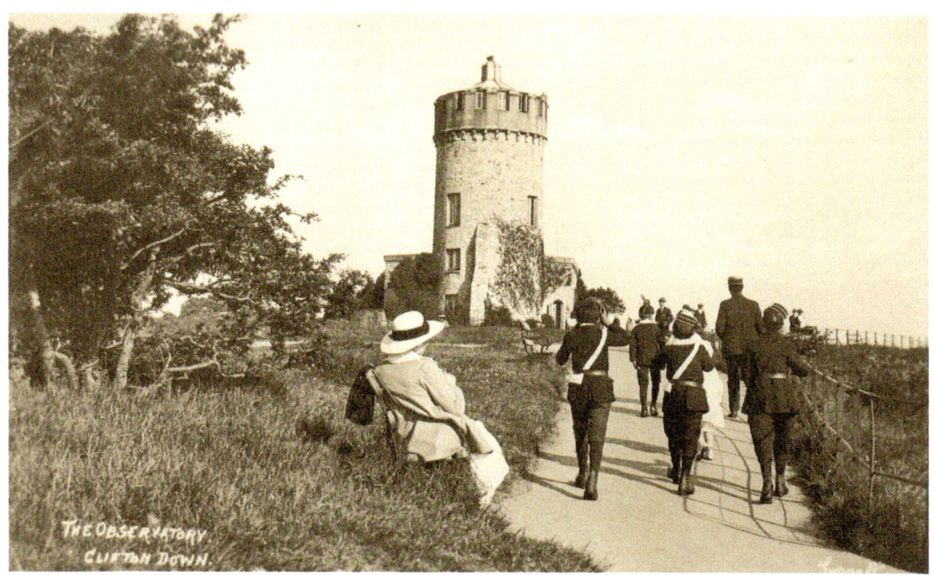

The Observatory, 5 October 1915

Built on the site of an Iron Age fort, the Observatory was originally a snuff mill which was destroyed by fire in 1777. The artist, William West, was fascinated by optics and engineering and in 1828 he leased the building to turn it into an observatory. In 1829, he replaced his telescope with a camera obscura – an arrangement of mirrors and lenses which enables a 360-degree external view. In 1837 he opened a tunnel, 61 metres in length, which he had excavated from the Observatory down to St Vincent's Cave on the cliff-face of the Avon Gorge. These are both open to the public.

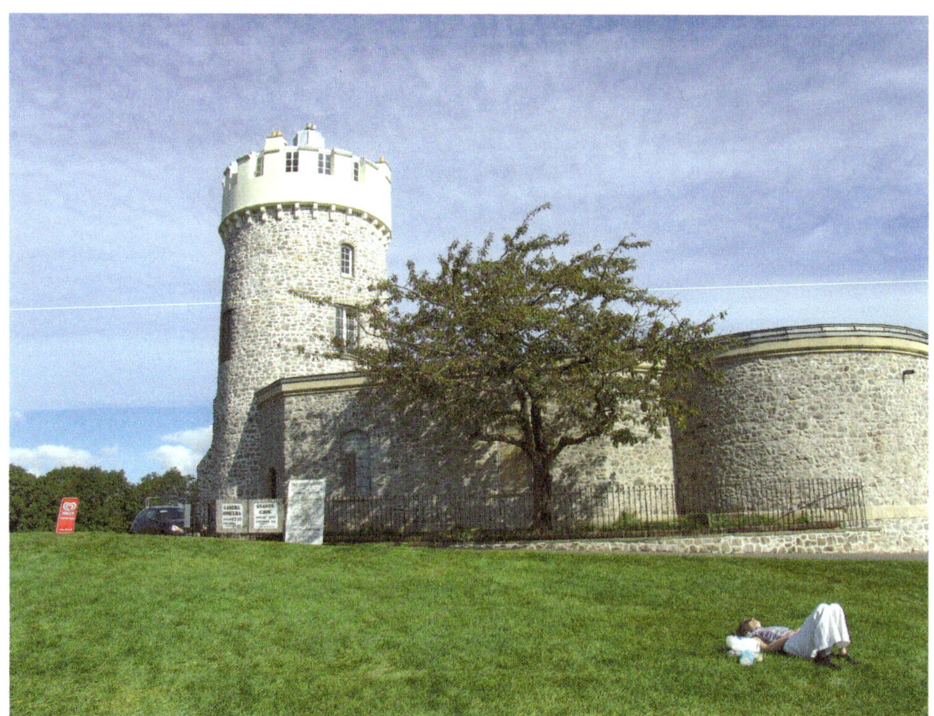

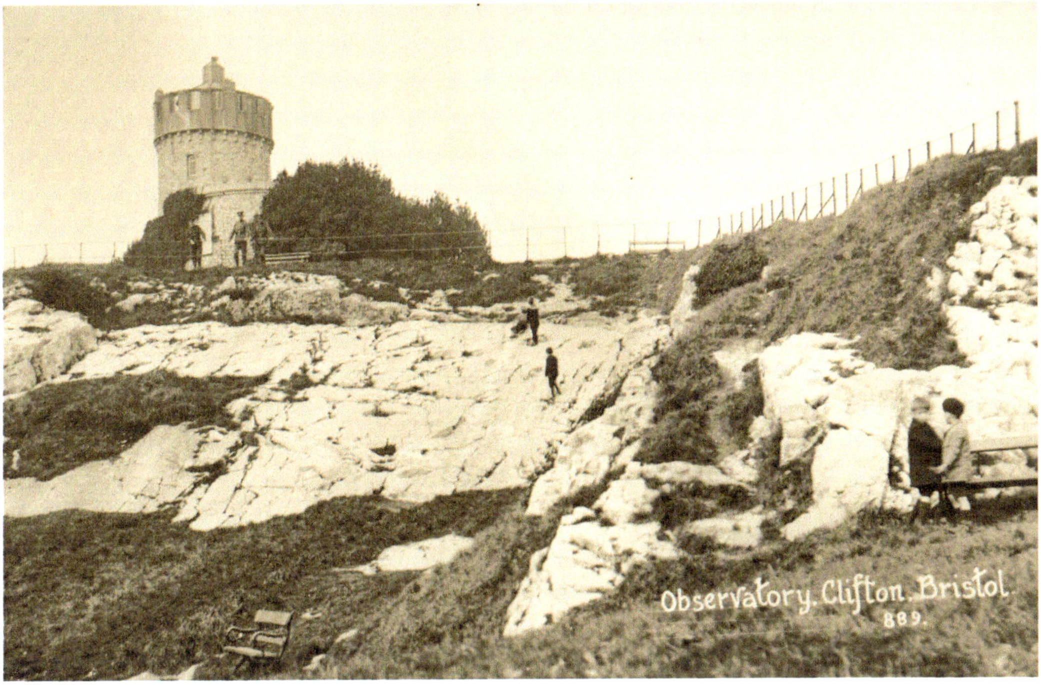

Rock Slide, the Observatory, 11 August 1916

Children (and adults) still enjoy playing on this natural slide on the side of the Observatory, although it is not clear when this pastime dates back to – probably not to the Iron Age, as the rock-face would have been part of the Clifton camp's defences.

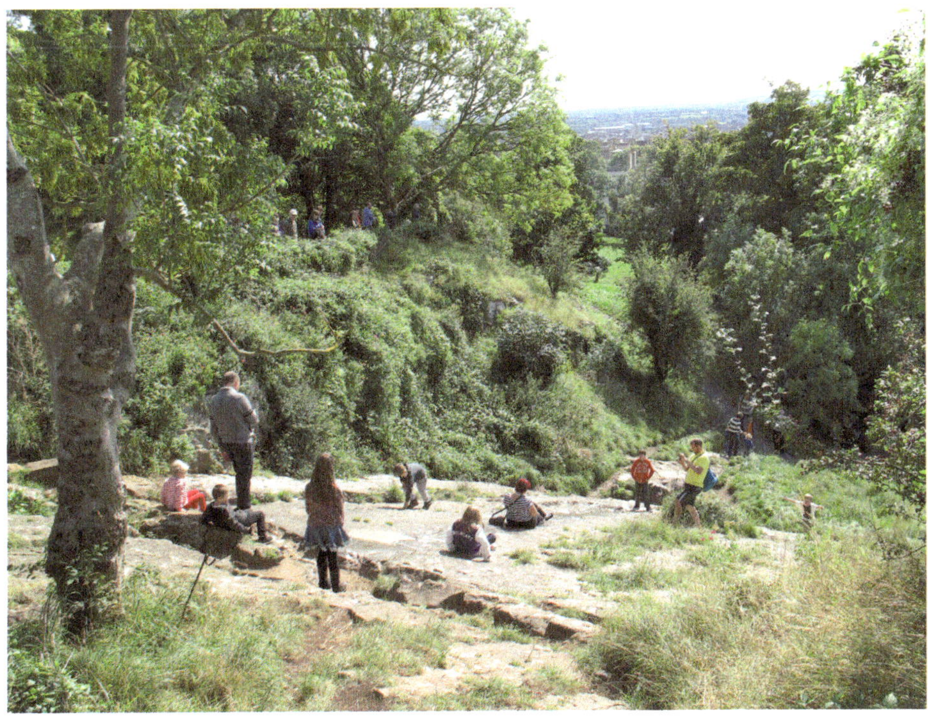

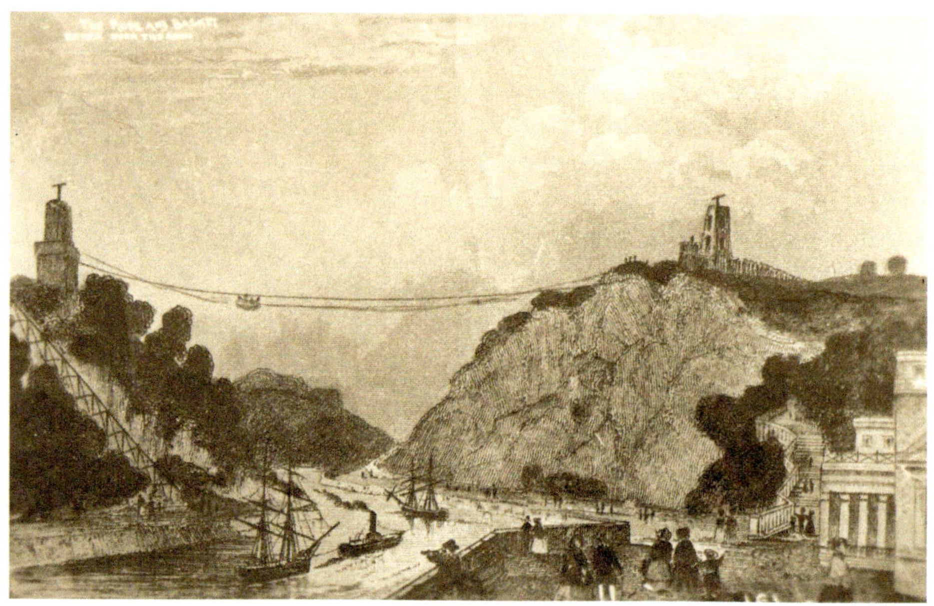

Clifton Suspension Bridge, 1840s

The world-famous Clifton Suspension Bridge, which spans the Avon Gorge, was designed by the renowned Victorian engineer Isambard Kingdom Brunel. Work began in 1831, but the project was dogged with political wranglings and financial disputes, and by 1843, with only the towers completed, the bridge was abandoned. Sadly, Brunel never lived to see his masterpiece in all its glory, dying aged only fifty-three in 1859, but the Clifton Suspension Bridge was finally completed as his memorial. It is seen here from St Vincent's Rock.

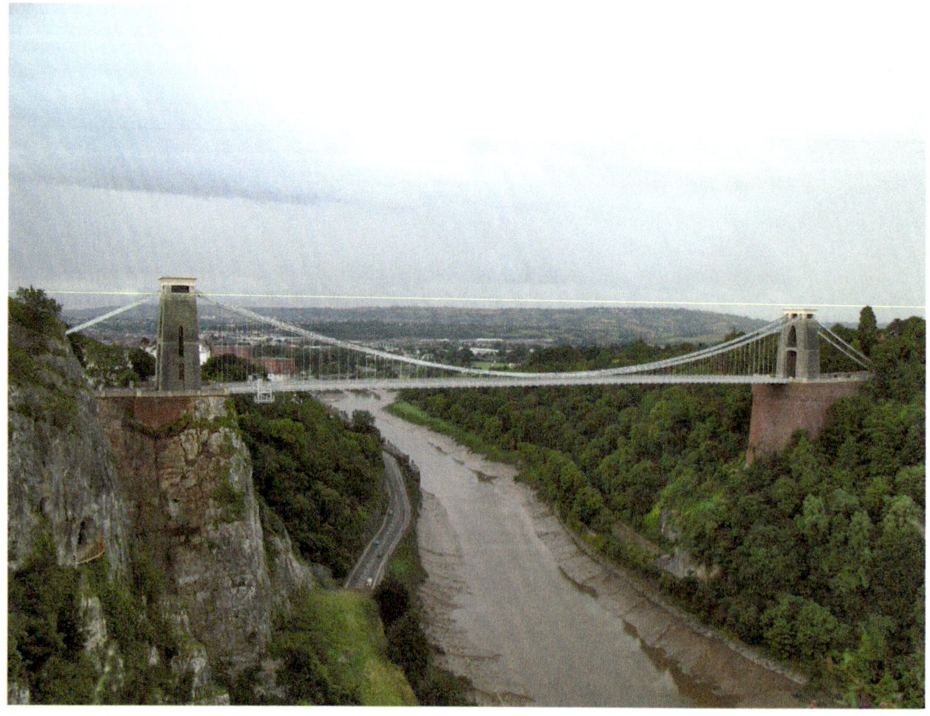

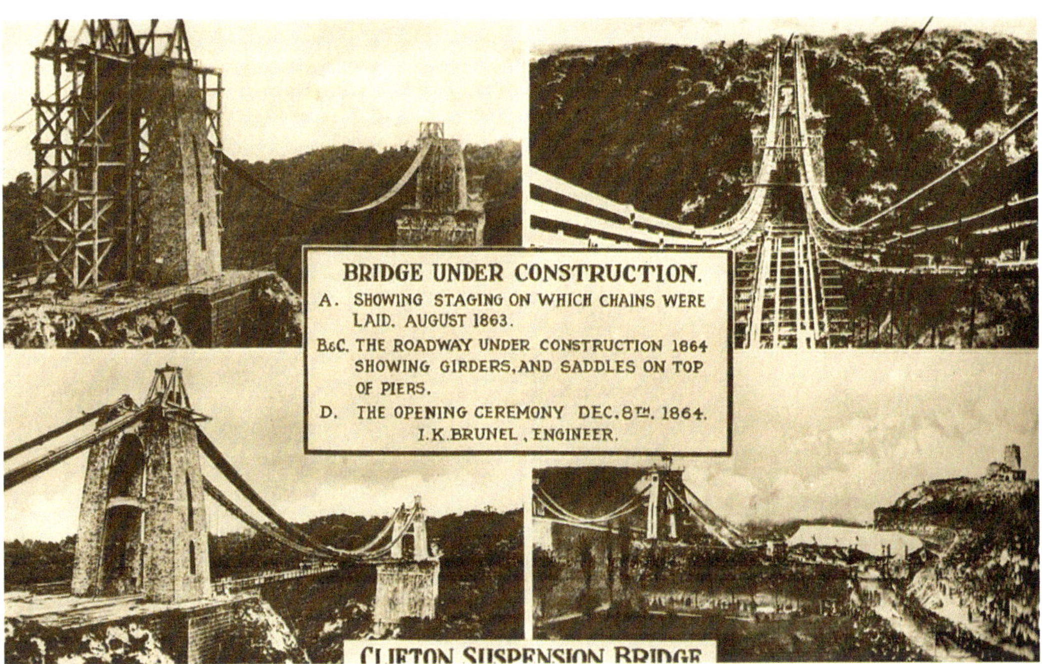

Construction of the Suspension Bridge, 1863–64

After the judge Thomas Telford had rejected all designs save for his own, the bridge committee finally announced in 1821 that Brunel's design had won the competition for a suspension bridge. Work started in 1836, and the towers were built by 1843. Then, inevitably, the funds ran out. To honour the memory of the recently deceased Brunel, his colleagues raised funds and completed the bridge in 1864. It was not quite to the original design – the Egyptian theme was largely dropped and they recycled the chains from Brunel's Hungerford Bridge.

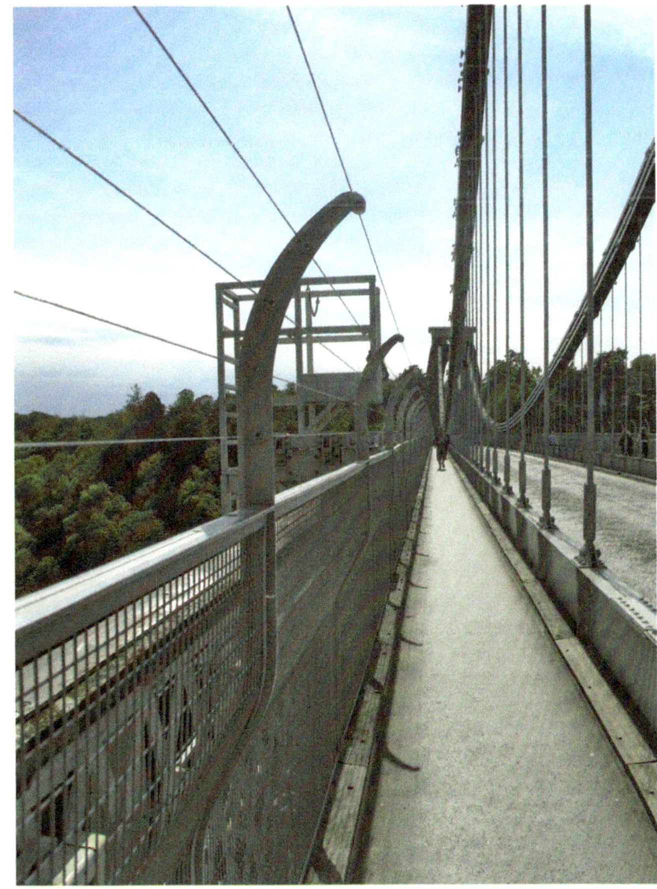

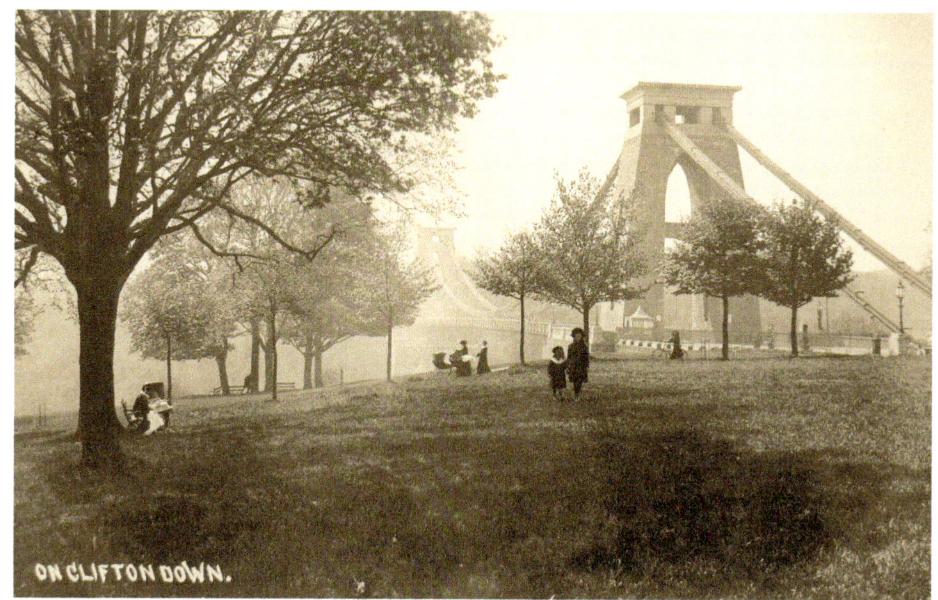

Suspension Bridge from Sion Hill, 1910s

It is not surprising that over 500,000 people visit this bridge every year. Its sturdy but elegant design and the fascinating story behind it are as captivating as ever. It was announced in 2011 that a new visitor centre would be built across the bridge on the Leigh Woods side which, it is hoped, will be opened for its 150th anniversary. It is a huge tribute to Brunel that, although the road across was only for horse-drawn vehicles, it meets the demands of twenty-first-century commuter traffic, with 11,000–12,000 cars crossing it every day.

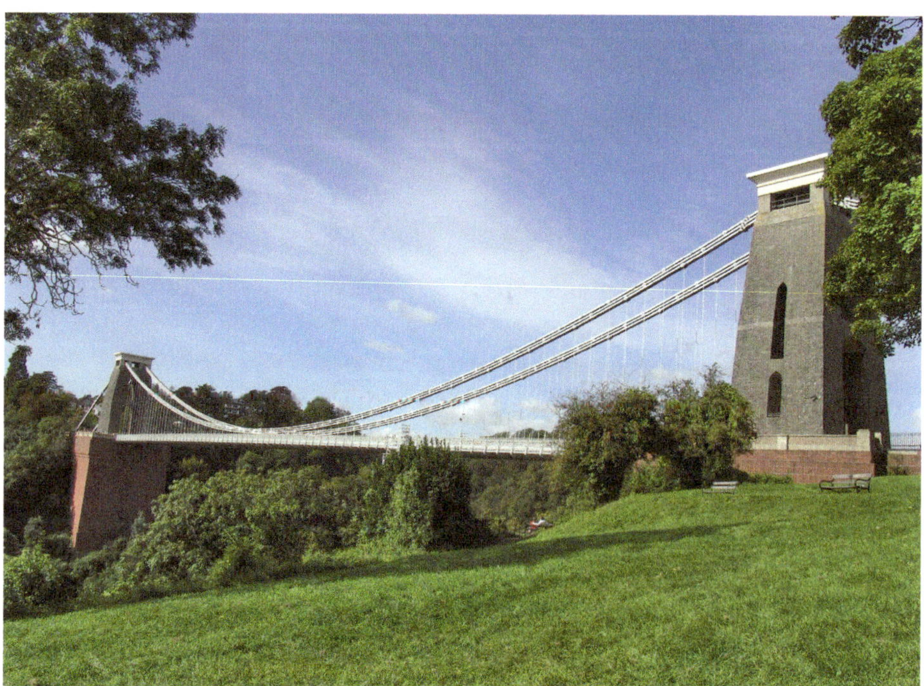

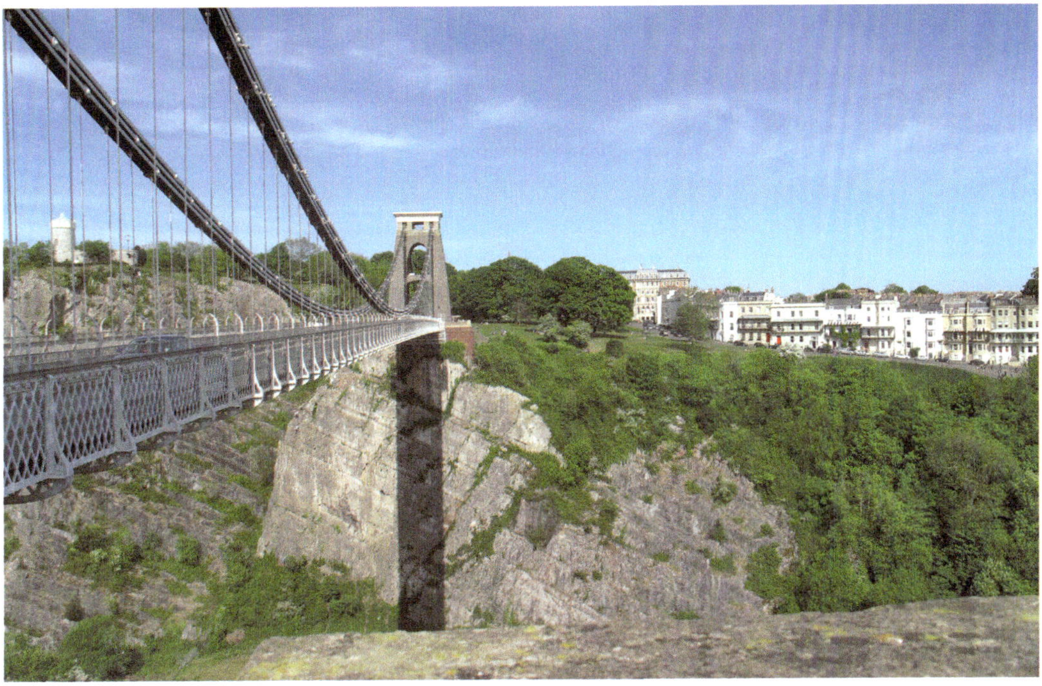

Sion Hill, 1900s

The views of the gorge and the proximity of Sion Spring must have been the reason for the somewhat haphazard development of Sion Hill between 1780 and 1790 by Thomas Morgan. These elegant, balconied four and five storey houses are as individual now as they were in the eighteenth century. As seen from the modern photograph, taken from the Leigh Woods end of the Suspension Bridge, Sion Hill stretches from the former Downs Hotel at the centre to the former St Vincent Rocks Hotel at the bottom right (the Observatory can be seen on the left-hand side).

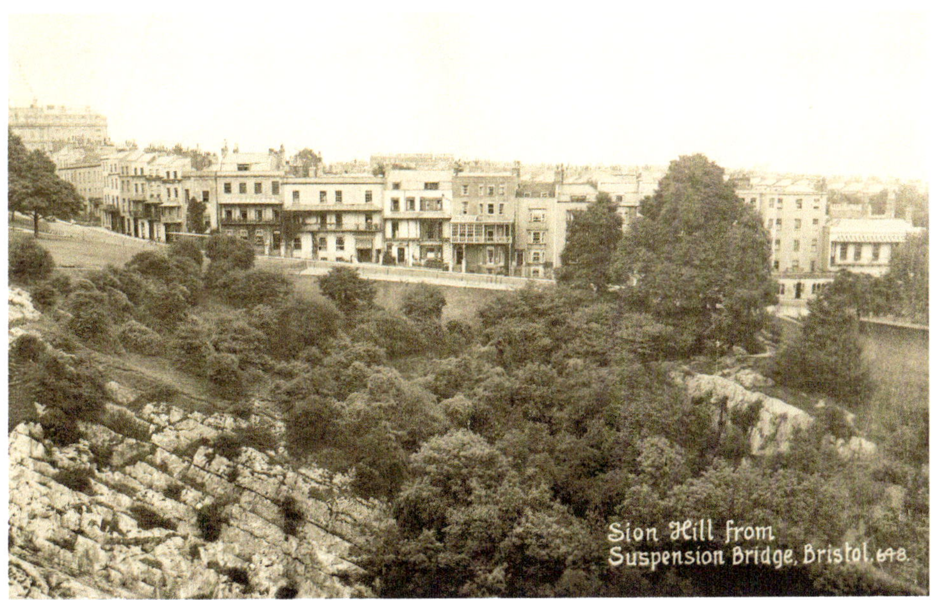

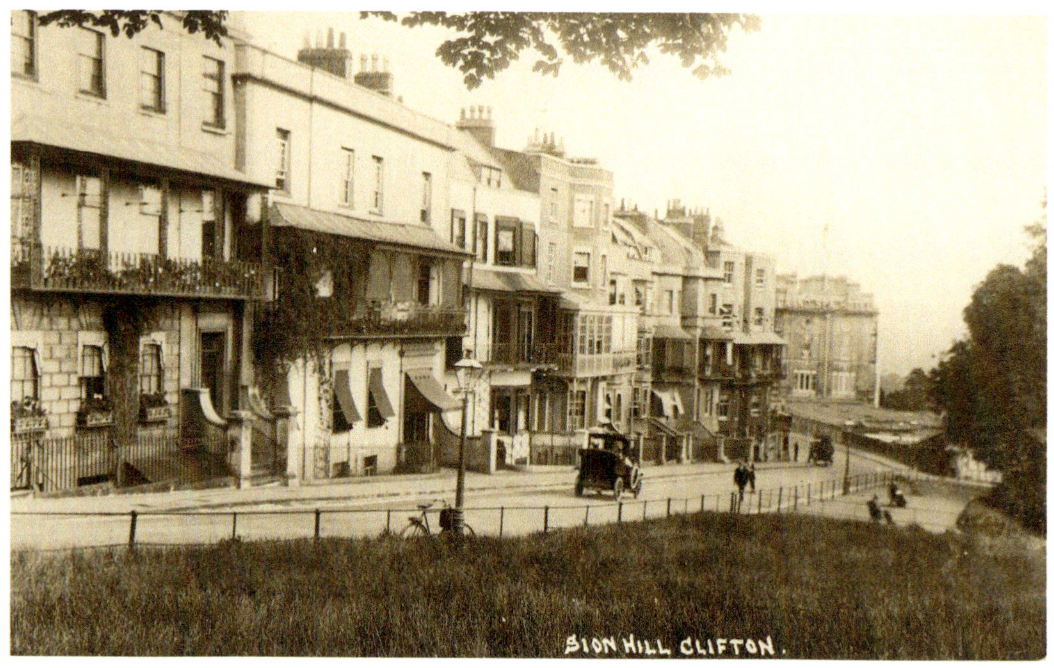

Sion Hill, 1900s

These two pictures are looking down Sion Hill towards the Avon Gorge Hotel (with its terrace lights shining in the colour photograph) and the St Vincent Rocks Hotel on the corner. The Sion Spring, discovered in the 1780s by boring 250 feet into the rock, produced 33,560 gallons a day, and as well as serving as a bath house (then part of the Rock's Hotel), the water was sold at a penny a bucket. Some of the houses in nearby Caledonia Place still have iron traps in the pavement, giving access to water cisterns where they stored the Sion Spring water.

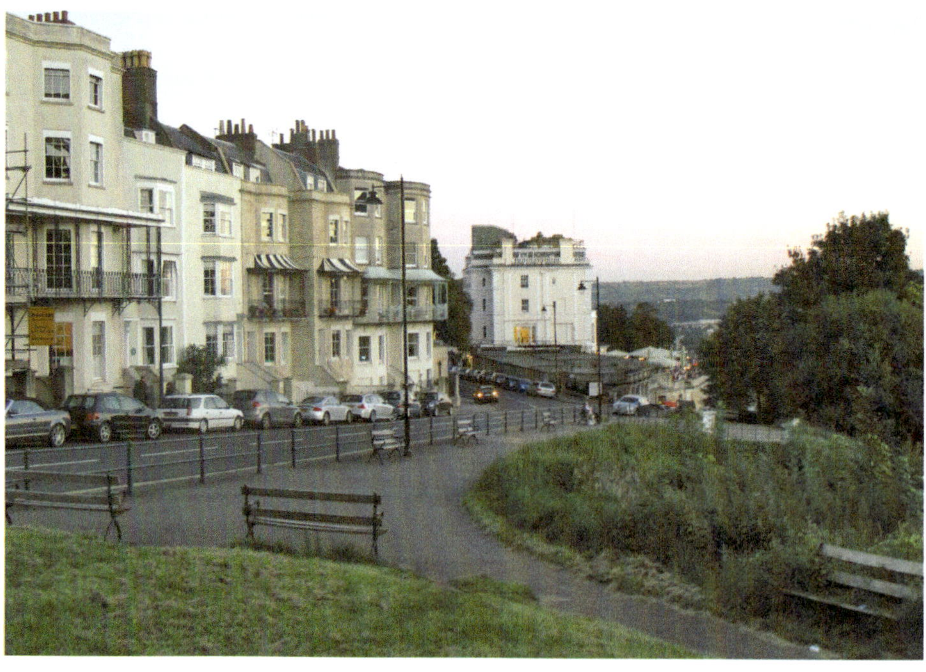

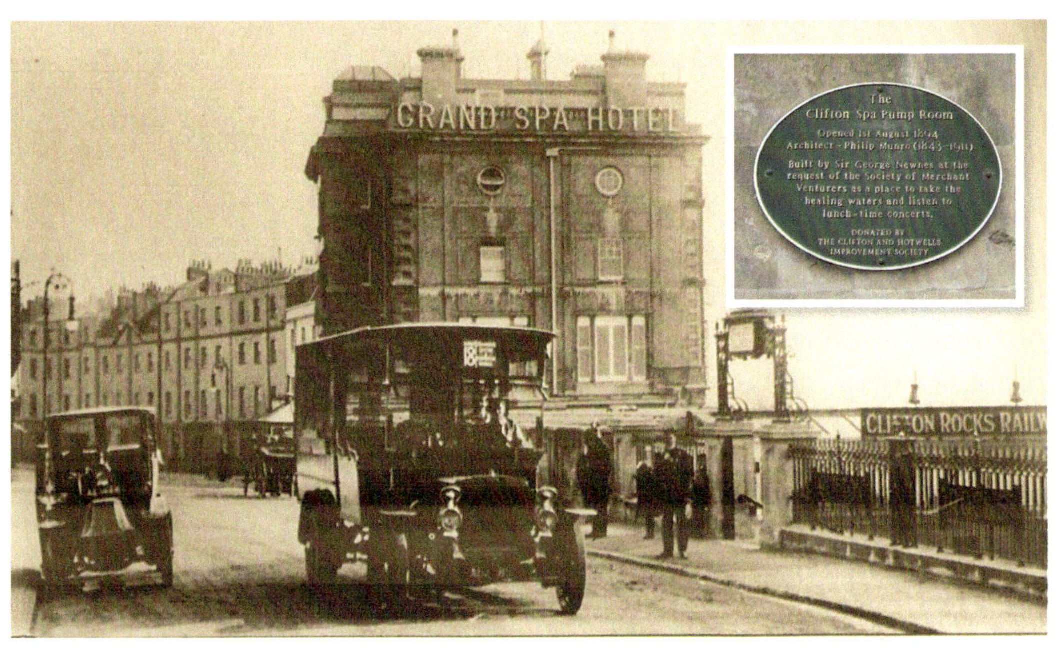

Avon Gorge Hotel (Formerly the Grand Spa Hotel), 1900s

These pictures reflect the passing of time. The 1900s postcard shows an old bus going up past the top of Clifton Rocks Railway, which is clearly still in use. The hotel opened in 1898 with the hope of gaining popularity as a spa resort. The elegant Pump Room was opened in 1894 to dispense 'health-giving' spa water. Just beyond the black car in the modern photograph is the entrance to the hydro-therapeutic rooms. There was a brief period of popularity, but times and tastes changed. The Pump Room and the baths remain but are unused.

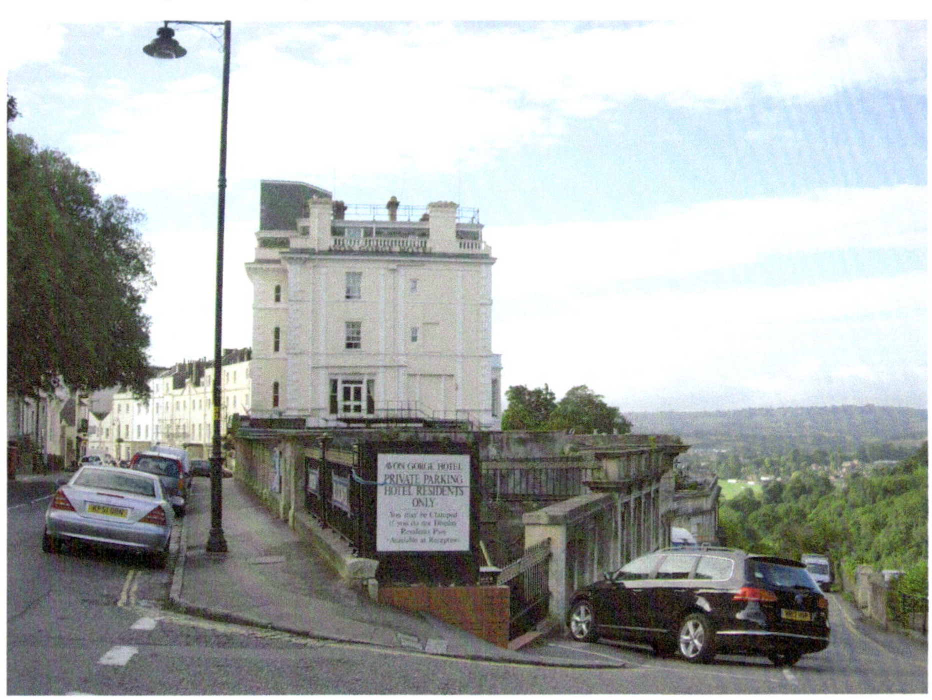

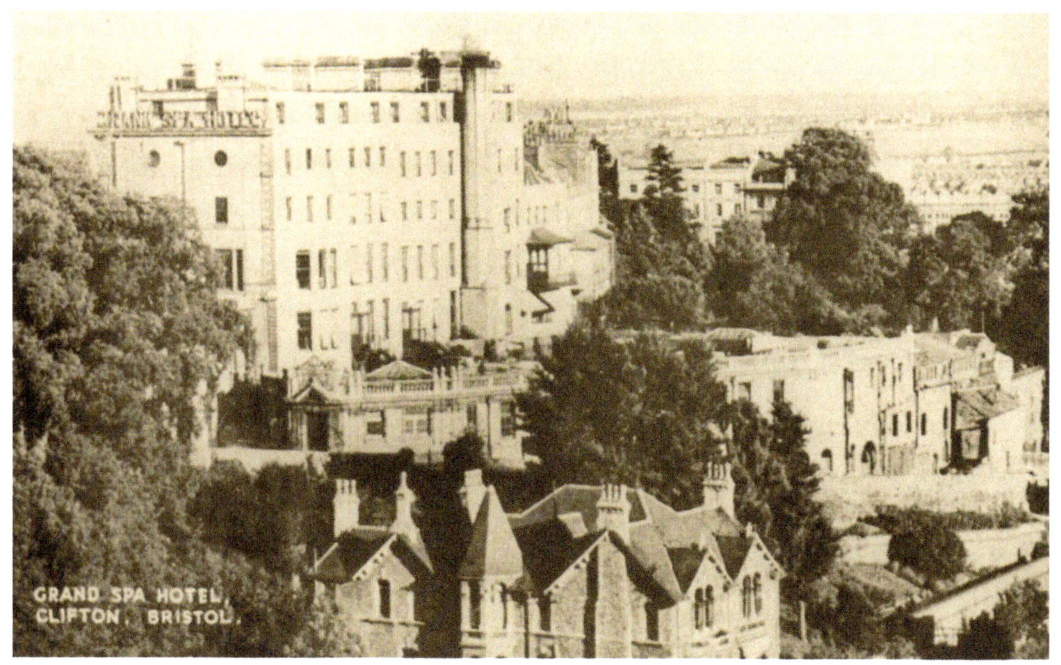

Avon Gorge Terrace, 1900s

Much of this side of the Avon Gorge was developed by the Grand Spa/Avon Gorge Hotel, its Pump Rooms and the Clifton Rocks funicular railway. The modern view puts the connection between Hotwells and Clifton into context. At the bottom of the gorge runs the Portway road, heading towards Portbury and Avonmouth Docks. The nearest two cars on the road are opposite the entrance to the Rocks Railway, which runs up to the hotel and the Hotwells spa complex respectively. Also visible are the steamer terminals beside the river, the entrance to the Floating Harbour and three Bond Warehouses.

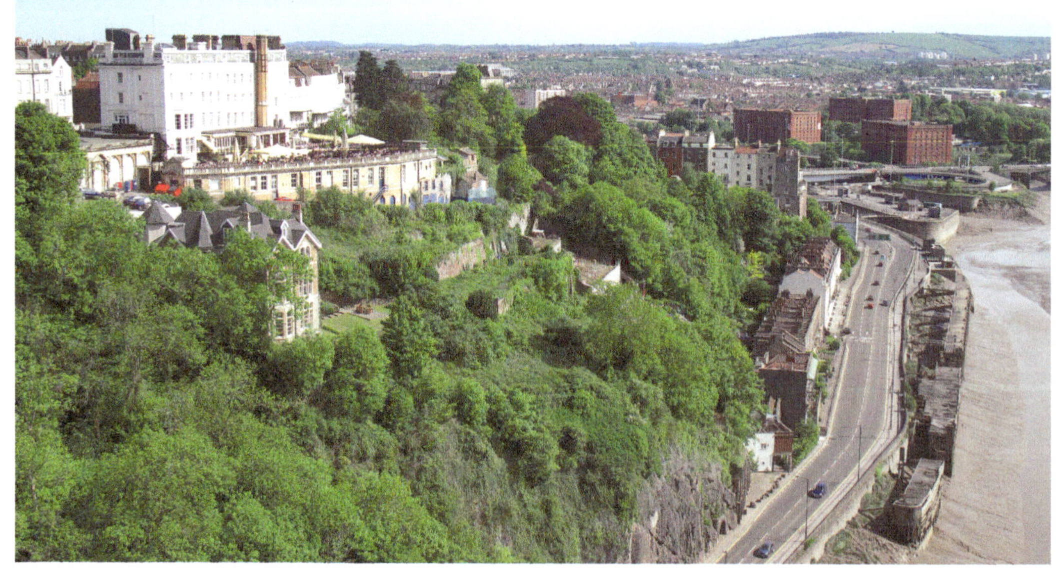

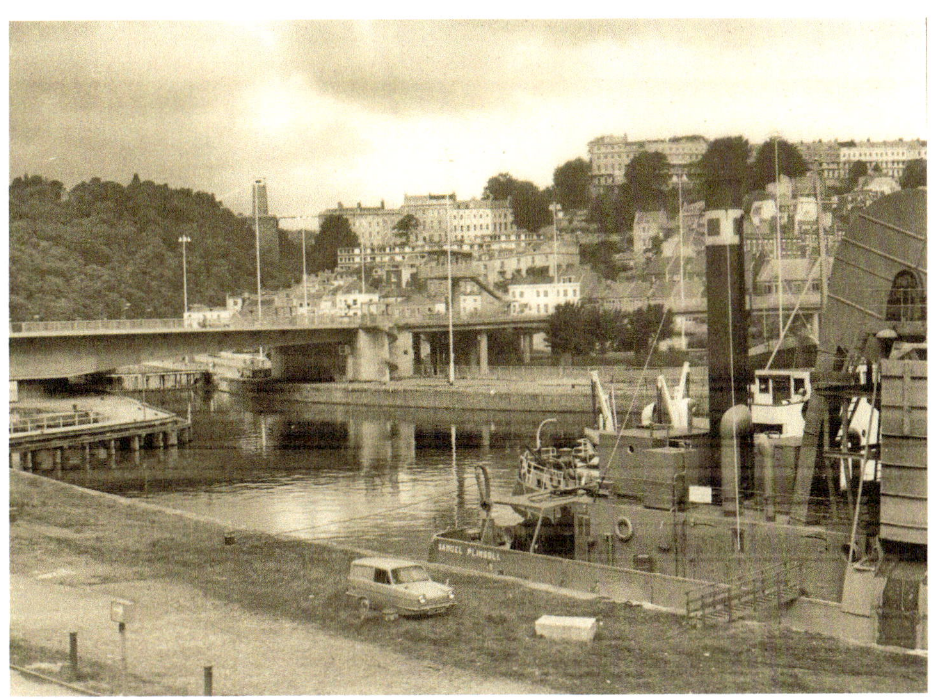

Floating Harbour, Hotwells, 1970s

This rather gloomy and claustrophobic image of the Floating Harbour from the early 1970s captures the spirit of the time nicely. In contrast, the returning affluence to the area is reflected in the more recent picture (with some help from the sunshine) and The Paragon and Windsor Terrace appear probably as their architects intended before they went bust.

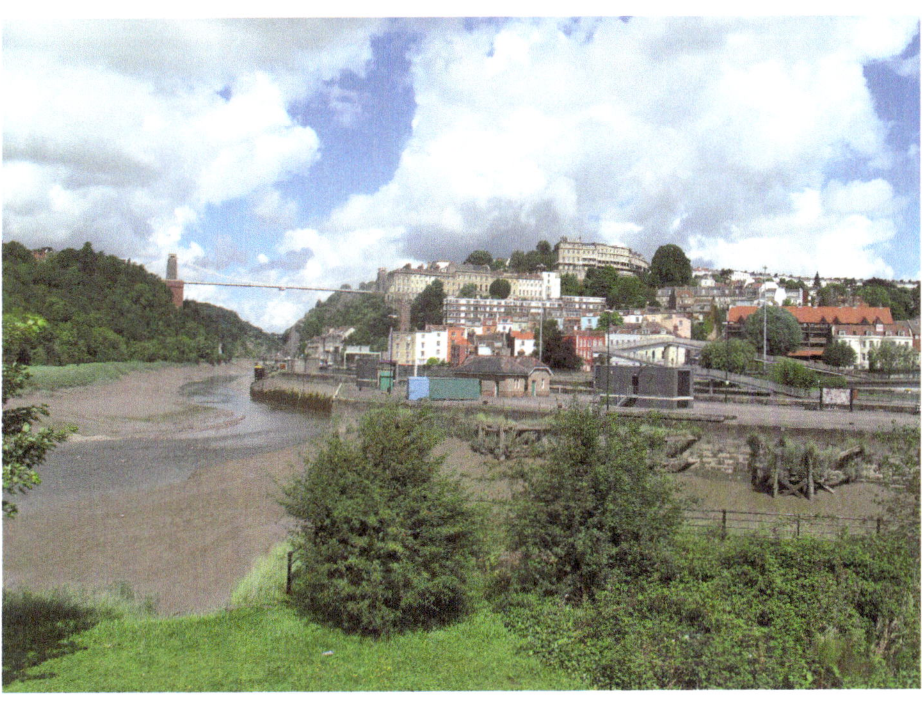

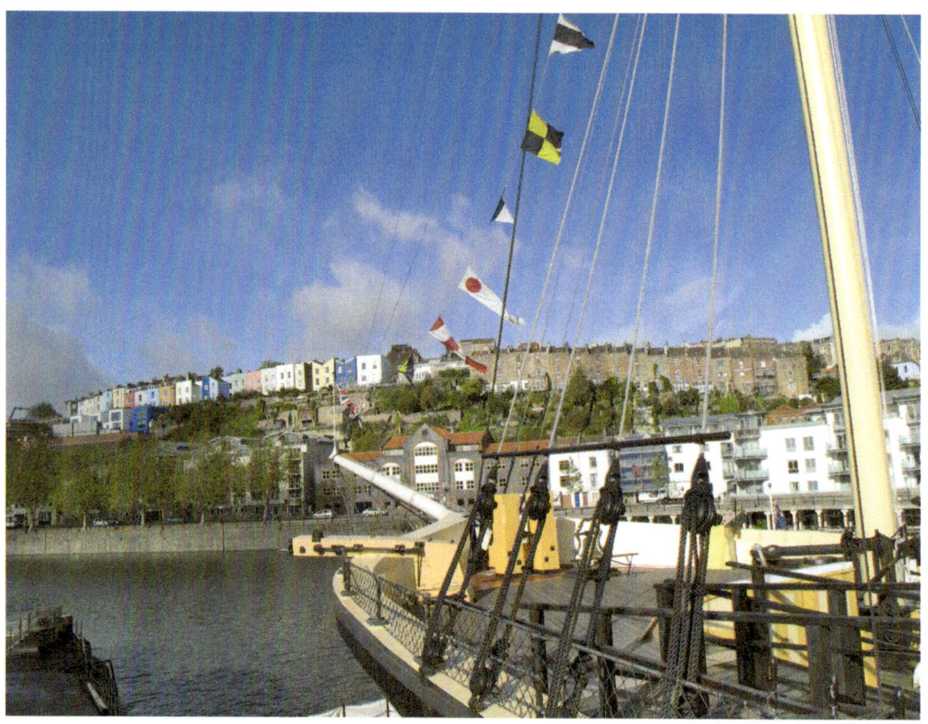

Mardyke Ferry and Cliftonwood, 1910s

Viewed from the bow of Brunel's SS *Great Britain* (which has been lovingly restored and now lives in a dry dock) Cliftonwood shows off its confidence in a profusion of brightly coloured houses. Along with Hotwells, with its numerous new accommodation buildings, Cliftonwood has been regenerated and is no longer under the shadow of its more illustrious neighbour. The drab appearance of the Mardyke ferry picture has long since gone.

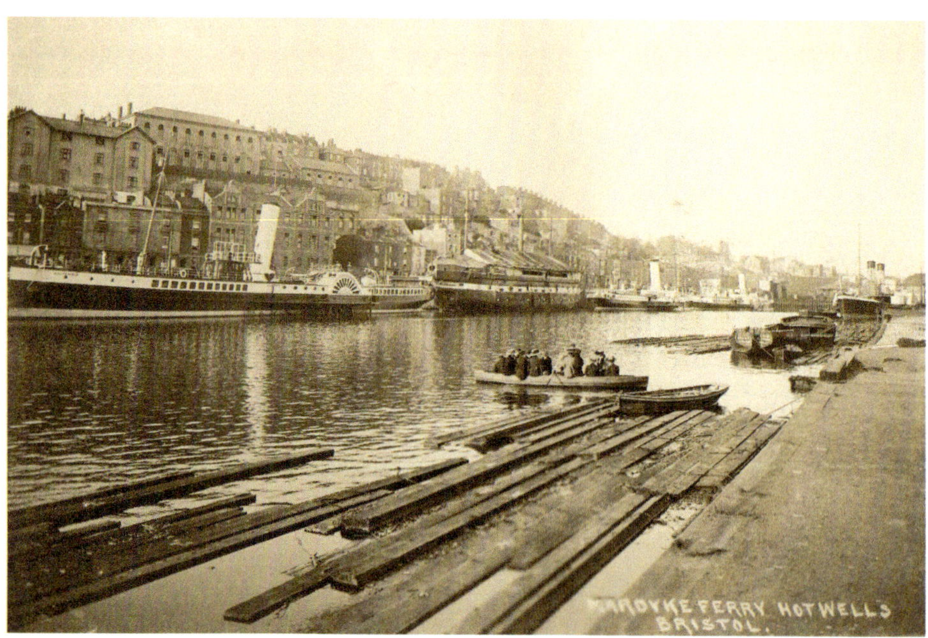

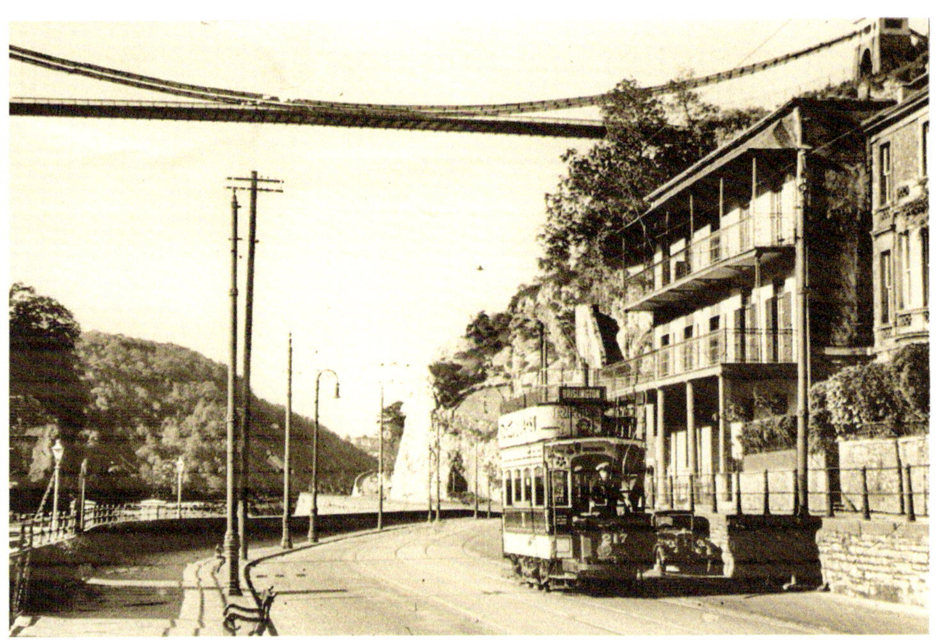

Hotwells Spa, Early 1900s

The colonnade was built in 1786 by Samuel Powell, lessee of the Hotwell, as shops for spa visitors, and is now almost all that remains of the fashionable Hotwells spa. The main buildings were demolished in 1867 after Hotwells failed to halt its decline. In the recent picture (obscured by the tram in the old one) can be seen the lower entrance to Clifton Rock Railway. In 1900 the electric trams reached here, giving a quick connection from other parts of the city up to Clifton via the railway, and to the nearby landing stage of Campbell's Steamers, which began in 1887.

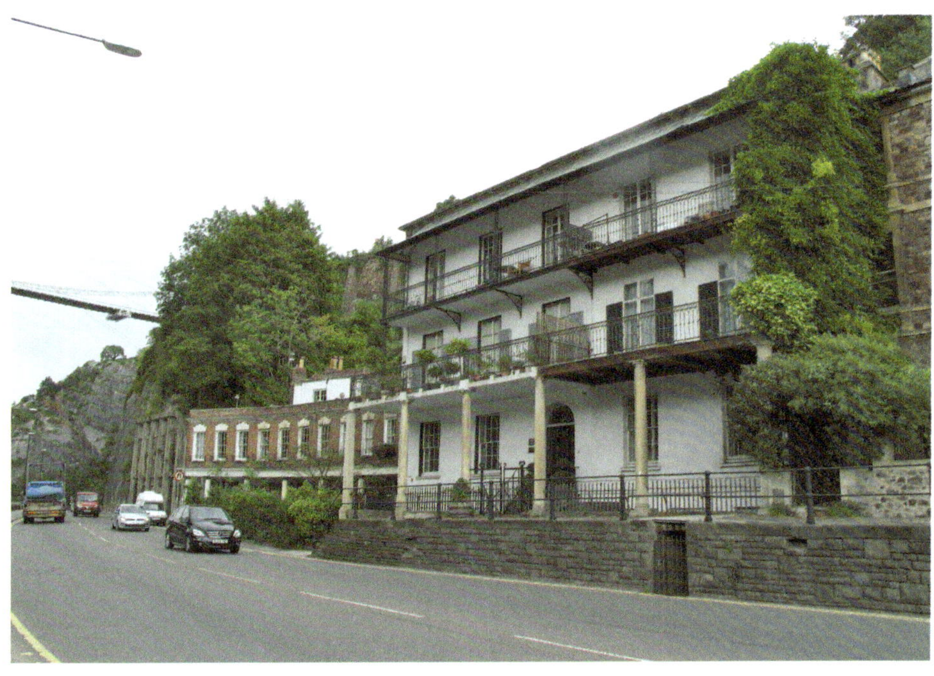

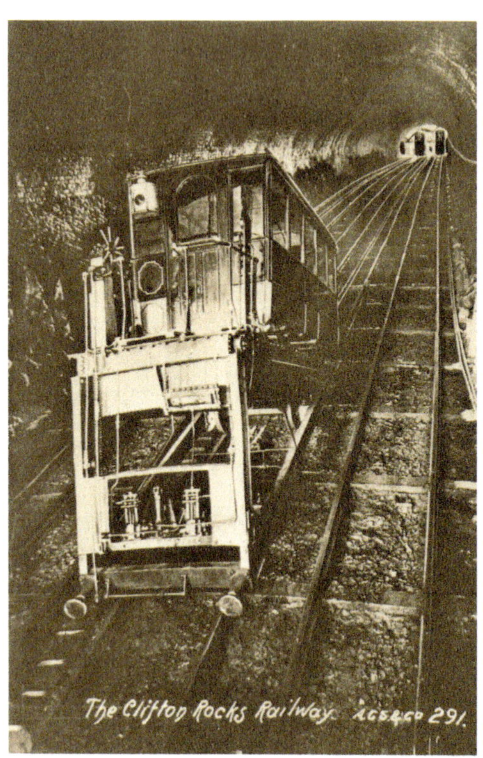

Clifton Rock Railway, 1900s

The funicular railway linking Hotwells to Clifton opened in 1893, with funds provided by the publisher George Newnes and engineering work undertaken by George Croydon Marks. The 500-foot journey took a sprightly forty seconds. It was closed in 1934 due to continued losses, but was used during the Second World War as offices by BOAC, as a relay station by the BBC and as an air-raid shelter. The BBC continued to use part of the tunnel until 1960. A group of local enthusiasts cleared the tunnel and now arrange to take parties down.

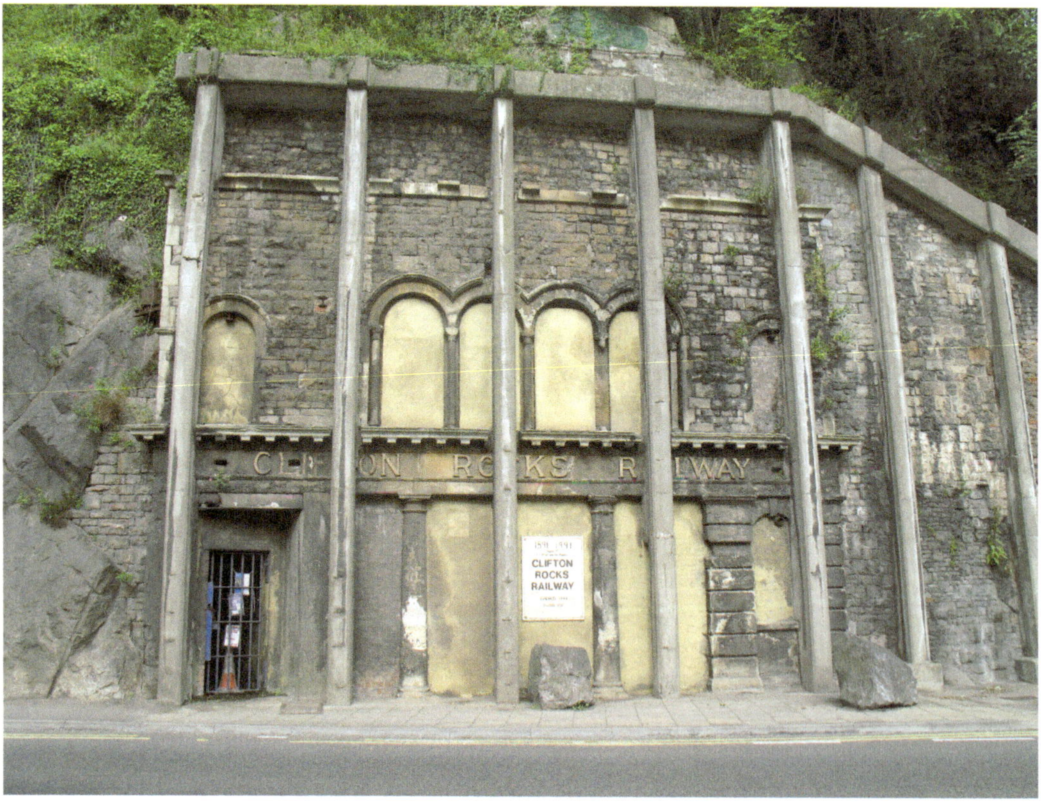

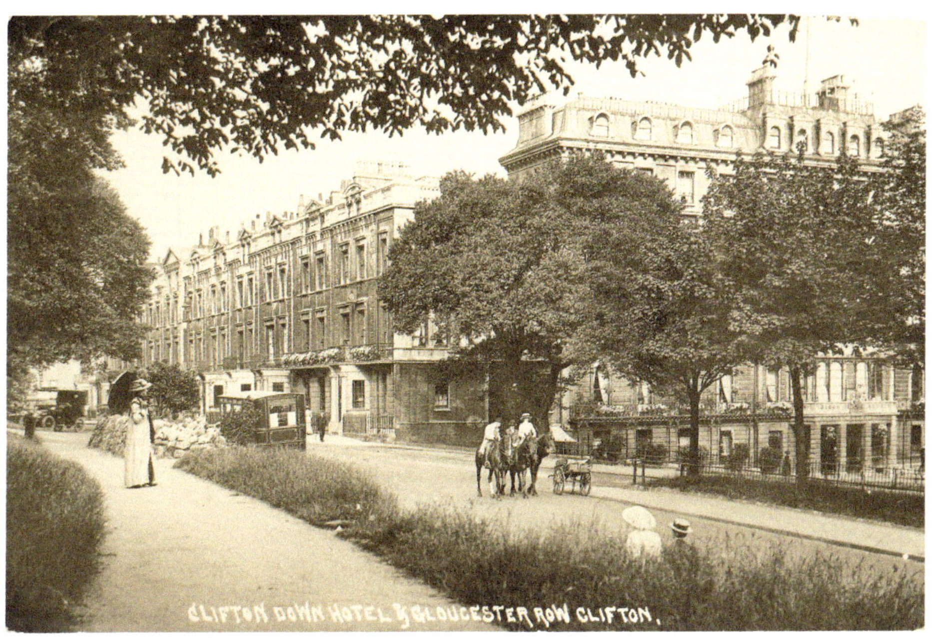

The Downs Hotel, Gloucester Row, 15 August 1919

Opened in 1865, one of the key functions of the Downs Hotel was catering for visitors to the newly opened Suspension Bridge, and it was said to be the largest hotel in Bristol. An advertisement in 1905 proudly boasted it had 'a lavatory on every floor'. At about the same time, the owner complained to the Downs Committee that the sheep grazing on the Downs disturbed his guests at night. Converted in 1939 to offices, it remained as such until 2007 when it became luxury apartments. At the bottom left of the old photograph is one of the early buses which ran from the Victoria Rooms to the Suspension Bridge.

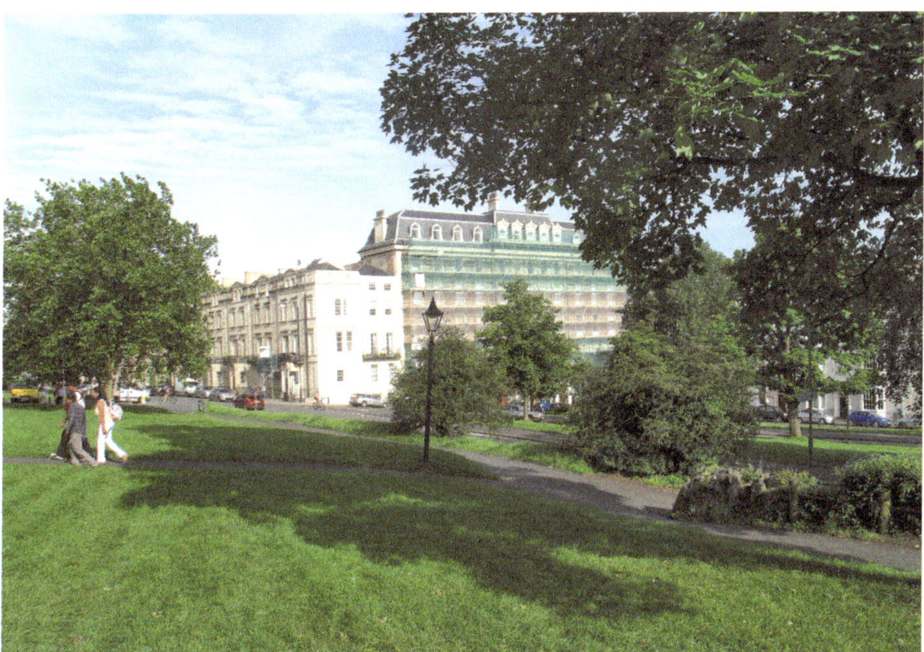

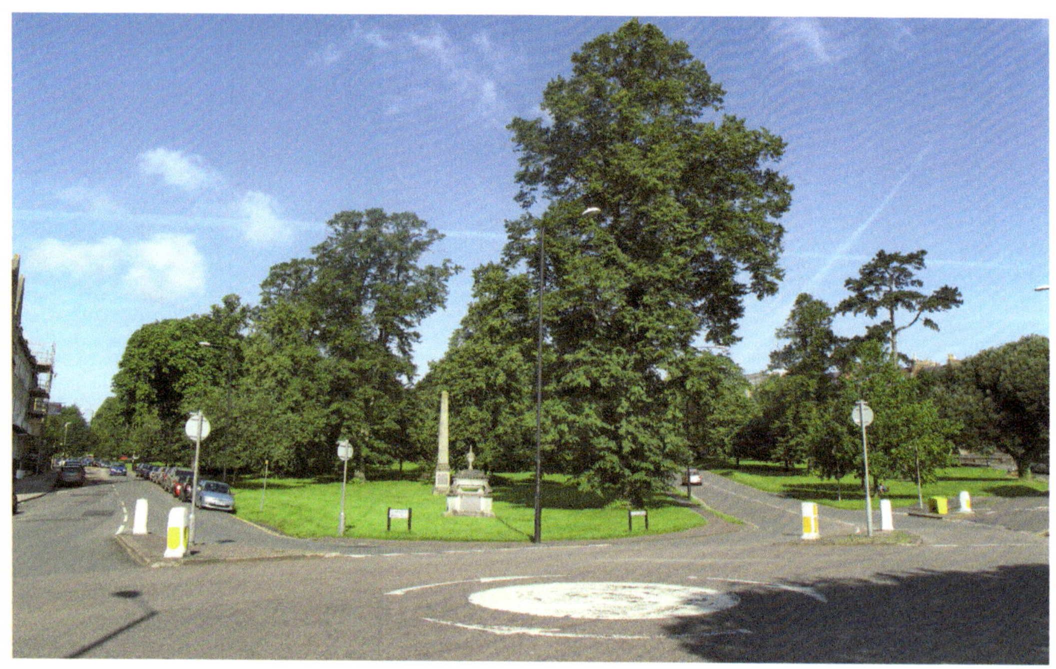

Clifton Down Road, 1900s

The scenes here are of three main roads dividing: to the left is Suspension Bridge Road, in the middle Clifton Down Road leads to The Promenade, and Christchurch is just out of view on the right. The monuments seen in the recent photograph were moved there in 1882 when Manilla Hall, where Sir William Draper once lived, was demolished. The obelisk is his personal tribute to William Pitt, Earl of Chatham. The cenotaph honours the officers and men of the Queen's Own Cameroon Highlanders who fell in India fighting the French in 1758–61.

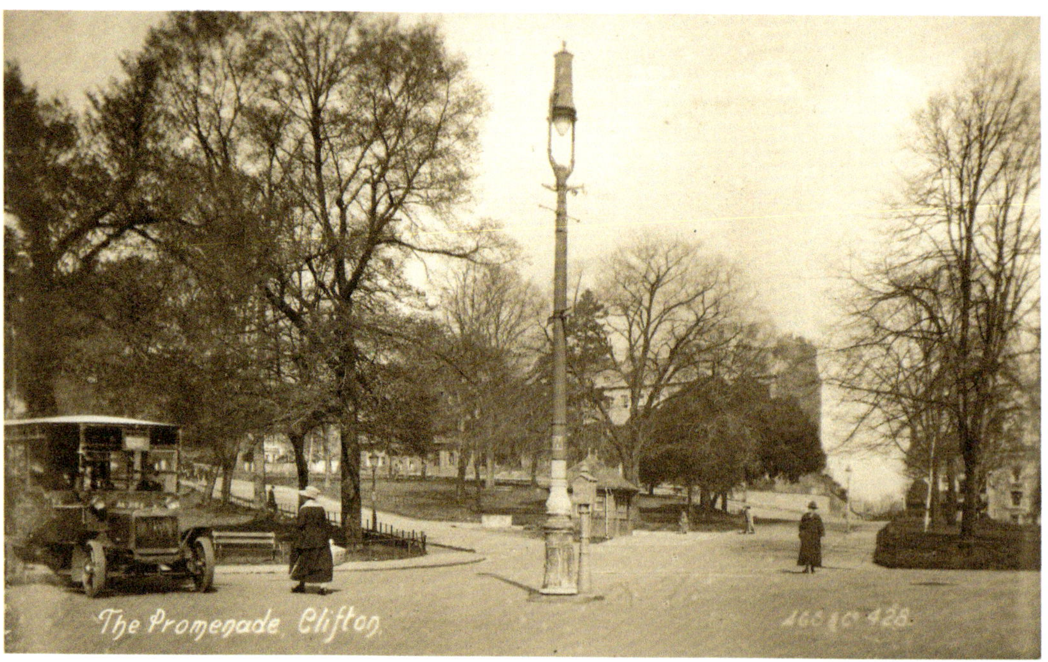

Lamp Lighting, 1960s

Gas lighting in Clifton started surprisingly early, with a few gas street lamps installed in 1824. The Victoria Rooms were illuminated by three lamps in 1847 and private houses followed suit shortly afterwards. Once a familiar sight, lamplighters sadly are no more (although nearby Canynge Square still has the facilities to operate gas lighting). Here, one of the last lighters is at work on Christchurch Green (Christchurch can be seen in the modern picture).

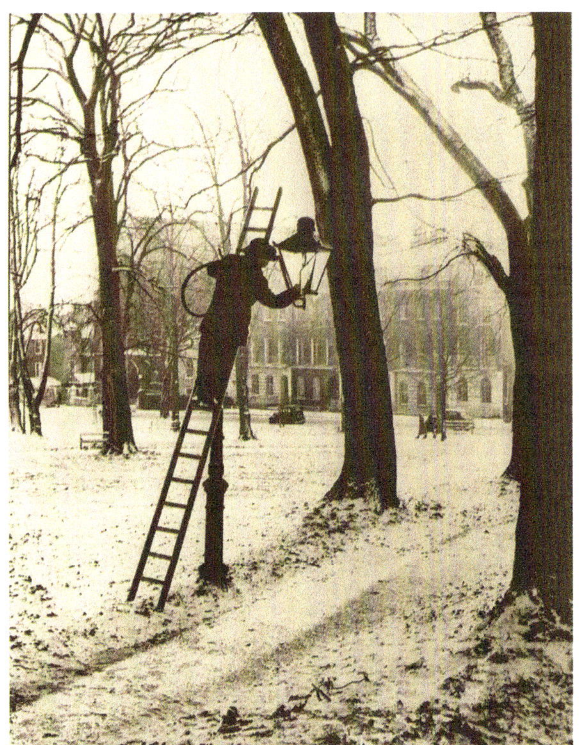

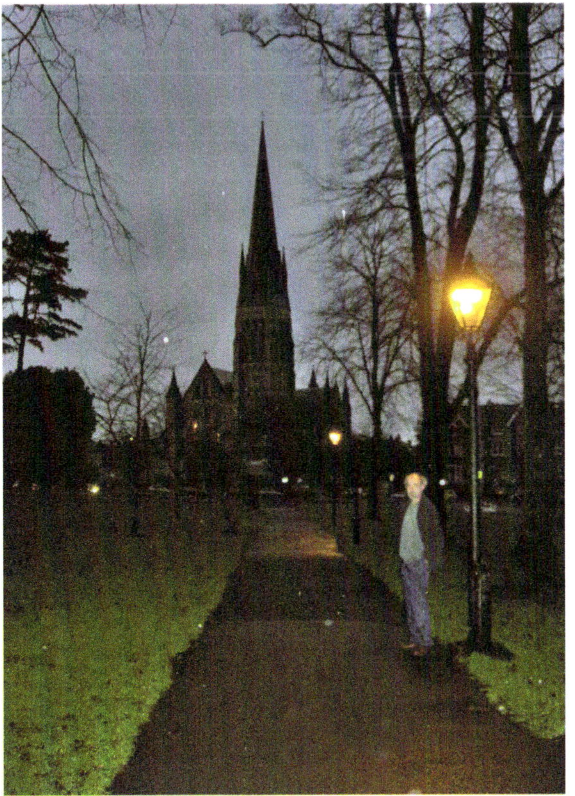

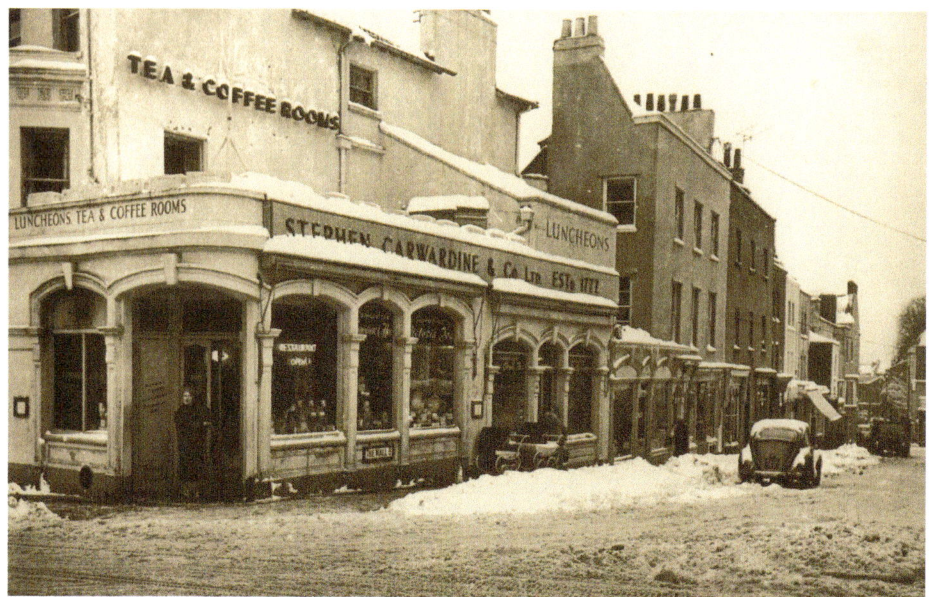

Carwardine's, The Mall, 1960s

This snowy shot of the top of The Mall nicely captures the refined character of old Clifton village. Carwardine's was a family business that imported its own teas and roasted its own coffee beans. In the twentieth century their coffee and tea shops spread from central Bristol to suburbs like Clifton. Unfortunately, this leisurely service could not compete with the major chains (it is very unlikely they would have sunk to selling takeaway coffee in paper cups). In 1981, Carwardine's seven coffee and tea houses joined Madisons, an expanding coffee enterprise, and disappeared from Clifton's landscape.

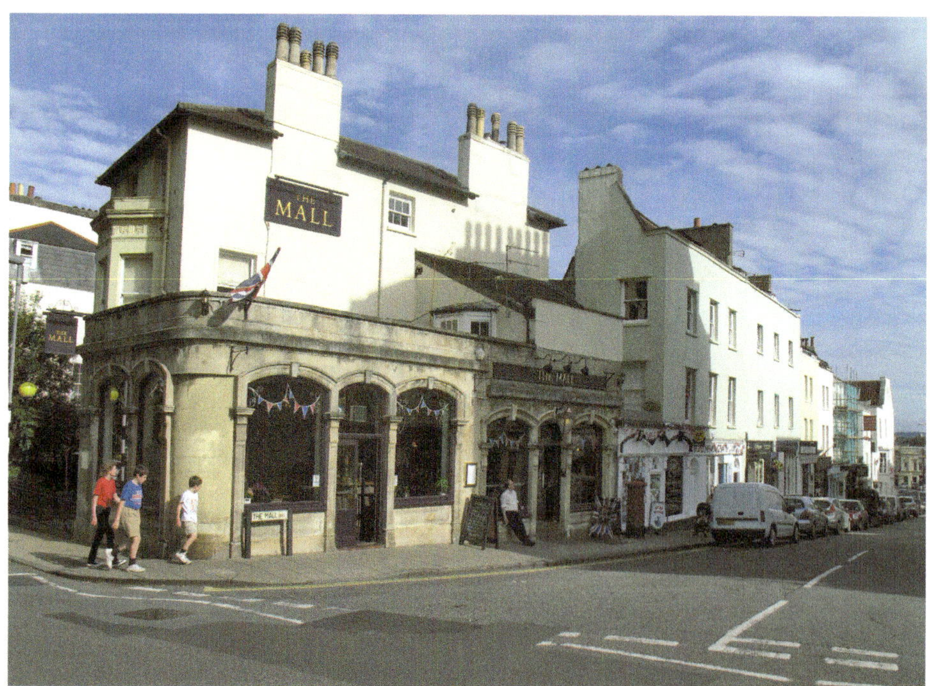

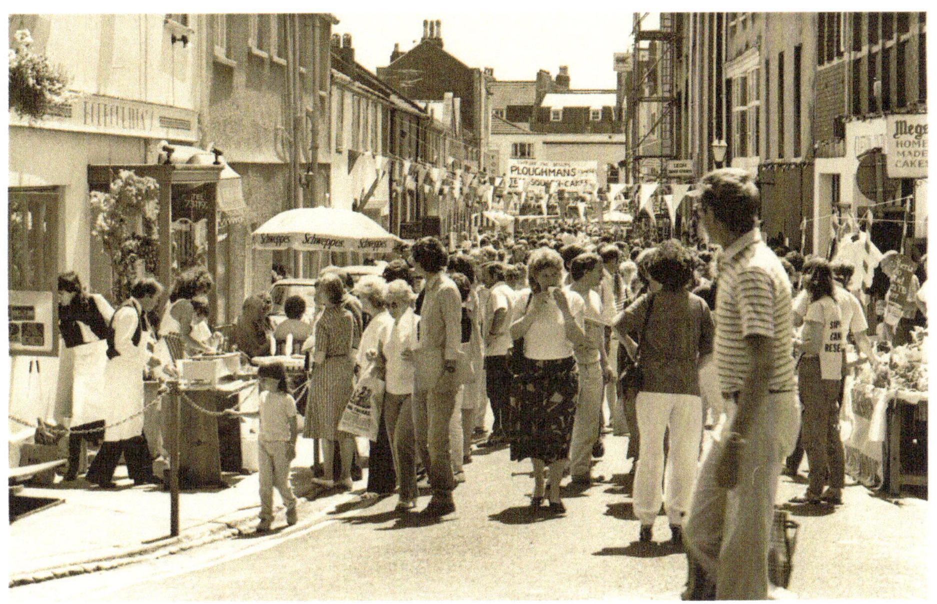

Waterloo Street, 1970s

This is a picture taken at the top of Waterloo Street of one of the Clifton Fairs of the late 1970s. These ambitious and successful communal events ran for a few years to raise money to replace and restore the railings around The Mall Gardens. Food and drink stalls did thriving business and musicians, games and rides entertained the public (some of whom donned fancy dress to enter into the spirit). More than thirty years later, people still remember them with fondness.

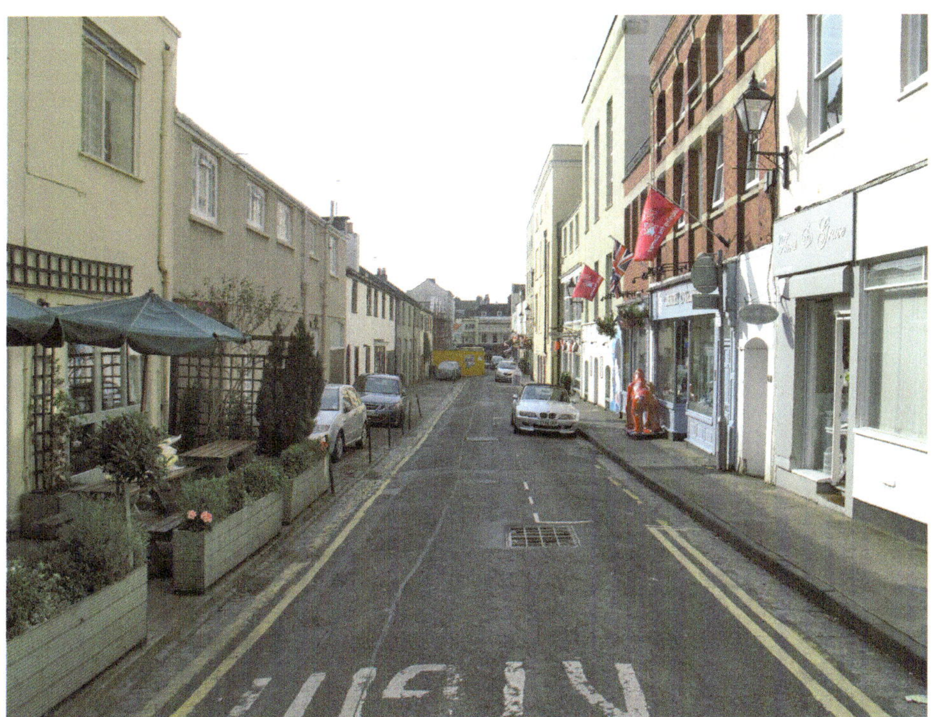

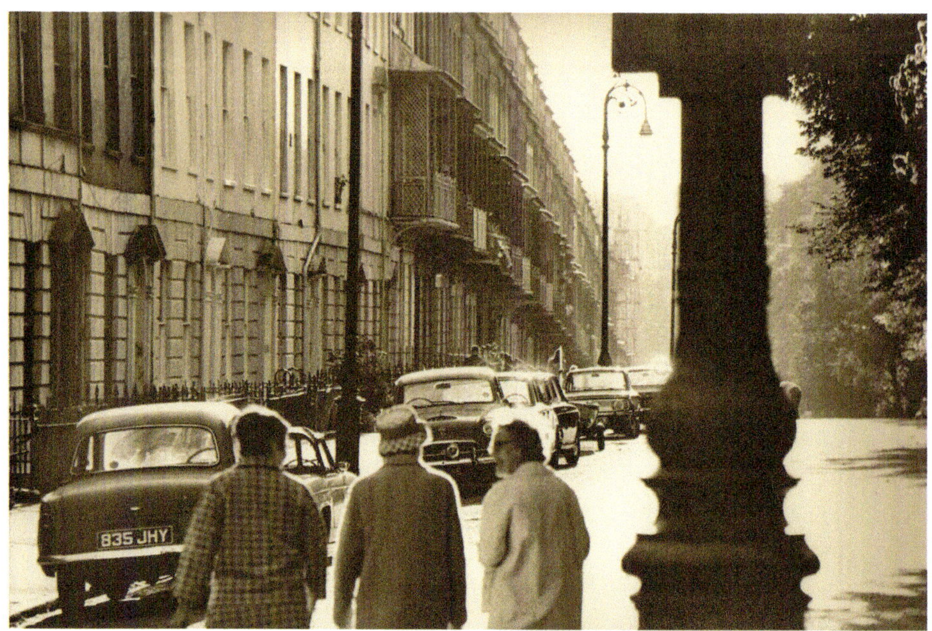

Caledonia Place, 1960s

The 1960s image shows some venerable ladies of Clifton walking down the terrace towards the Avon Gorge Hotel. Caledonia Place and its sister West Mall, which runs parallel across the central gardens, were built to a design by Foster & Okely in 1833–40. The bank on the corner started business as the National Provincial Bank in Mall Buildings adjoining the Clifton Club. In 1921, larger premises were needed and it moved across The Mall to the present building. Great care was taken to preserve the classical design of the building, built in 1788.

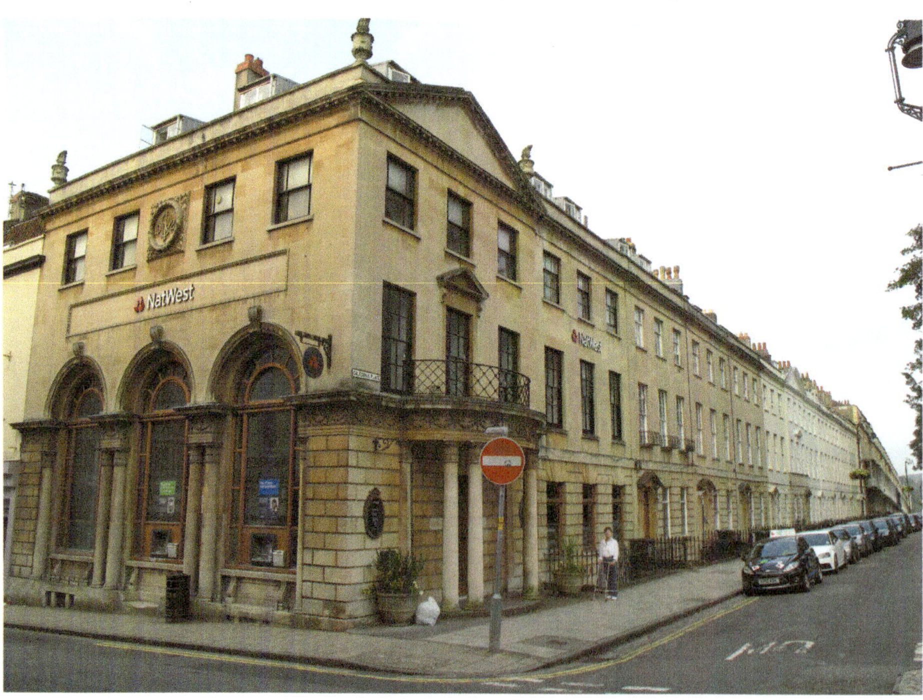

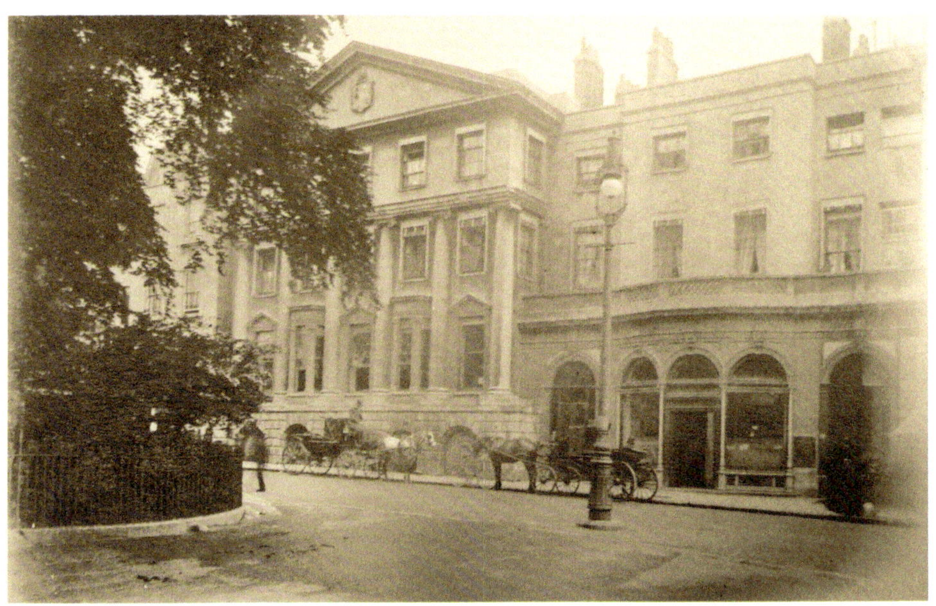

The Assembly Rooms, The Mall, Late 1800s

The frontage of this fine building at the centre of The Mall was designed by Francis Greenway in 1805. Greenway subsequently became known as the 'Father of Australian Architecture' after being convicted for fraud and forgery in a building dispute and transported. On 20 October 1830, Princess Victoria stayed in the attached Clifton Hotel (now gone) with her mother when being 'shown off' to her future subjects. The Clifton Club (an exclusive gentleman's club) was founded in 1818 and moved into these premises in the 1850s.

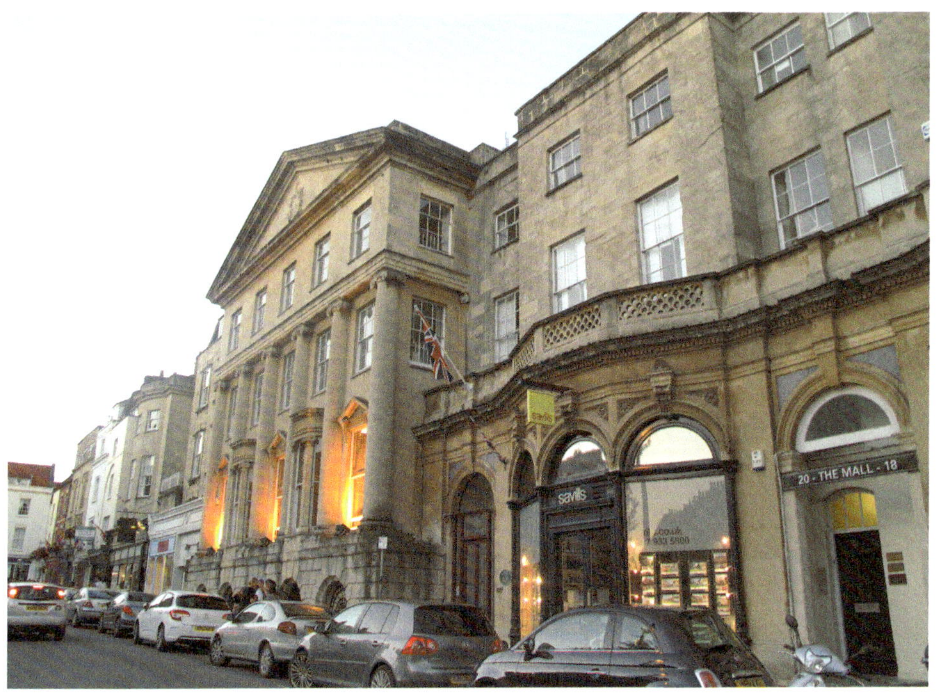

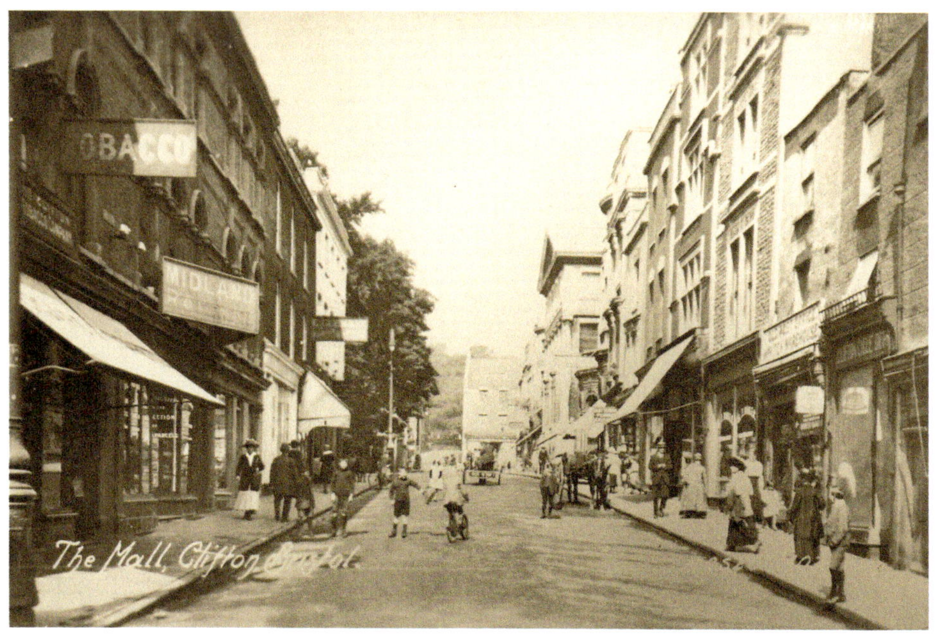

Princess Victoria Street

Looking up The Mall, it appears not much has changed, but although the older picture appears as busy as its modern counterpart this is partly because today the road is part of a one-way system. Halfway up on the right-hand side is the Assembly Rooms and further up on the left, on the corner with West Mall, was an 'old-school' pharmacist (now, inevitably, an estate agents).

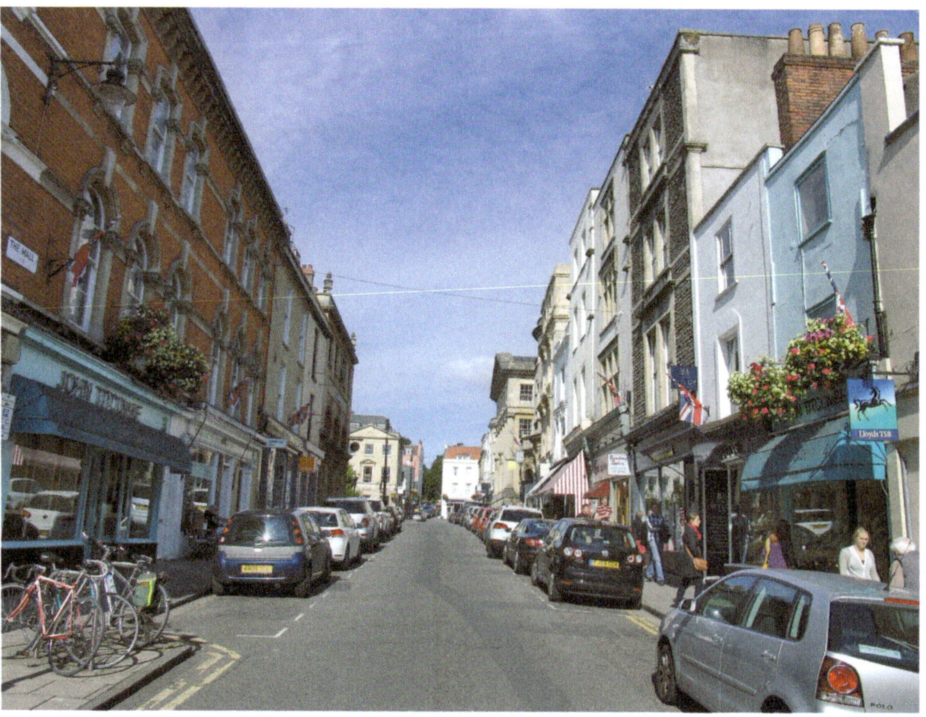

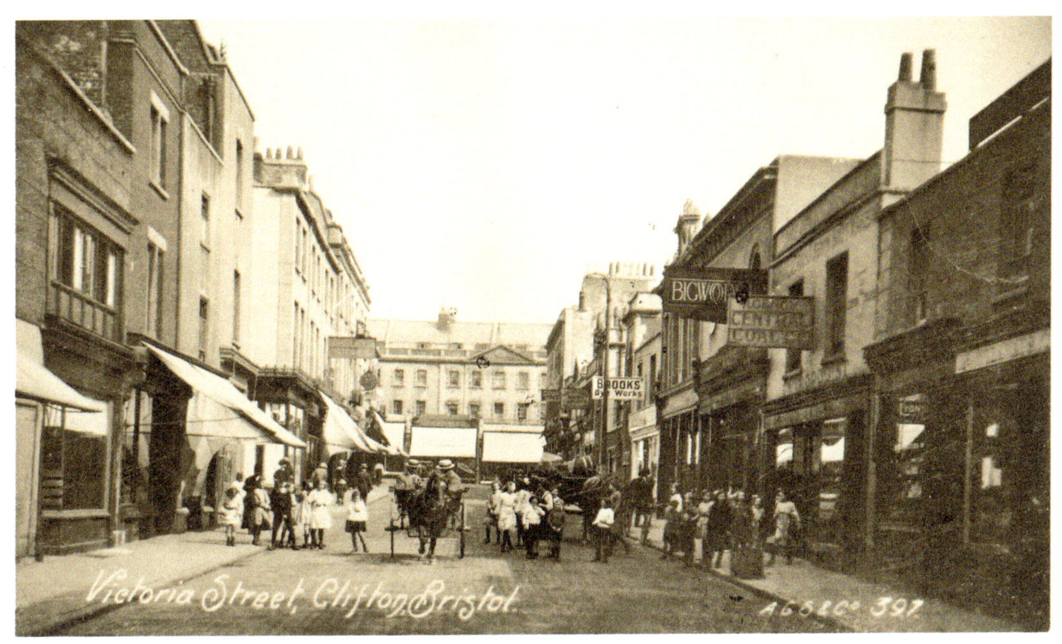

Princess Victoria Street, 1920s

Originally called Nelson Buildings, it was renamed in honour of Queen Victoria. The 1900s photograph shows a street with small shops, which it still is, but many have changed from selling domestic to luxury goods. The terrace of houses across the top of the street is Boyce's Buildings, built by William Boyce in 1793. This was the first terrace in Clifton, providing accommodation for visitors to the spa. There was a formal garden in front, with stabling behind.

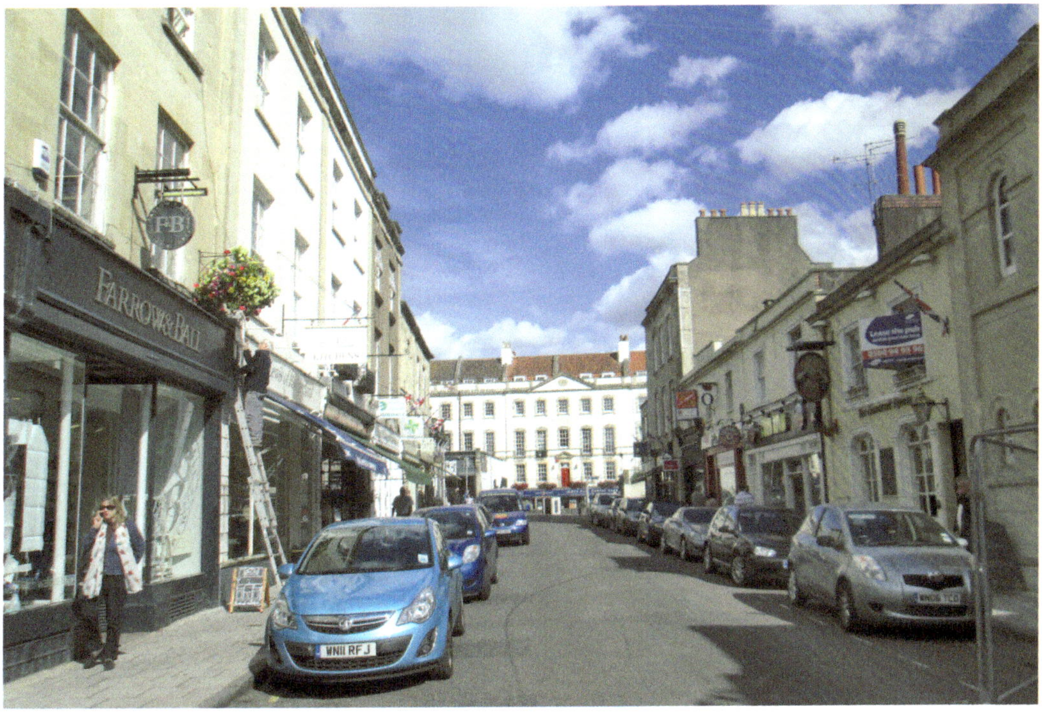

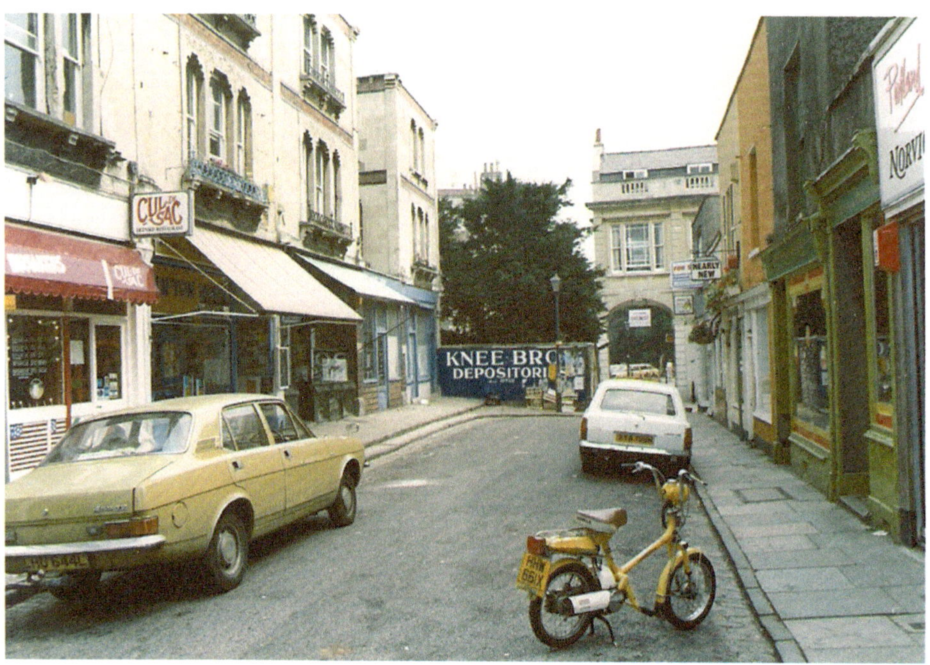

Boyce's Avenue, 1970s

Nearly forty years divide these two photographs, and the changes in this small street neatly sum up how Clifton has altered since the 1970s. Only the greengrocer remains; the butcher, baker and grocer shops have long since lost the battle with metro supermarkets. There are five new cafés and since it was pedestrianised in 2011, they have spread into the road. It has become a more sociable place, but at the cost of local shopkeepers.

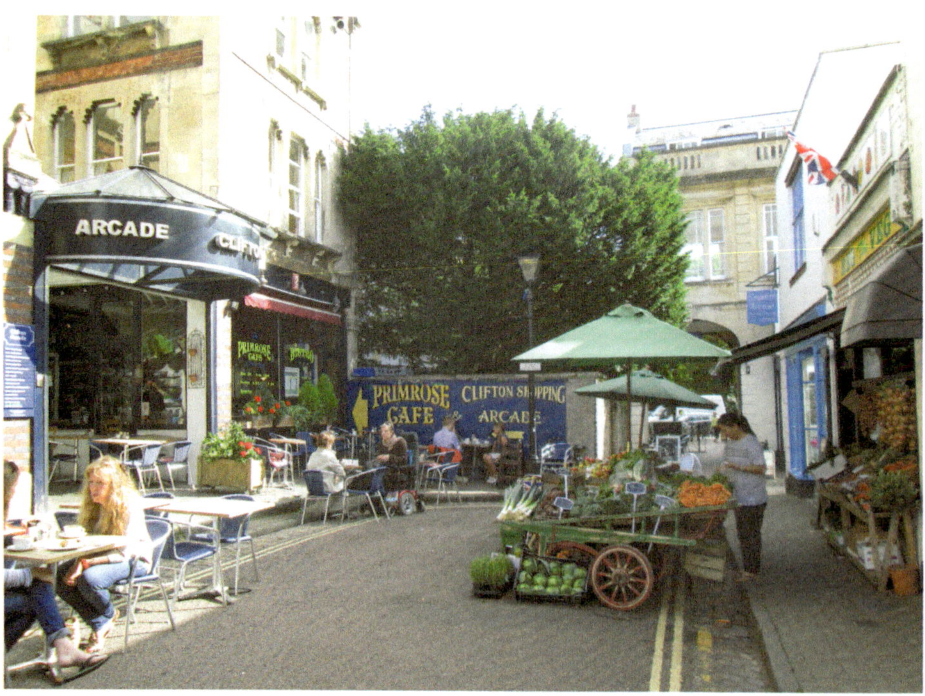

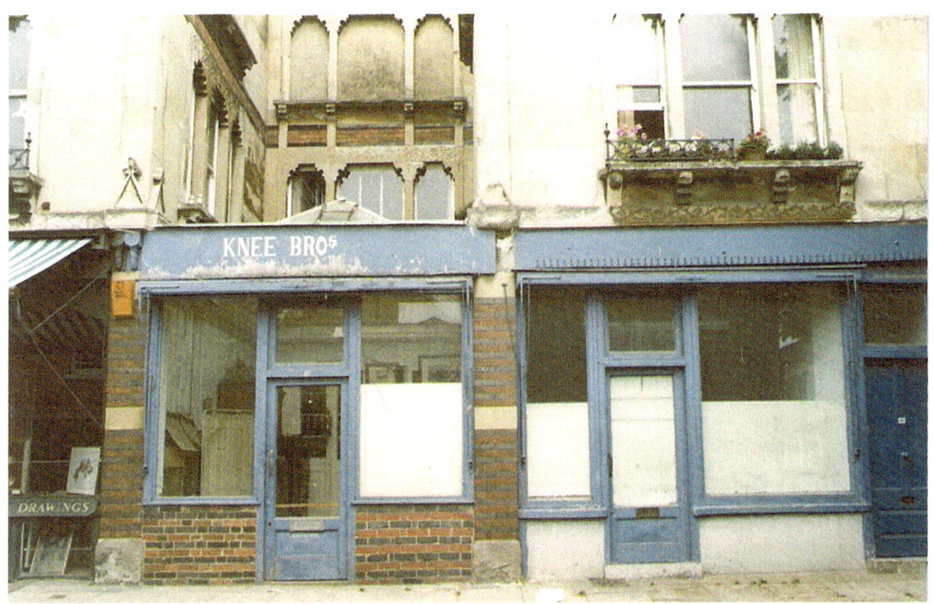

The Clifton Arcade, Boyce's Avenue, 1970s

The pictures clearly show the change since the 1970s. The arcade, originally known as King's Clifton Bazaar and Winter Garden, opened in 1878. It was an ambitious exotic extravaganza, with a stuffed tiger gazing through tropical plants. It was also an instant flop. In 1880, Knee Brothers bought the property as a furniture warehouse. Following the death of Edward Knee in 1985, the whole arcade was found to be unsafe, having largely been untouched since its original construction. Moorpoint Ltd acquired the arcade and undertook the restoration of those parts of the building that could be saved. By 1998, the Clifton Arcade was finally opened the way Joseph King had envisioned (minus the tiger).

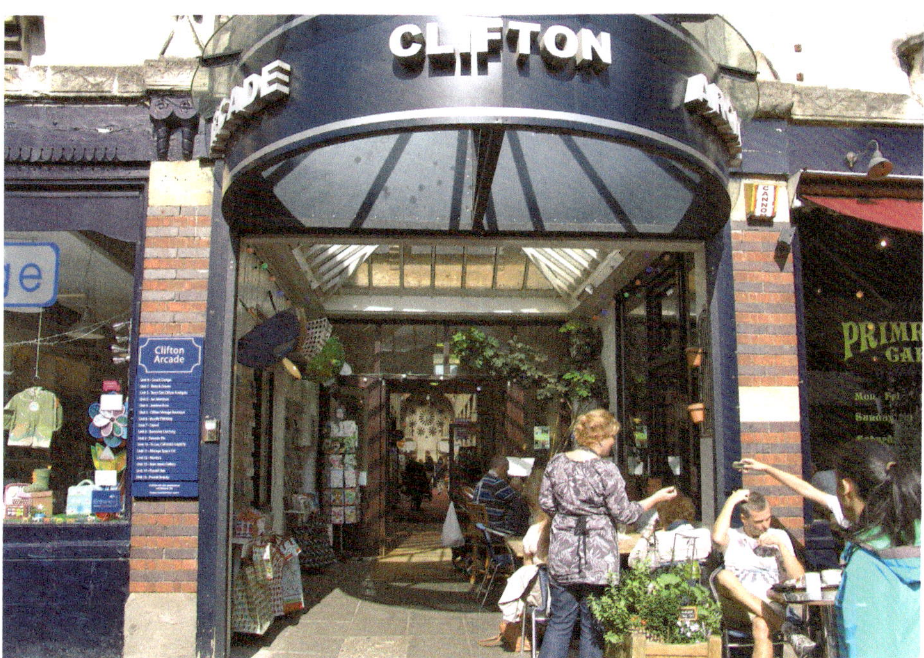

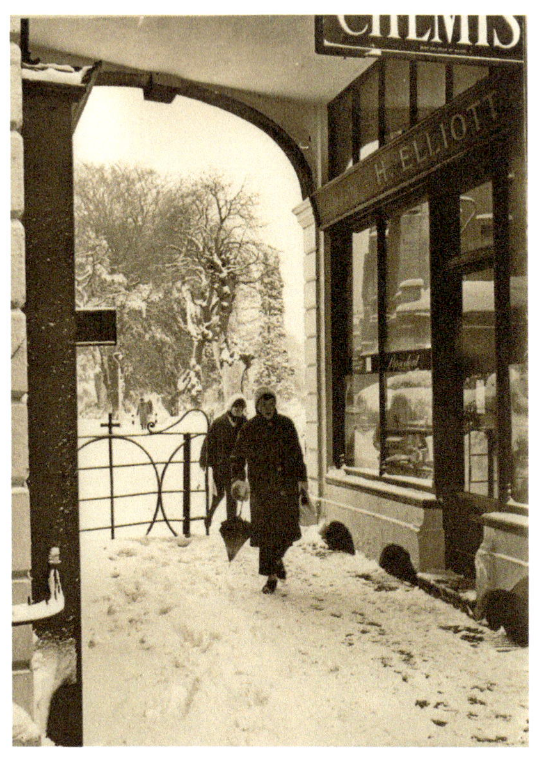

The Archway, Boyce's Avenue, 1960s

A cantankerous man, William Mathias (nephew of Thomas Boyce), owned the properties either side of the pathway that ran through Victoria Square to Boyce's Avenue. In order to stop any wheeled vehicle taking this route, he built the archway in 1837 and put in a gate. The present gate (see old photograph) is from one of the sheep pens that were on the Downs. The carved head in the centre of the arch is the same as the portrait used on the world's first adhesive postage stamp – the penny black.

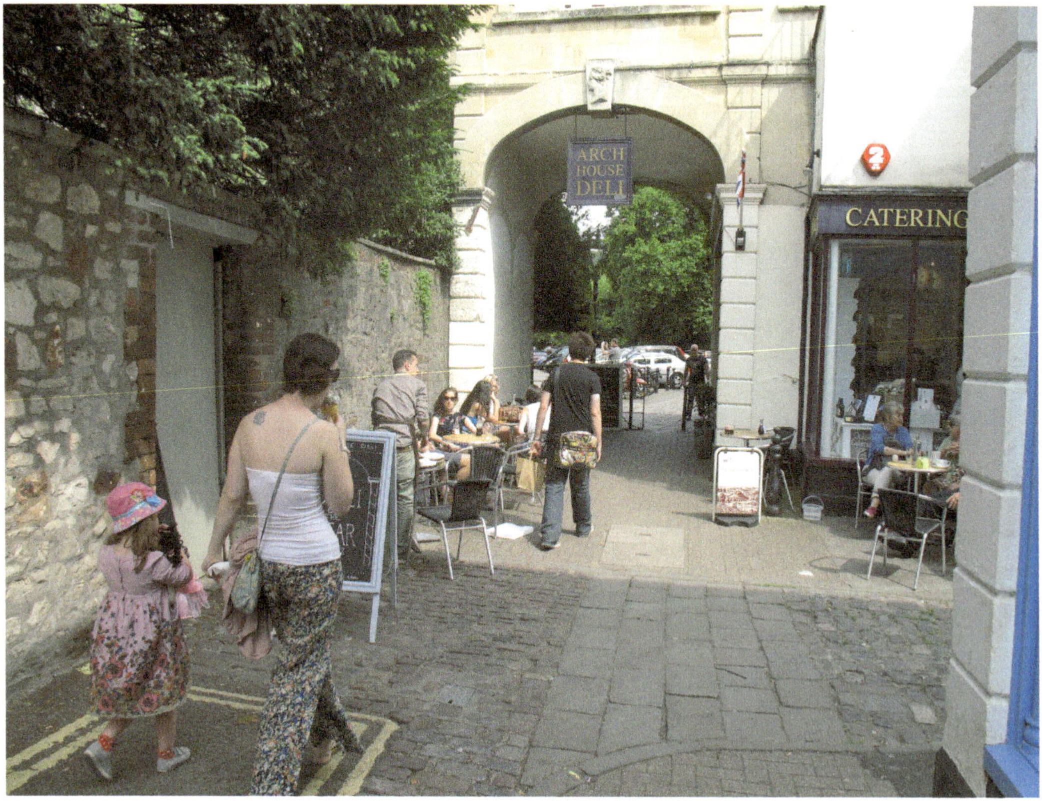

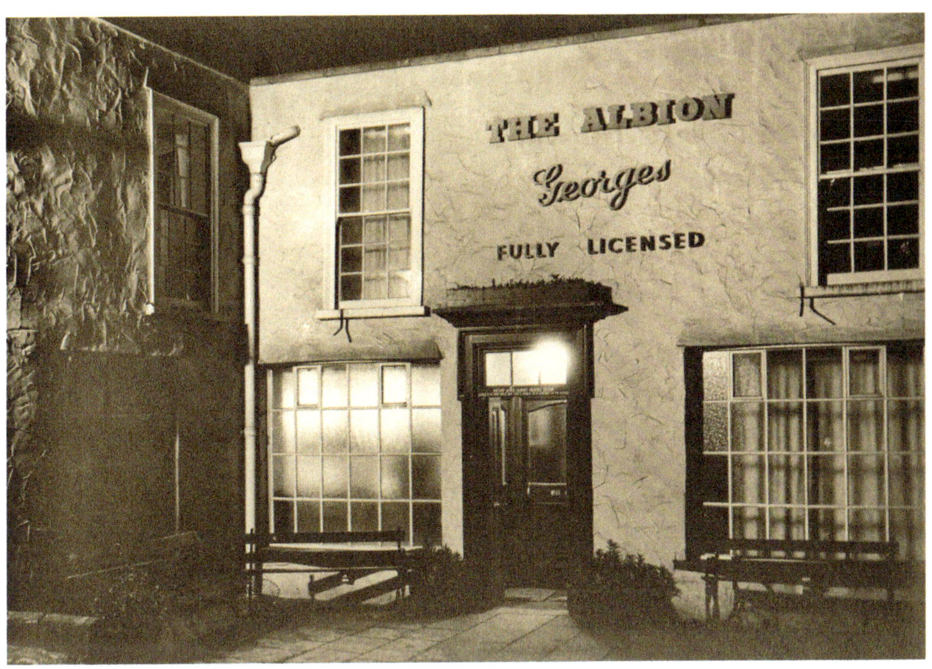

The Albion, Boyce's Avenue, 1960s

Tucked away down a short, cobbled lane at the end of Boyce's Avenue is one of Clifton's many popular public houses, the Albion. It is a late eighteenth-century inn and was probably built at the same time as the nearby Boyce's Buildings. The 1960s picture captures its snug appeal on a winter's evening, while James, a local resident, entertains passers-by with his harmonica-playing on a recent sunny day.

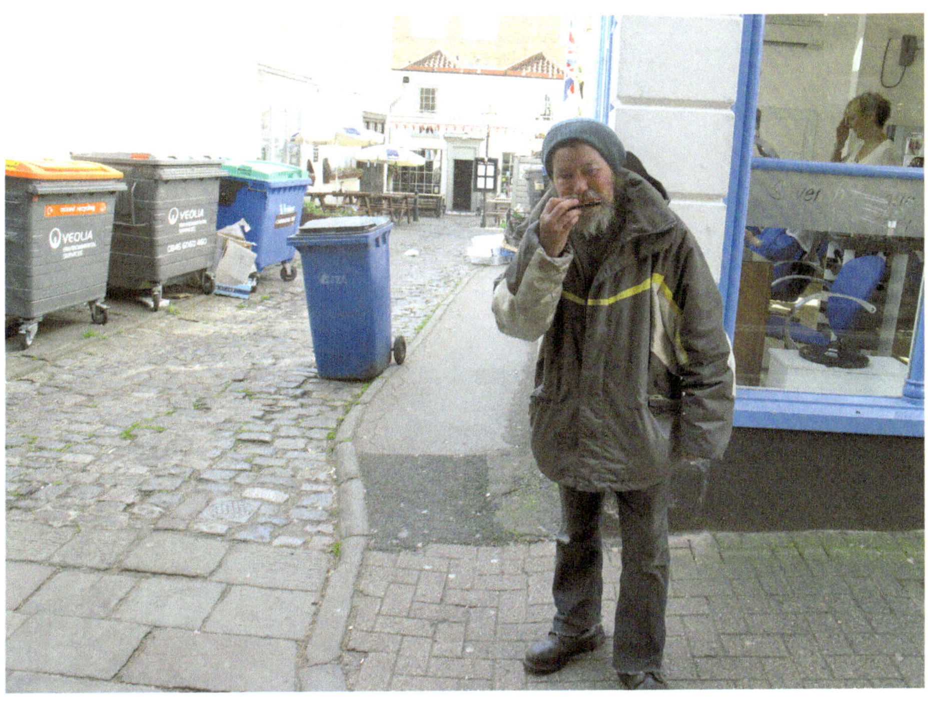

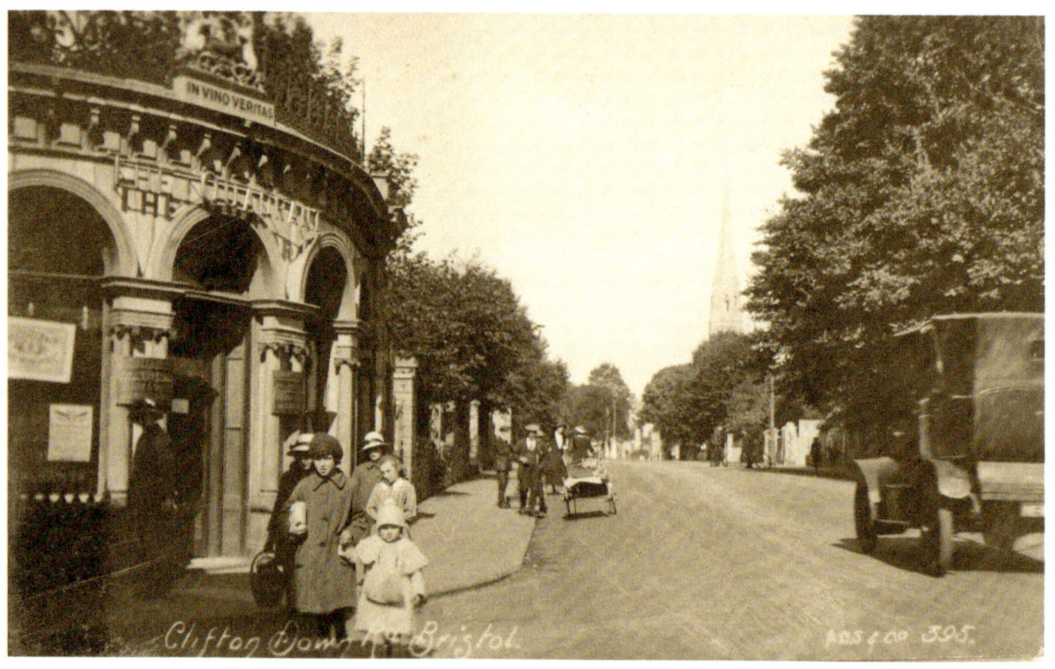

Clifton Down Road, 1940s

The Quadrant on the left is another well-known local pub, sitting on the corner of Princess Victoria Street and Clifton Down Road. W. H. Smith stands on a 1950s building infill, which has 2012 planning permission for a new small shopping complex. In the distance is the spire of Christchurch (at 212 feet it was the highest point of Bristol's skyline until a hospital chimney was built). The church was built to the designs of Charles Dyer in 1843–44 and the tower and spire were completed in 1859.

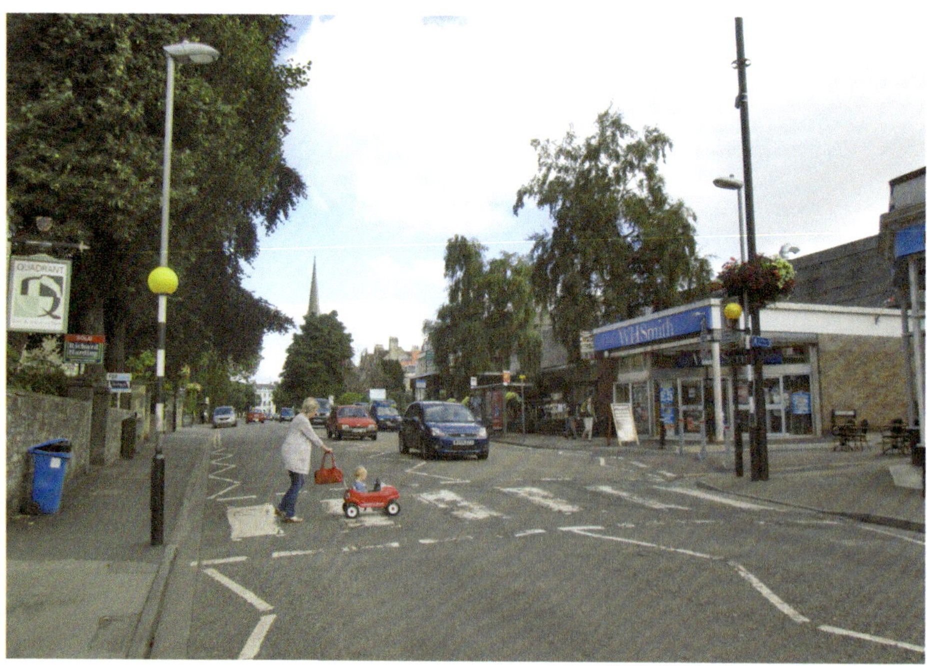

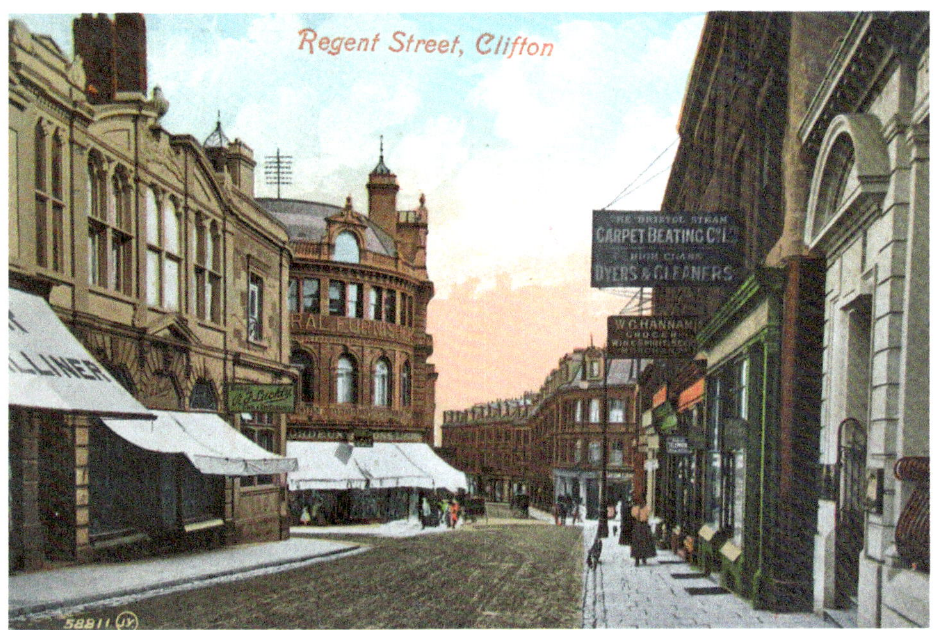

Regent Street, 24 November 1909

Regent Street was the main Victorian shopping street in Clifton. John Cordeux & Sons (bottom left of the above photograph) was one of the first large multiple stores. A special horse bus, subsequently a motor bus, carried customers from the Victoria Rooms to Cordeux (Clifton village never had trams). In 1928 the store became Bobbys. This corner was badly blitzed and all the shop buildings are now offices or flats. Today, a supermarket and coffee shops cater for university students (there are three halls of residence about 300 metres away).

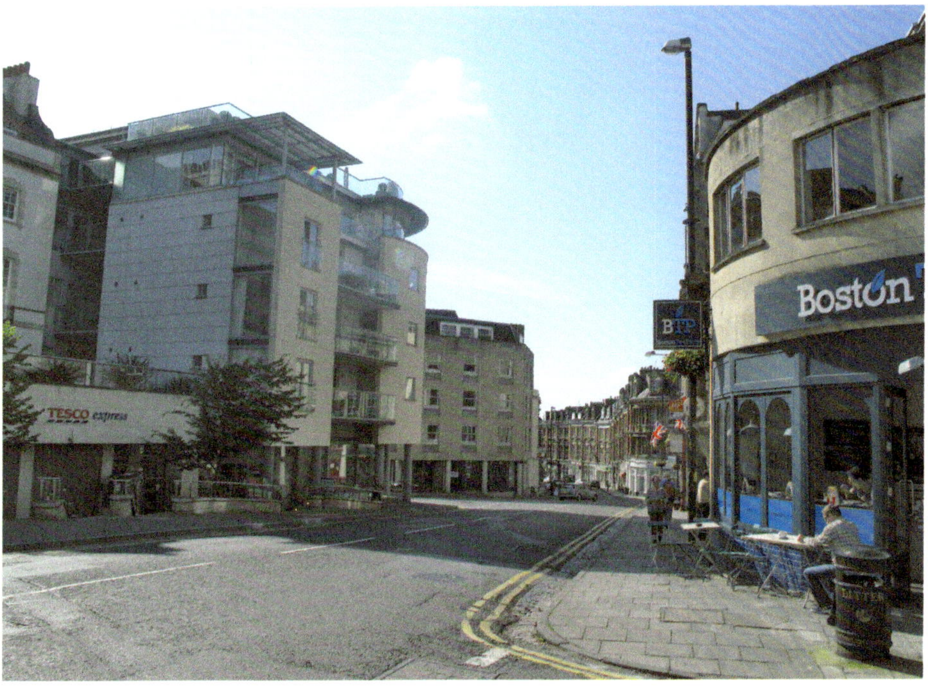

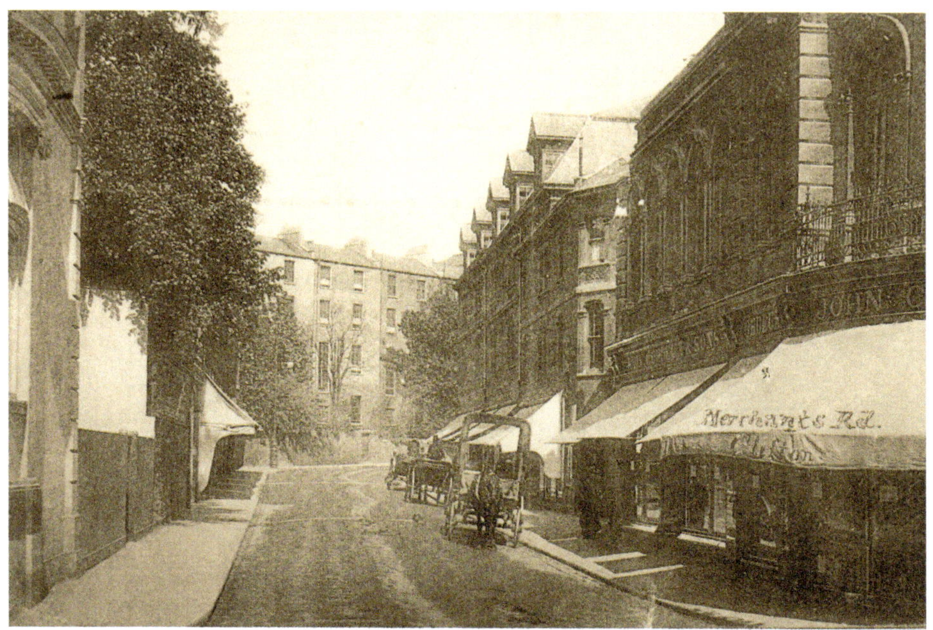

Merchants Road, 18 June 1904

In the 1860s, the Merchant Venturers were persuaded to have a road put through their land so that there was a direct route from the Victoria Rooms to Clifton. The area of these photographs suffered severe bomb damage. For many years there were shops on both sides of the road, then Hartwells Garage moved in and built a link bridge over the road. Now, apart from the first buildings on either side, this whole stretch is residential.

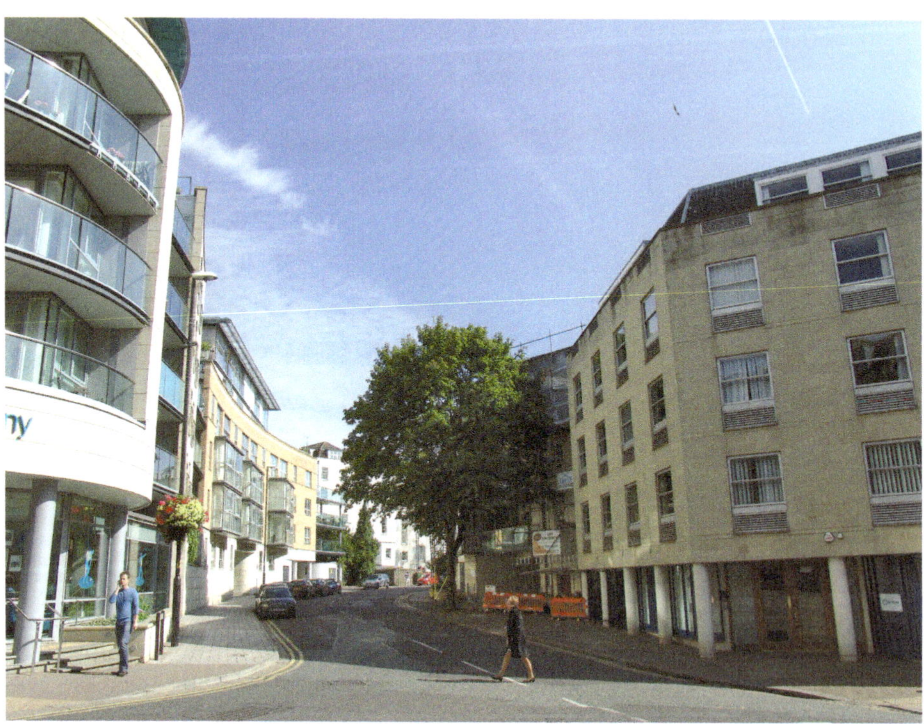

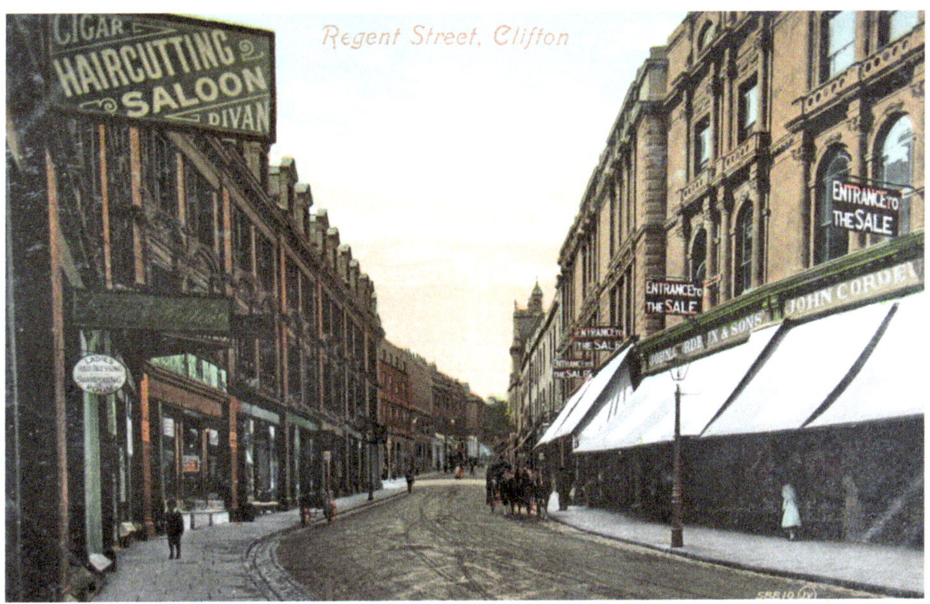

Regent Street, 1900s

Another part of the Cordeux empire is seen on the right. Later there was a large salerooms (Cowlins), which adapted to the changing times: in the second half of the twentieth century, many of the terraced and large houses were being divided into independent flats so furniture had to be disposed of. At the same time, the owners of new flats needed furniture. In the 1990s it was transformed into Pizza Express. This part of the street remains mainly utilitarian, still with hairdressers, a hardware shop and a pharmacist, interspersed with restaurants.

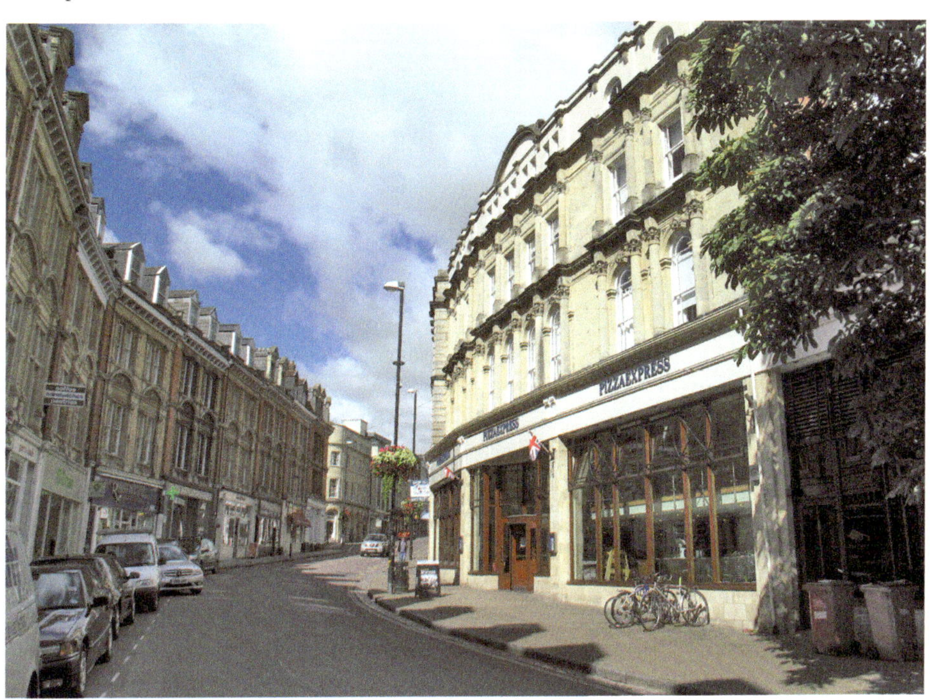

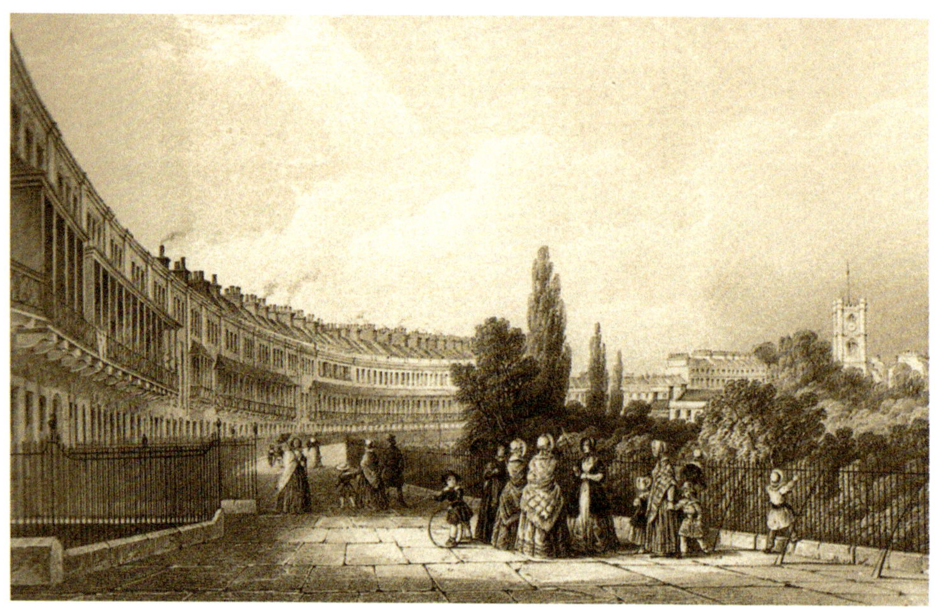

Royal York Crescent, 1800s

Reputed to be Europe's longest terrace, Royal York Crescent stands as a rival to Bath's Royal Crescent. Construction of the Georgian terrace over gardens and orchards began in 1791, and was eventually completed in 1820. This prolonged building period was a result of Clifton's property boom of the late eighteenth century coming to an ignominious end following the decline of the Hotwells spa and the prolonged Napoleonic Wars. Many houses were left derelict shells by bankrupt builders.

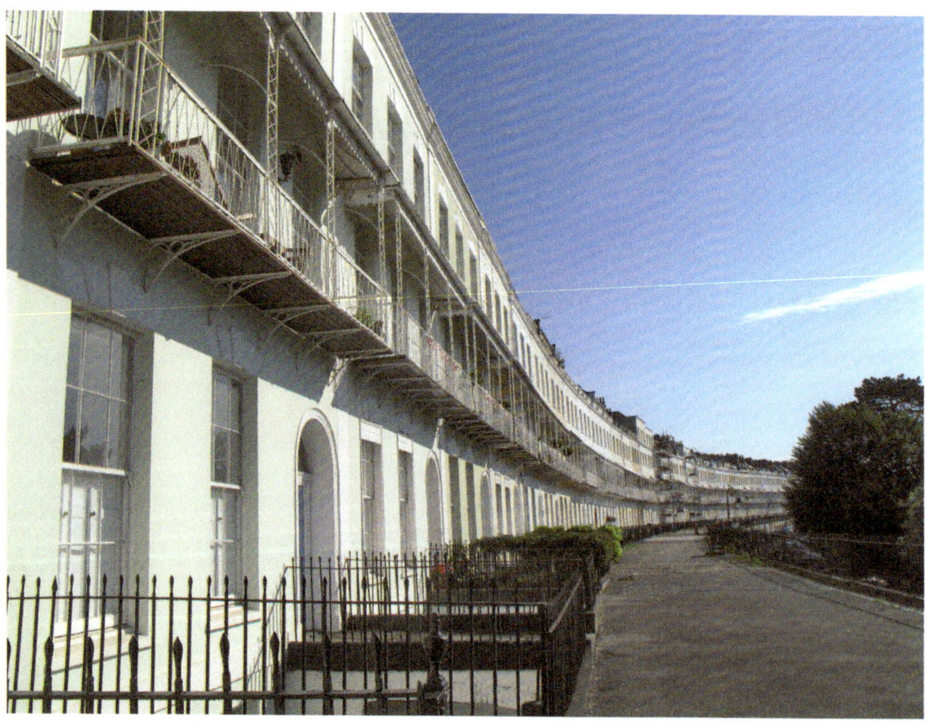

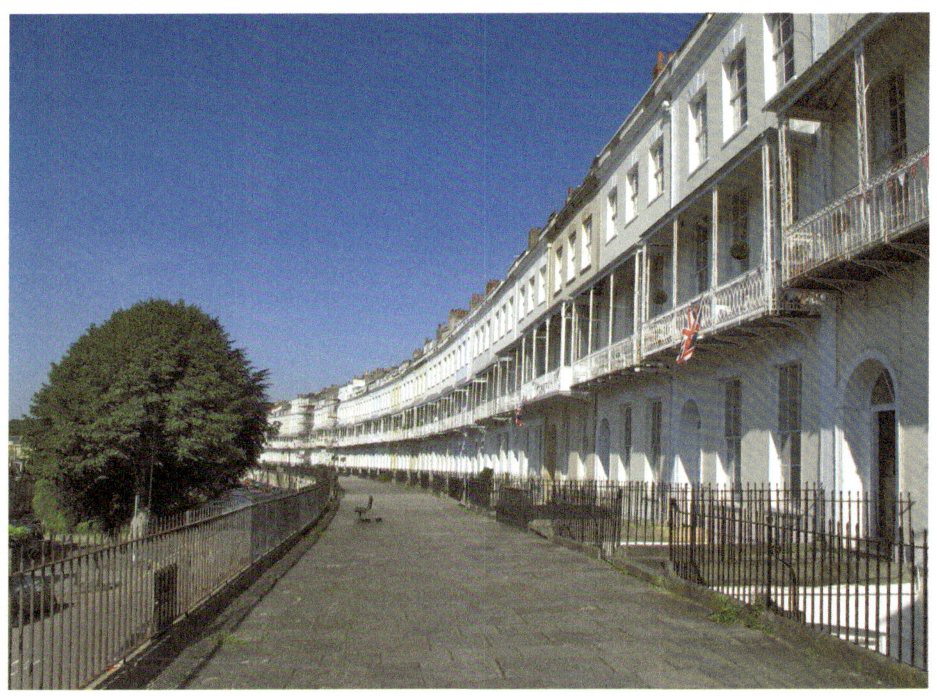

Both photographs show the magnificent sweep of the terrace just as it would have appeared once it had finally been completed. What has changed significantly are the occupants. A random look at six houses in the 1881 census showed that three were owner-occupied and three had two households. Today, most of the forty-six houses contain at least four households. During the 1950s and 1960s, many of these properties were student lodgings. As seen in this 1960s photograph, it was bordering on the shabby – a very different state of affairs to today.

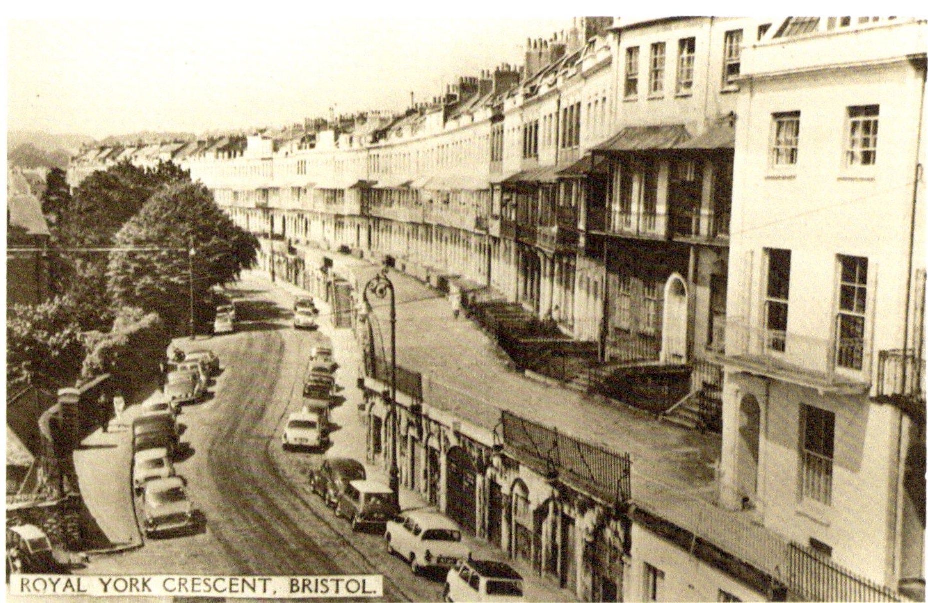

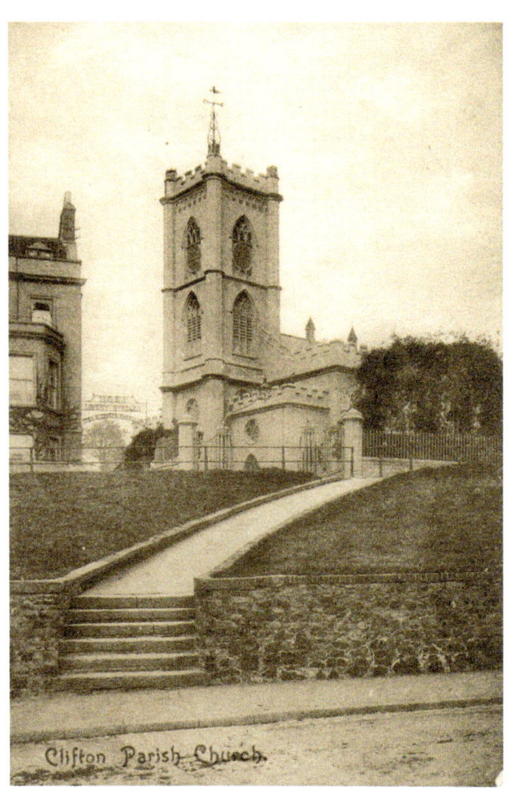

St Andrew's Church, 1800s

The old photograph shows the second parish church of St Andrew's in the nineteenth century. A twelfth-century church served the riverside community of Hotwells and the medieval hamlet of Clifton. As the population grew, the church had to be enlarged. Thus, in 1822, an even larger church was consecrated beside the small one, which was eventually pulled down. This in turn fell victim to German bombing on 24 November 1940. The path in the foreground is the old track up from Hotwells, which continues on down Lime Tree Walk.

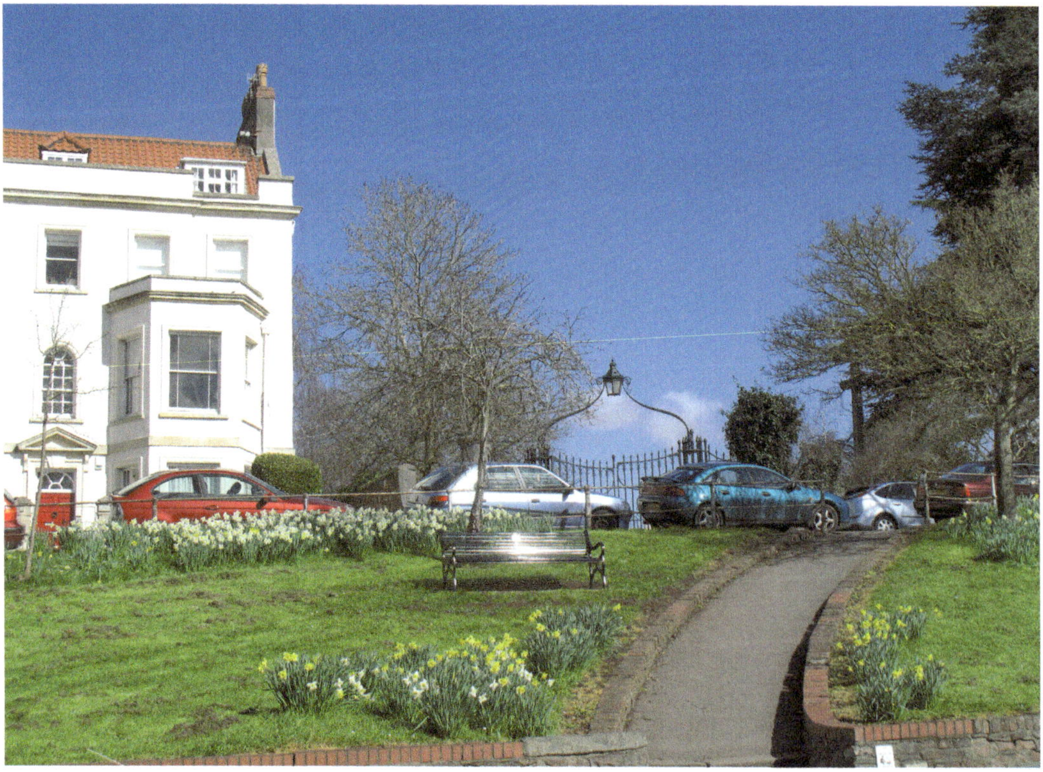

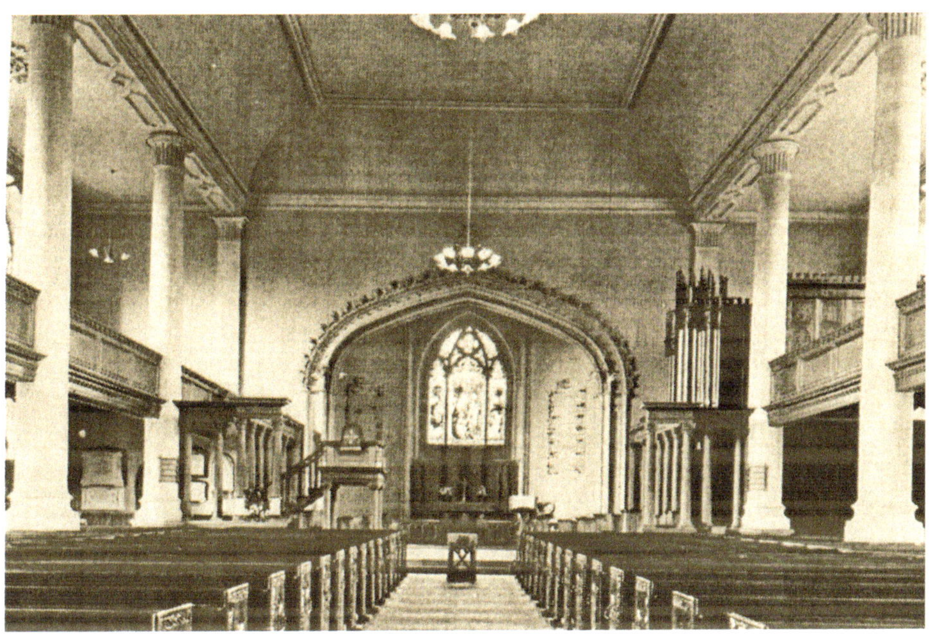

On 28 September 1954 the local press reported the demolition of the bombed shell of St Andrew's church. It said, 'When the final dust has cleared and the rubble emptied into the crypt to fill it, the remaining space will be laid out as a garden of rest.' The grass area is used mostly by children and sunbathers, both probably unaware of what lies beneath their feet. The house at the back is Bishop's House. It was designed by Isaac Ware and built in 1747, and until recently was the residence of the Anglican Bishop of Bristol.

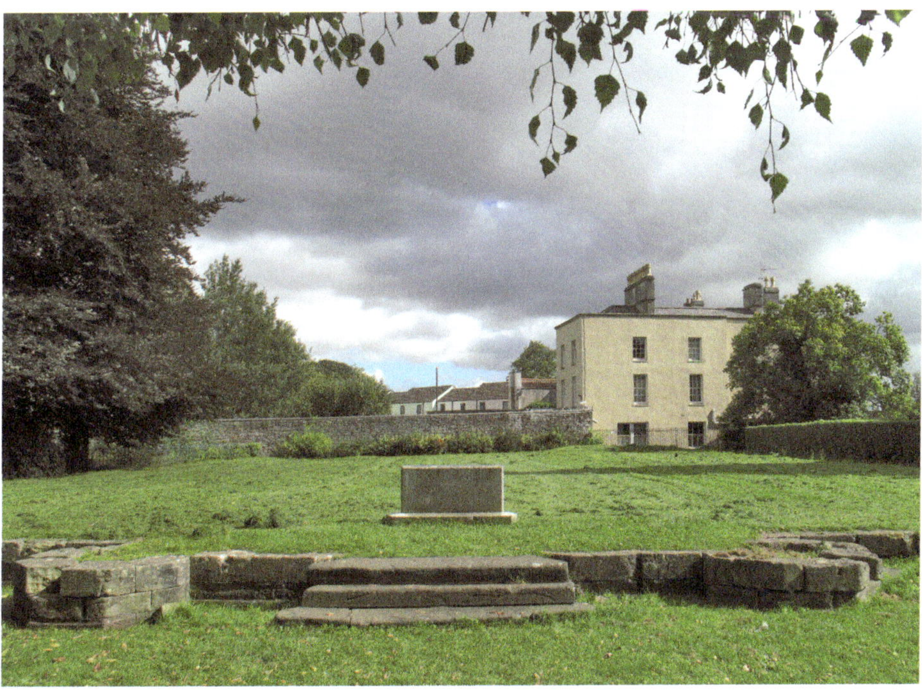

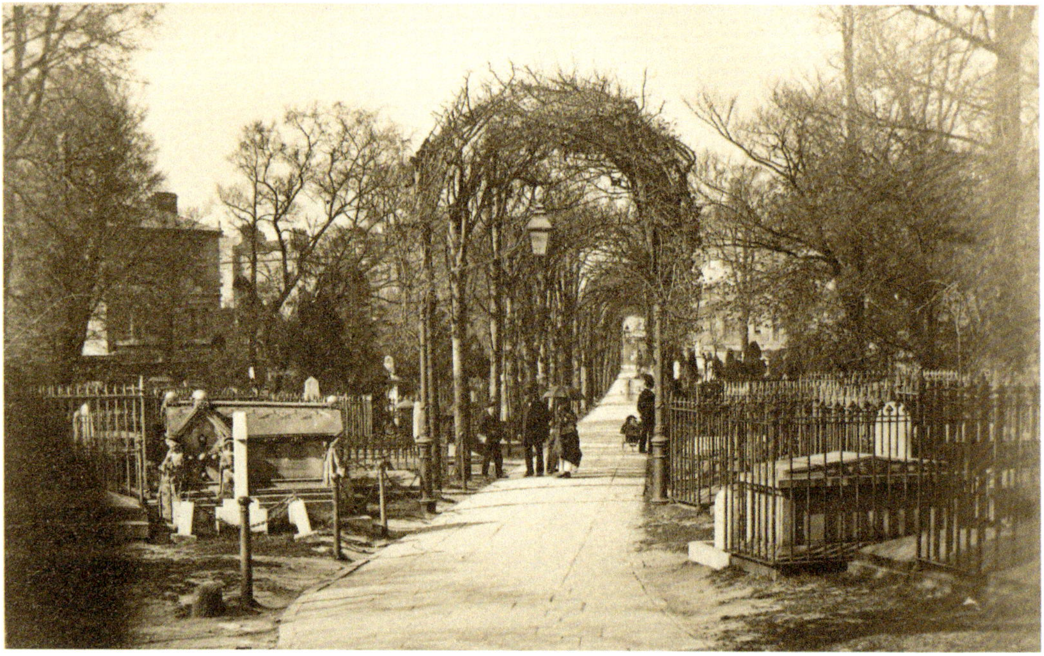

Lime Tree Walk, St Andrew's Churchyard, 1900s

This much-used walkway with its pleached lime trees goes through St Andrew's churchyard. The graveyard was only used from 1830 to 1871. The epitaphs reflect mid-nineteenth-century Clifton society, from peers of the realm and bishops to soap boilers and ropemakers. At that time a gravestone was a status symbol, with the nobler clustered near to the church.

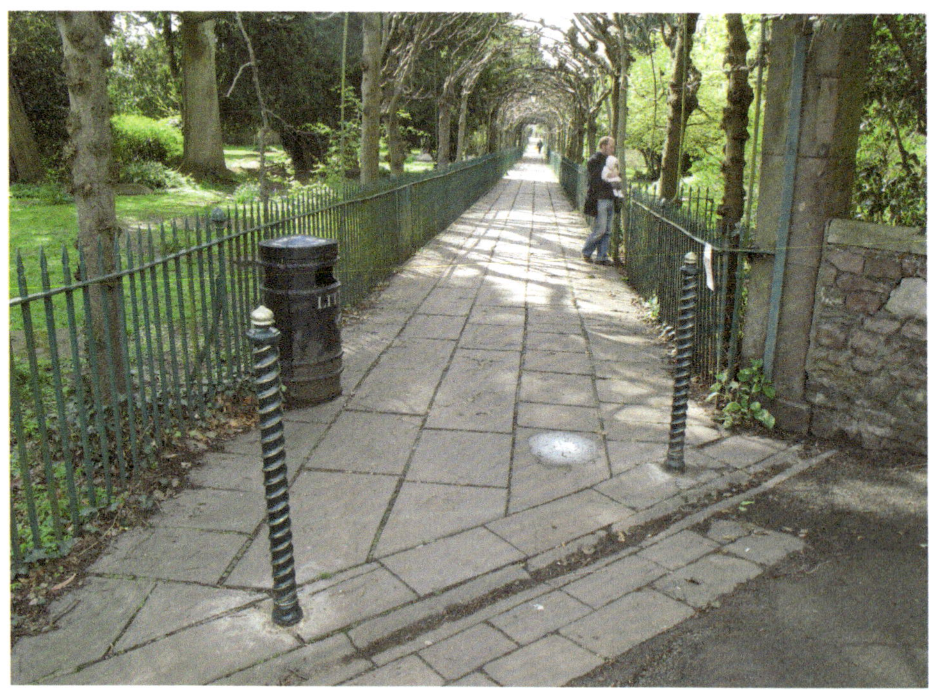

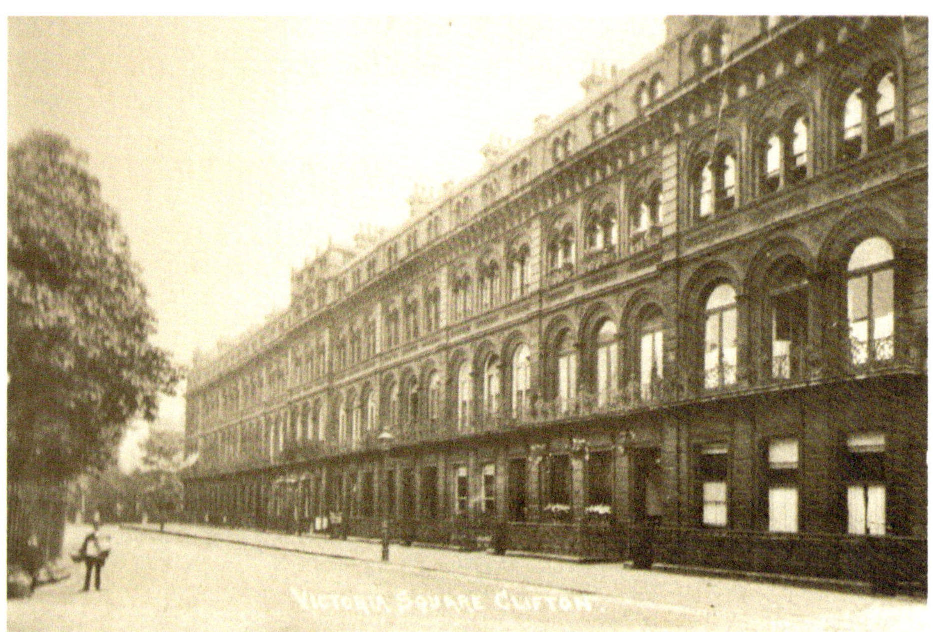

Victoria Square, 28 August 1907

Although square in shape, this is not a usual town square in that each side has individual architecture and an individual name. This north side, The Royal Promenade, was designed by James Foster & Sons in 1837 but not completed until the early 1850s. It is said that the central house (embossed with a royal coat of arms) was built with the hope that Queen Victoria would stay here if or when she visited Bristol. The epidemiologist William Budd, who proposed and proved that cholera was a waterborne disease, lived in the house facing us in Lansdown Parade.

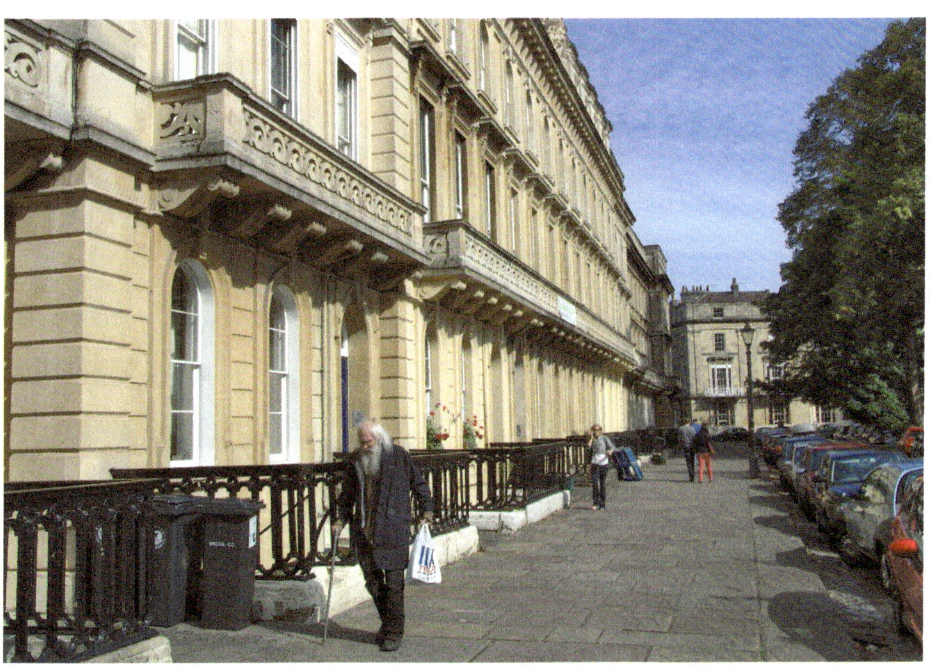

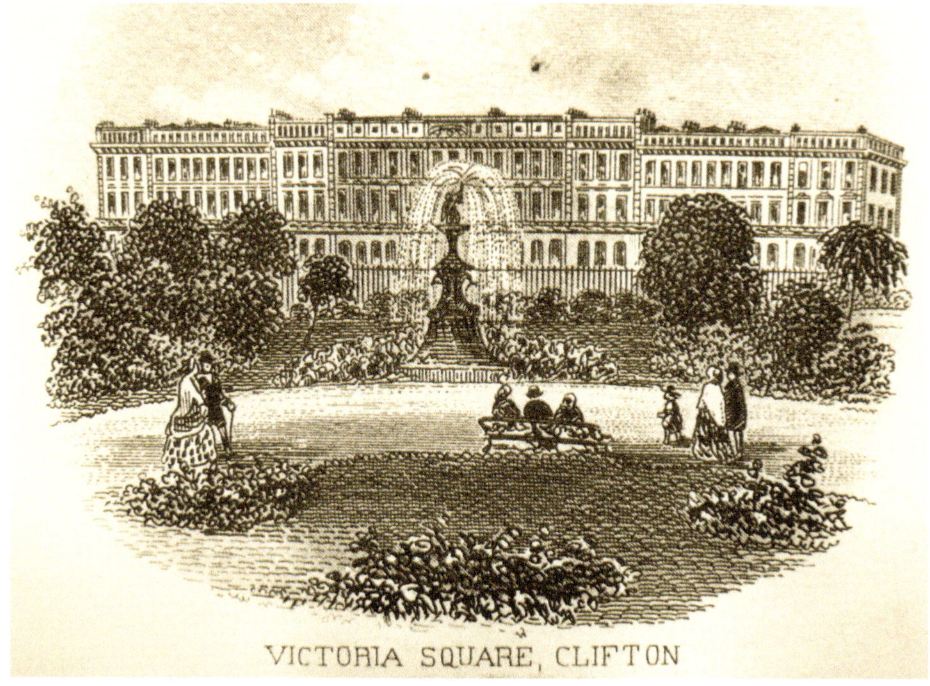

Victoria Square, 1800s

Not only would Victoria Square have looked different in the nineteenth century, it would also have sounded different – people placed their caged birds out to air along the central path that bisects the Square (originally called Birdcage Walk), whistles were blown by nannies to call in playing children and there is no longer the relaxing sound of a fountain to drown out the sound of cars and buses.

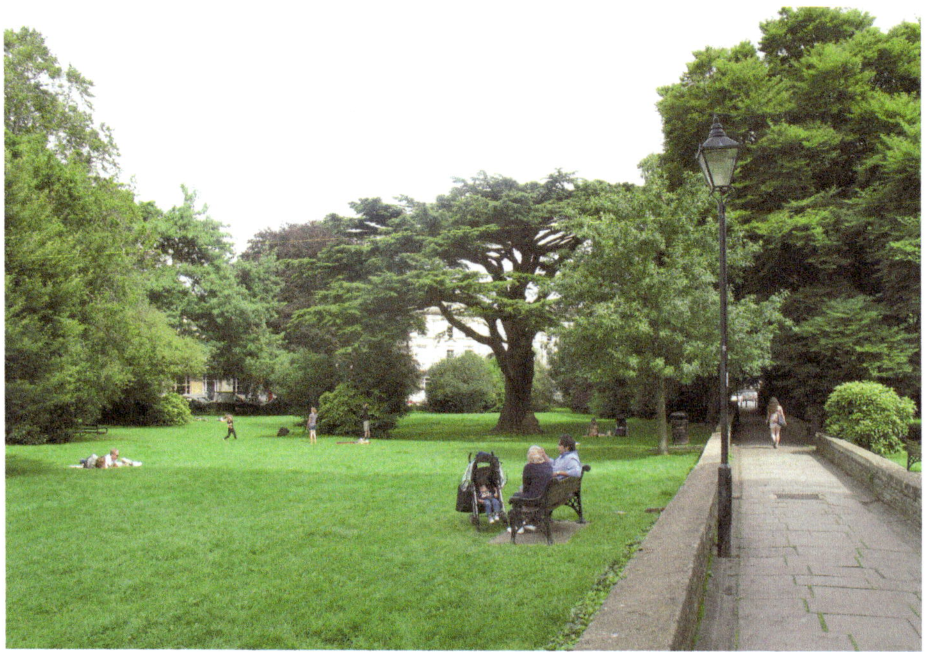

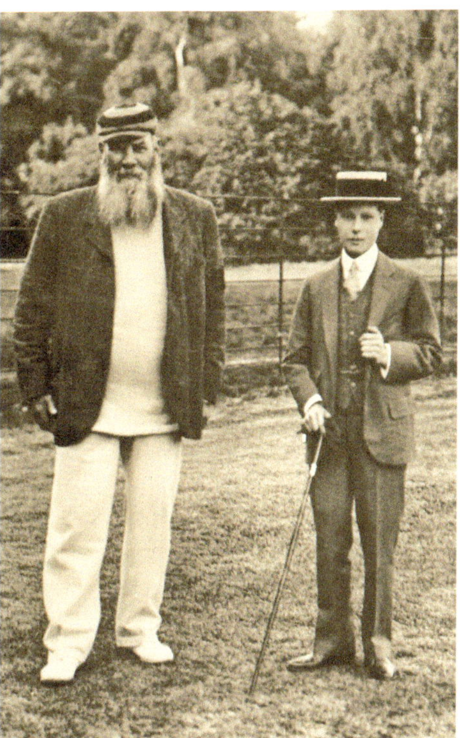

W. G. Grace, with HRH the Prince of Wales, early 1900s

Better known as possibly England's finest cricketer, rather than for his services to medicine, Dr William Gilbert Grace was born in 1848 in the Bristol suburb of Downend. He joined Gloucestershire County Cricket Club at fifteen and went on to play for England on twenty-two occasions. W. G. Grace's career tally included 126 centuries, 54,896 runs and nearly 3,000 wickets. He lived in Victoria Square in 1894–96.

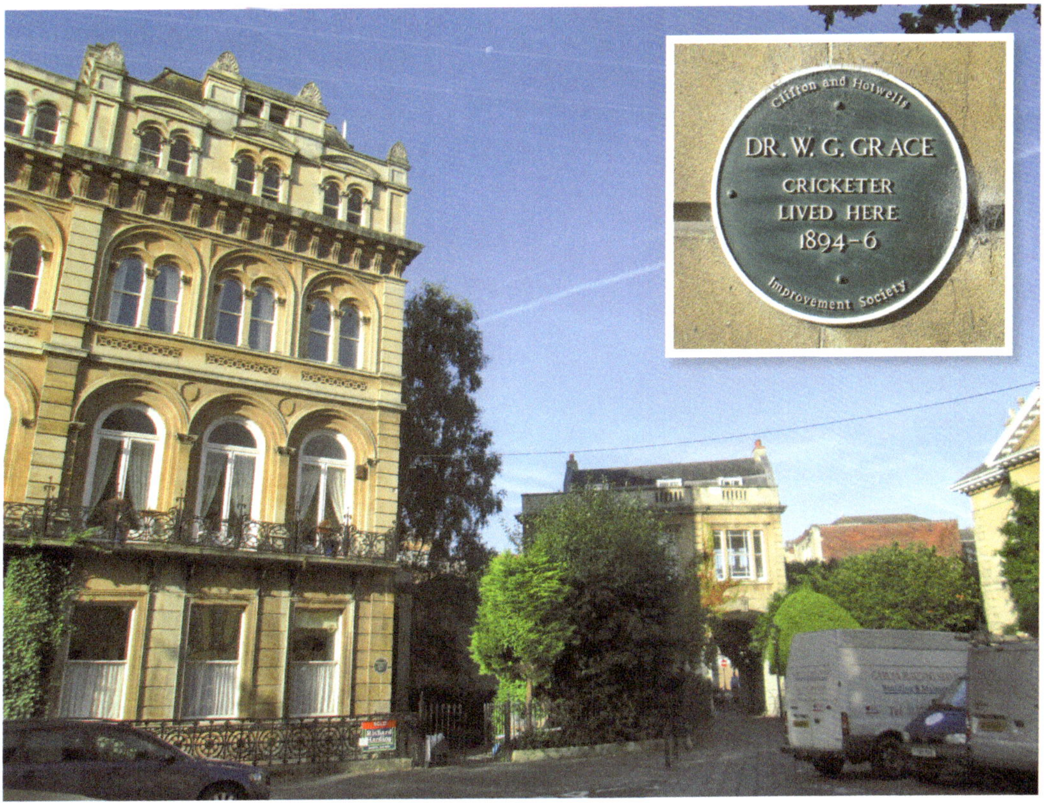

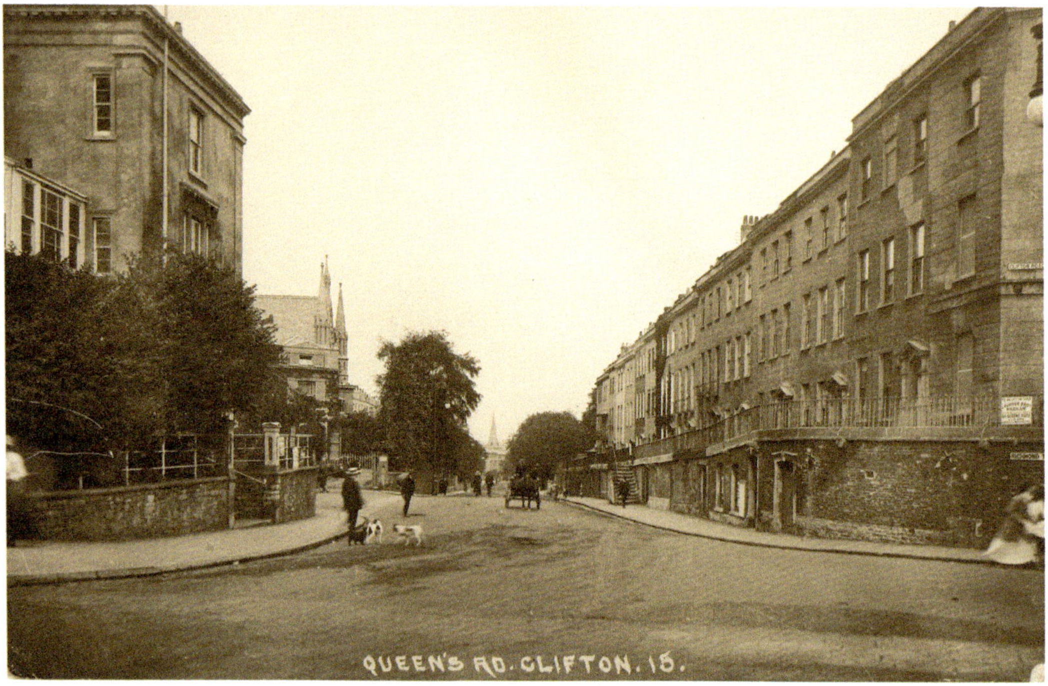

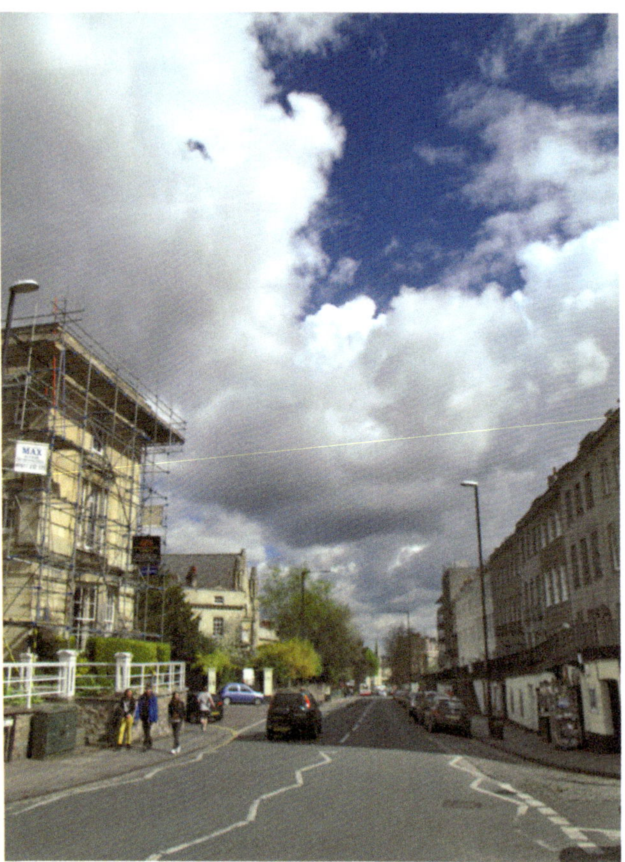

Queen's Road

The view is looking south-east down the top end of Queen's Road. On the right is Richmond Terrace, built around 1790, probably by William Paty. The space under the raised pavement which previously provided entry to the basements of the houses has now been turned into shops and a bar. Beyond this can be seen the University of Bristol Students' Building (now called Queen's Road Building). Built by Alec French & Partners and completed in 1965, it is currently undergoing a much-needed refurbishment. Facing it on the left is Buckingham Baptist Chapel.

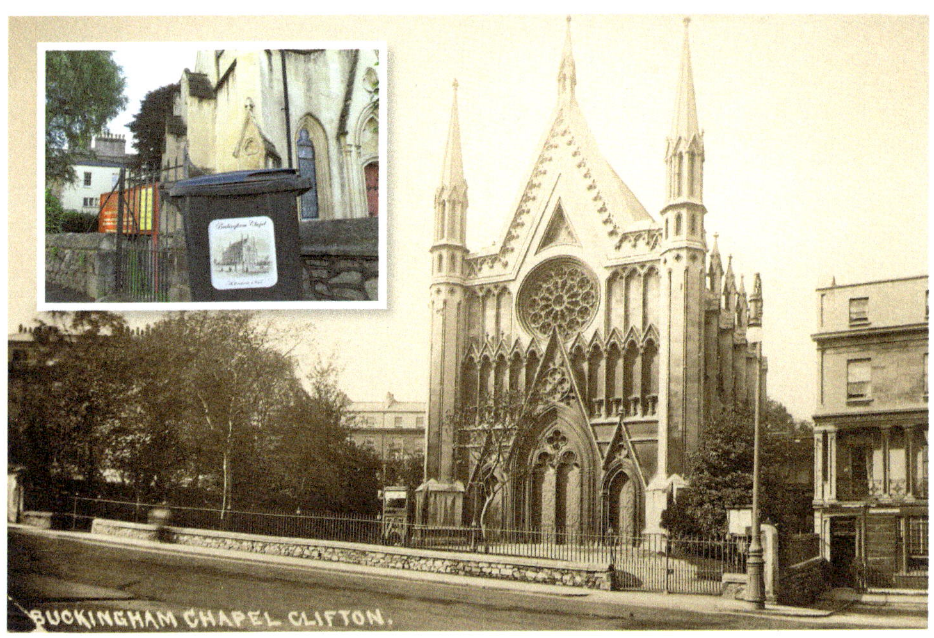

Buckingham Chapel, Queen's Road

Built in 1842 to the design of R. S. Pope, it is relatively unchanged, with just a few pinnacles missing here and there. In the 1840s, a group decided to form a Nonconformist place of worship; they felt a lack of evangelical teaching in the parish at the time and also formed the view that the Anglican church in Clifton offered little welcome to the poor. In 2010, it described itself as being 'independent evangelical baptist'. 'Independent' because, in 1972, the membership had taken the decision to leave the Baptist Union owing to a lack of clarity in the teachings on the deity of Christ. The congregation's appreciation of the history of the chapel can be seen in the picture of it attached to its wheely bin.

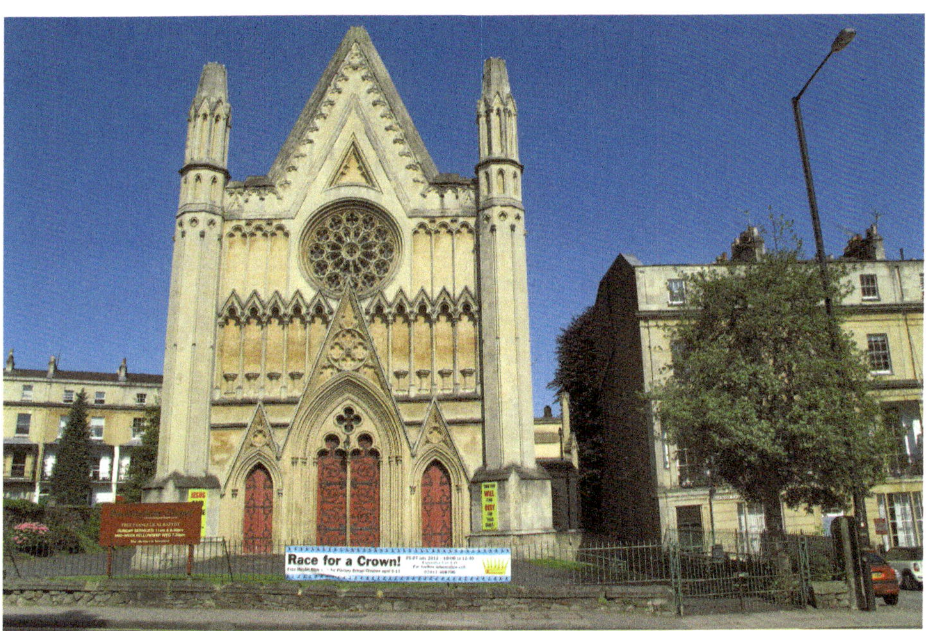

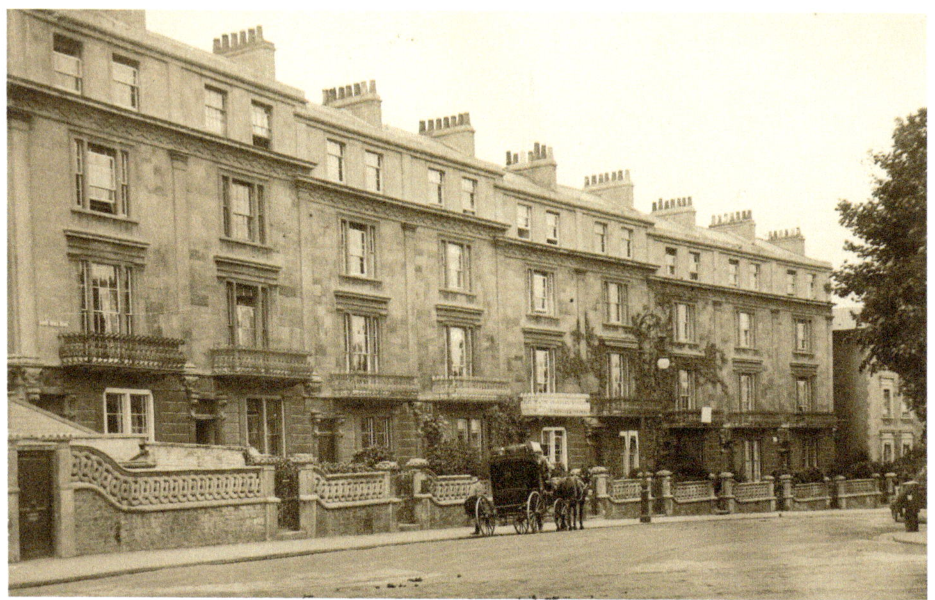

St Paul's Road, 1900s

At the top left of the 1900s photograph is the corner of the Clifton Music Club, which squats neatly between the end of Pembroke Road and St Paul's Road. Further down the road in the recent photograph can be seen the spire of St Paul's church by C. F. Hansom & Sons, replacing Manners & Gill's church of 1853, destroyed by fire in 1867. The greatest impact in the area was the building of Queen's Court in the 1930s – then a modern, prestigious block of service flats and now predominantly student accommodation.

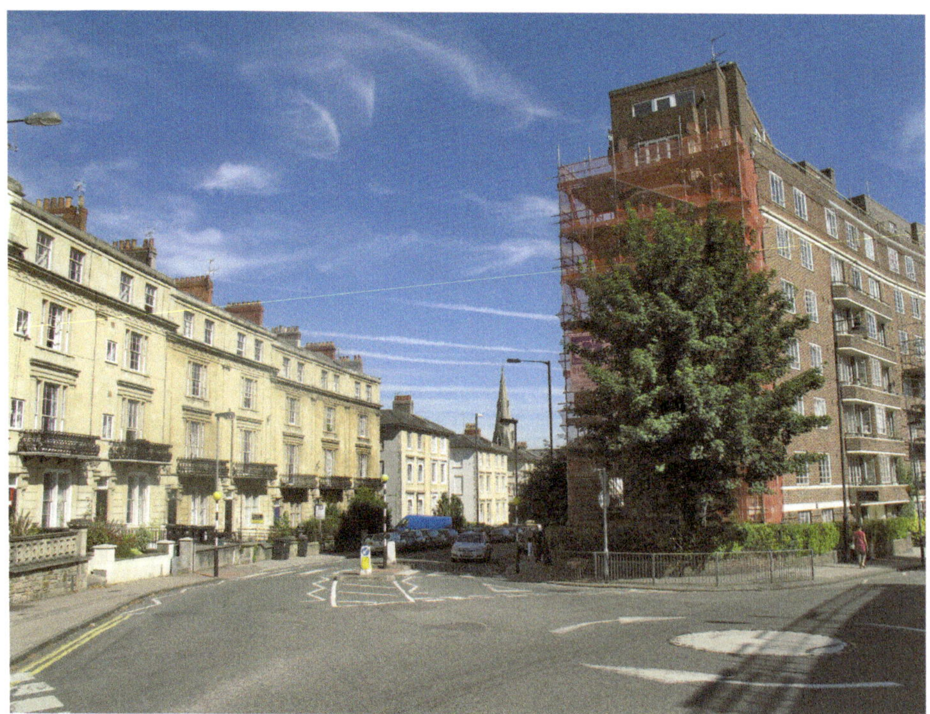

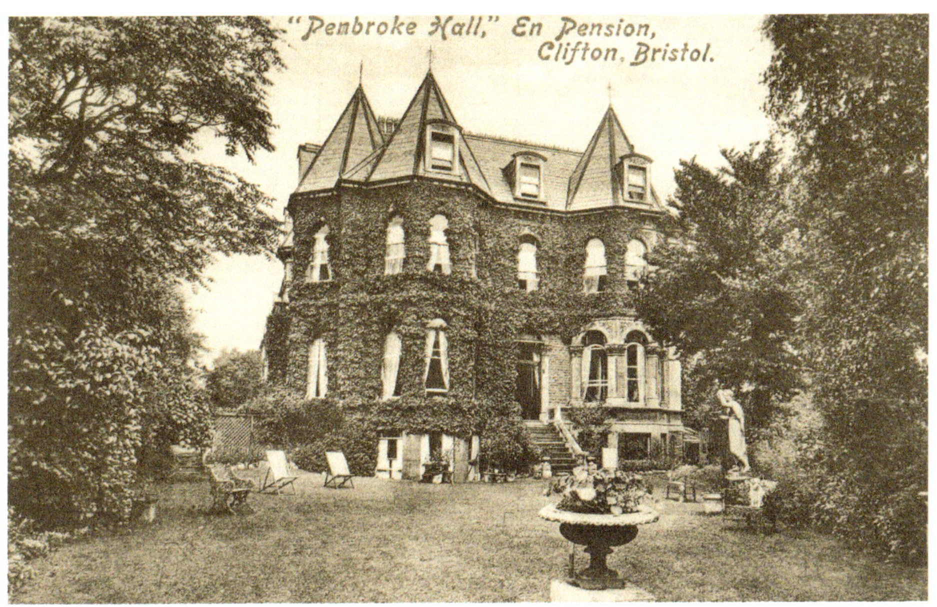

The Channings Hotel (Formerly Pembroke Hall), Pembroke Road, 1900s

The Channings is best known now for its bars and its suntrap garden, popular with students, locals and office workers alike. Rumour has it that it was built in 1879–82 by Thomas Nicholson as a potential home for one of Queen Victoria's ladies-in-waiting (evidence is hard to come by). The 1891 census records a lodge-keeper and his wife, three domestic servants, one female lodger with her lady's maid and one visitor. It still operates as a hotel.

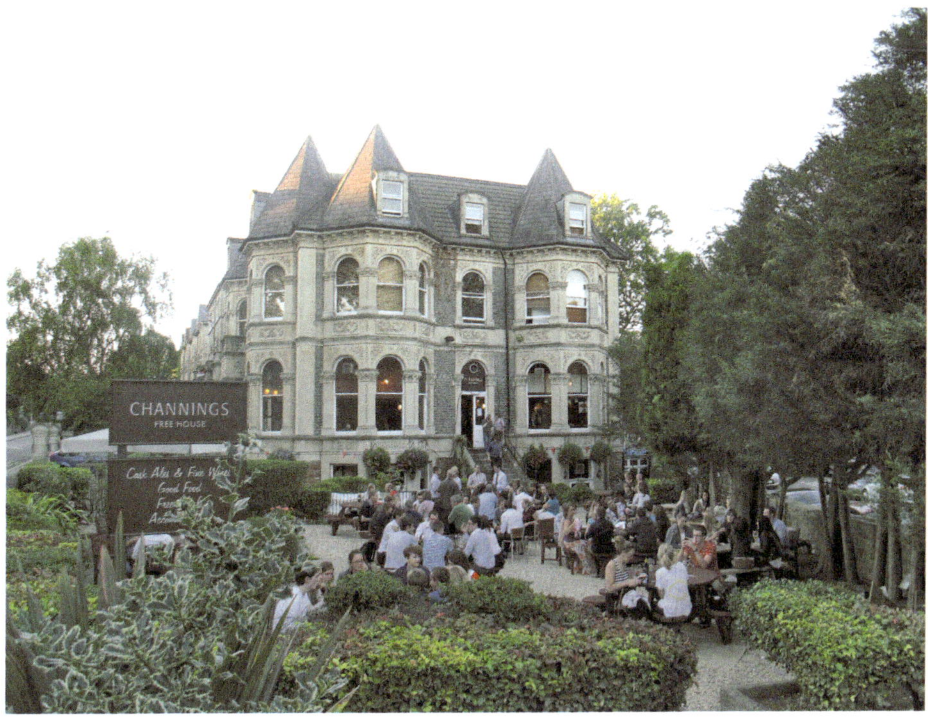

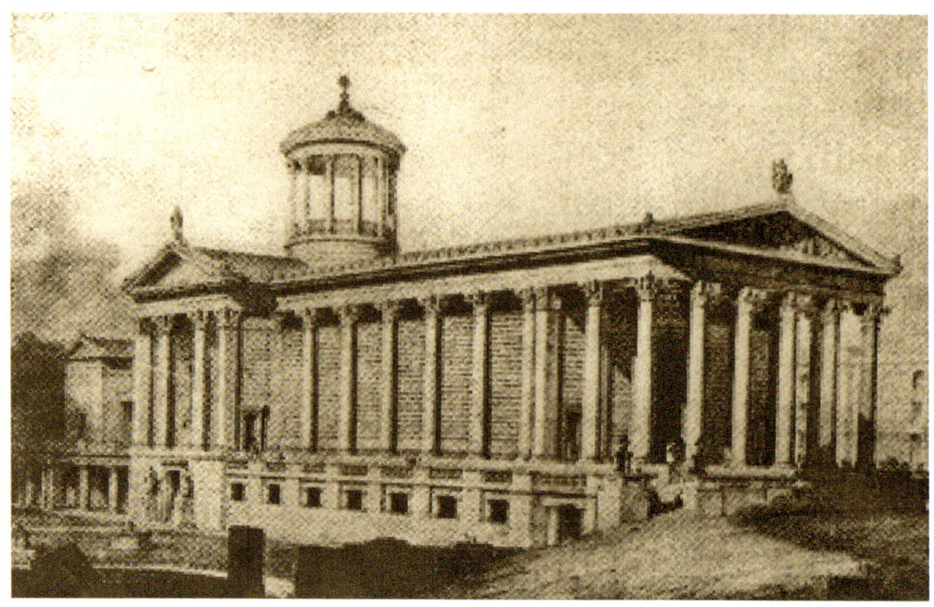

St Peter and St Paul's Cathedral, Pembroke Road

The Pro-Cathedral in Park Place was built in 1834 in response to Bristol becoming a Roman Catholic see. Its early existence was chequered with parts collapsing into the quarried hillside. After 1973 the building was turned into a school and is now student accommodation. The modern Catholic Cathedral was built on 4 acres of land where St Vincent's Hall had stood, close to All Saints church on Pembroke Road. It was designed by Percy Thomas Partnership and is an impressive example of modern architecture, with its exterior of panels of pink Aberdeen granite, and the tripartite spire is of reinforced concrete.

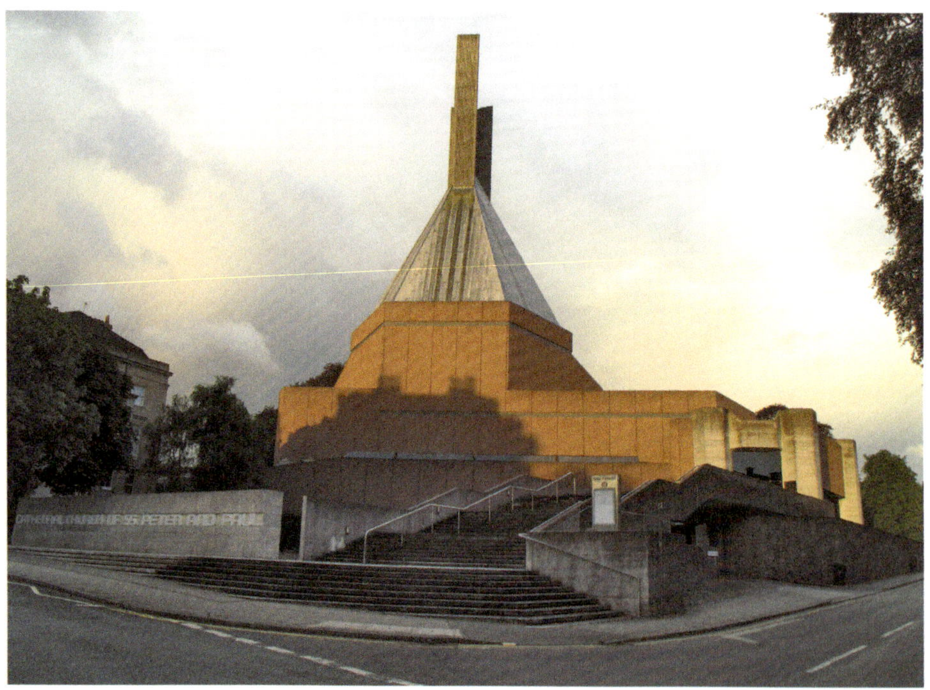

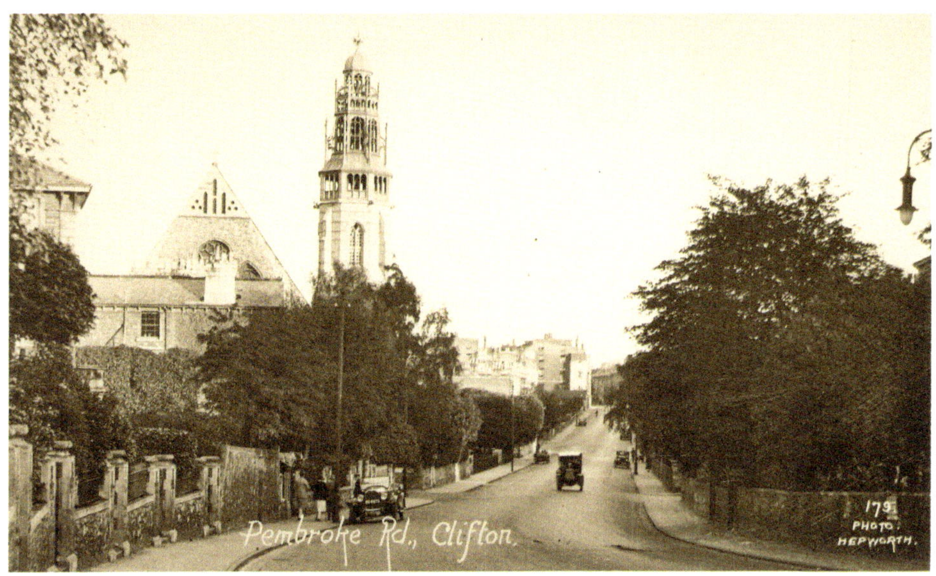

All Saints Church, Pembroke Road, 1900s

Dominating the eastern side of Pembroke Road, All Saints church has undergone a dramatic facelift during its lifetime. In the 1860s the architect, George Edmund Street, was commissioned to design a large church for the poorer residents of Clifton, or those who were non-evangelical. This was consecrated in 1868. In 1928, a dramatic tower was added with a Flemish, lead-covered lantern, designed by F. C. Eden. It was bombed in 1940 and rebuilt (using Europe's then-largest mobile crane to put on the 77-foot steeple) to a modern design by Robert Potter.

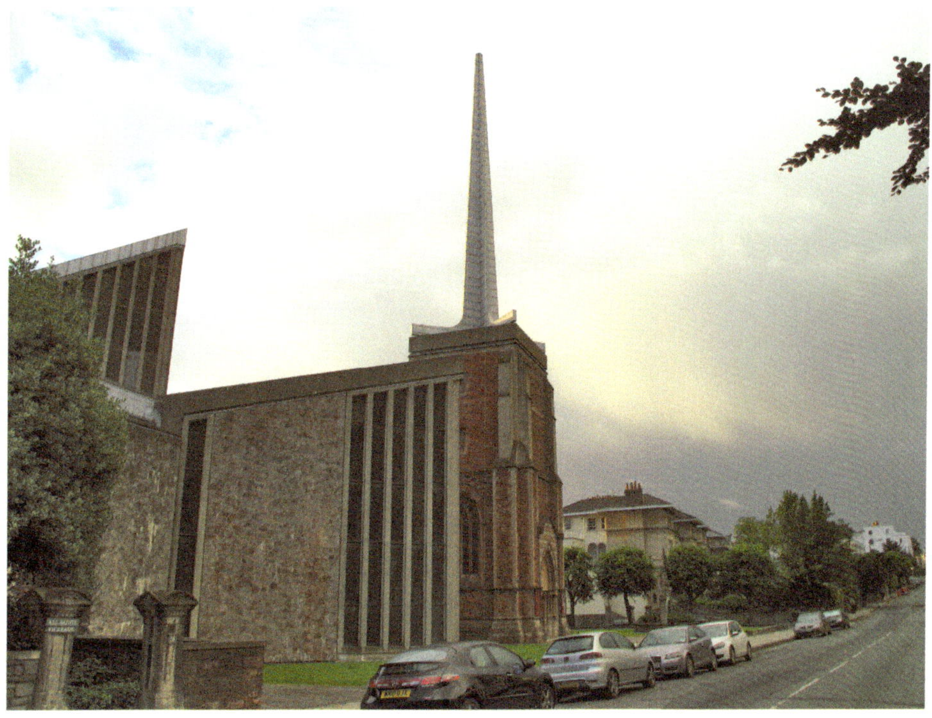

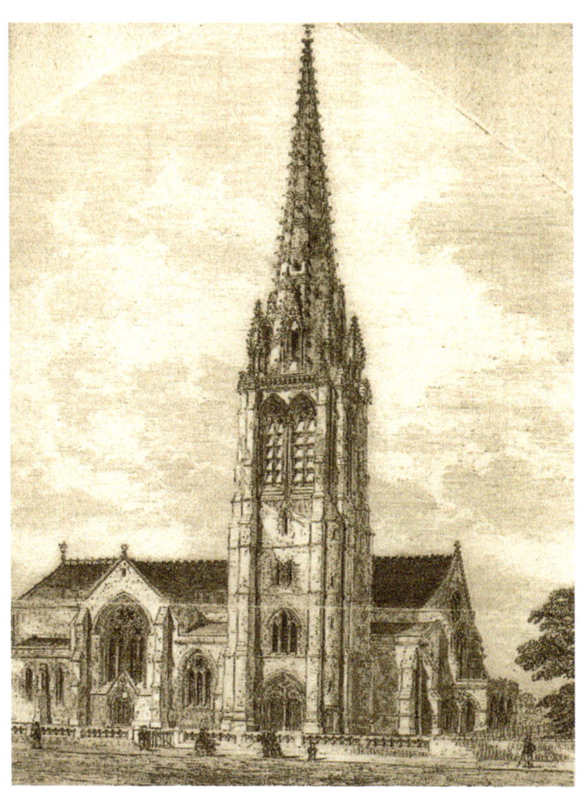

Emmanuel Church

Situated on Guthrie Road, just off Pembroke Road, Emmanuel church was an Anglican church for a 'low church' congregation (in 'opposition' to the 'high church' of All Saints around the corner). Designed by John Norton and consecrated in 1869, the imposing 108-foot tower was subsequently added but plans for a steeple were never realised. Most notably, an aspiring crime writer Agatha Miller married Lieutenant Archibald Christie here on 24 December 1914. The church was demolished in 1977 and sixty-six flats for the elderly were built on the site, incorporating the tower as a landmark.

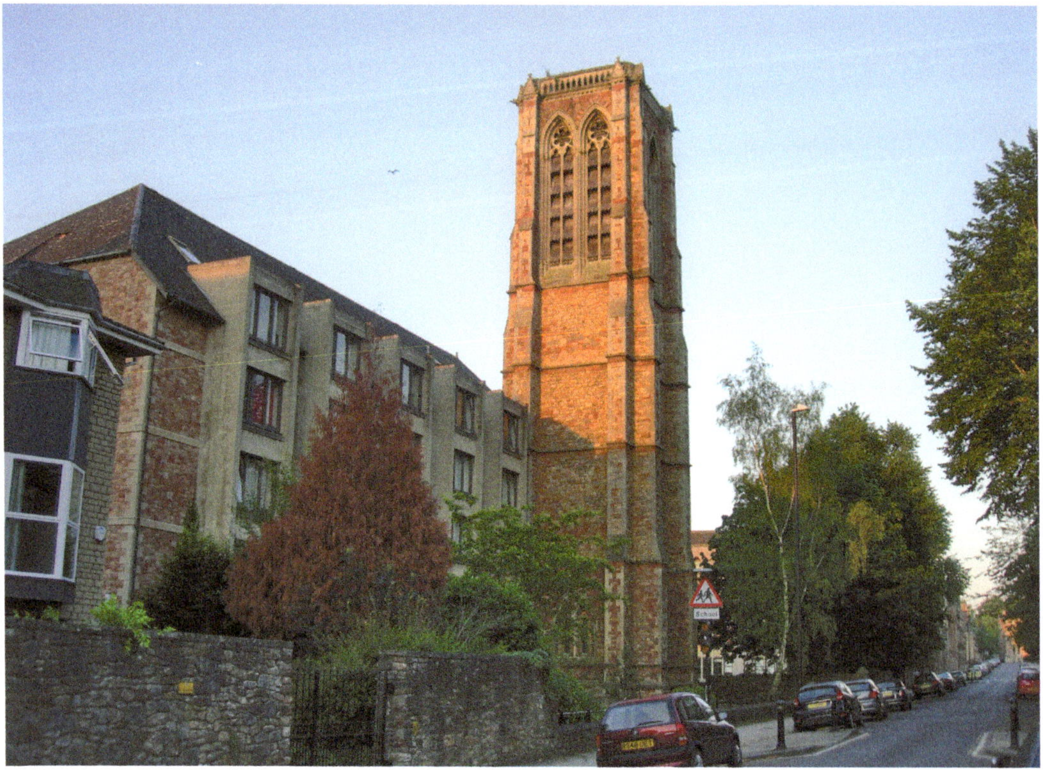

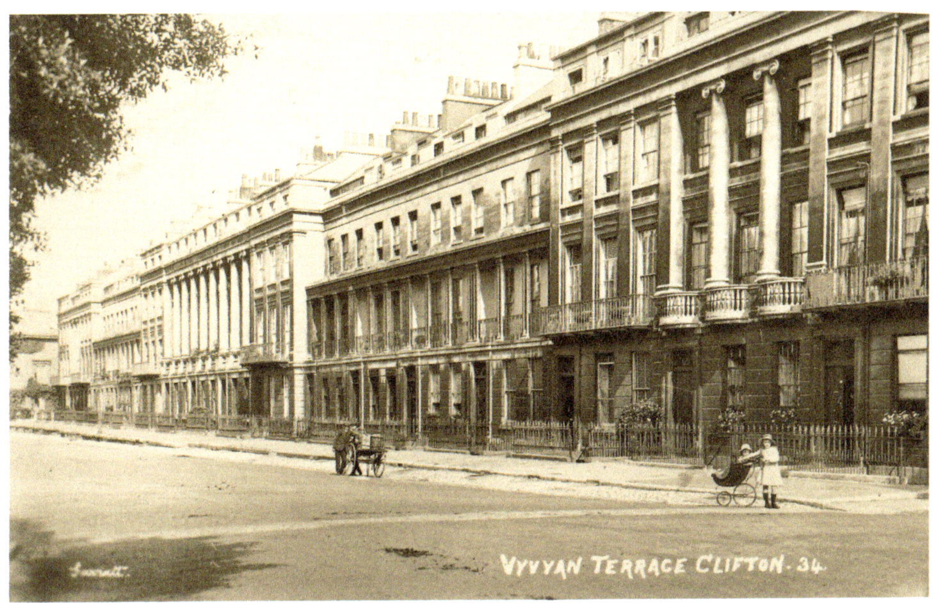

Vyvyan Terrace, 20 April 1924

Parking your car was clearly not such a problem in 1920s Clifton. This residential terrace, named after Sir Richard Vyvyan (Tory MP for Bristol in 1832) was built piecemeal in 1838–47. The 1891 census shows that of the nineteen houses, twelve were lived in by one family; of those, six were widows with children (often daughters of a marriageable age); six were lodging houses; one stood vacant. All had at least two servants living in.

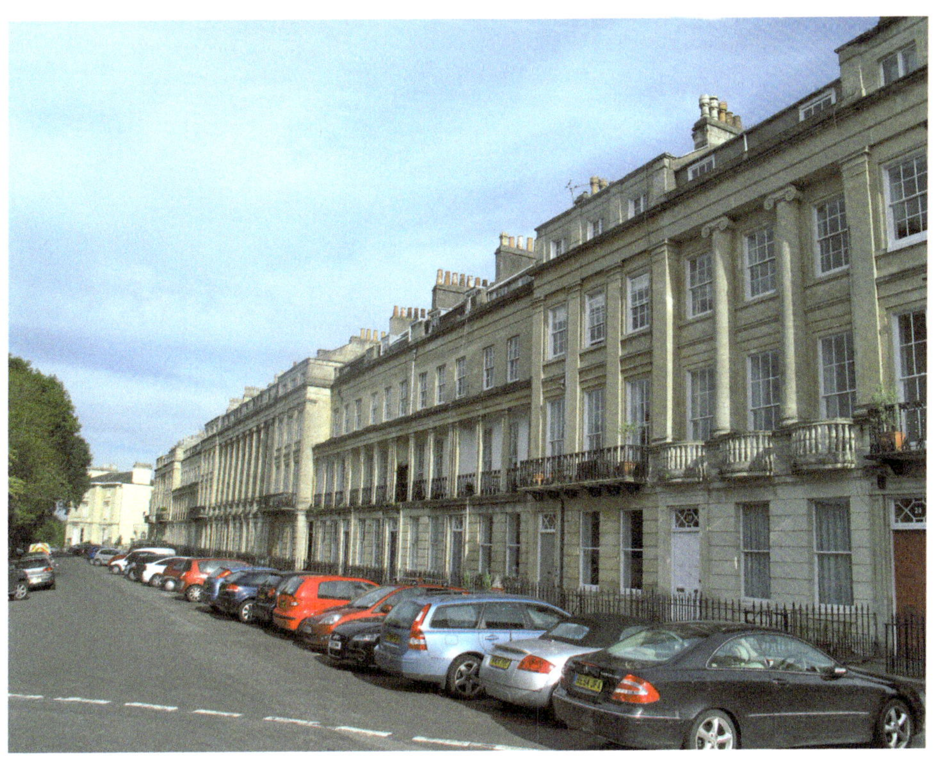

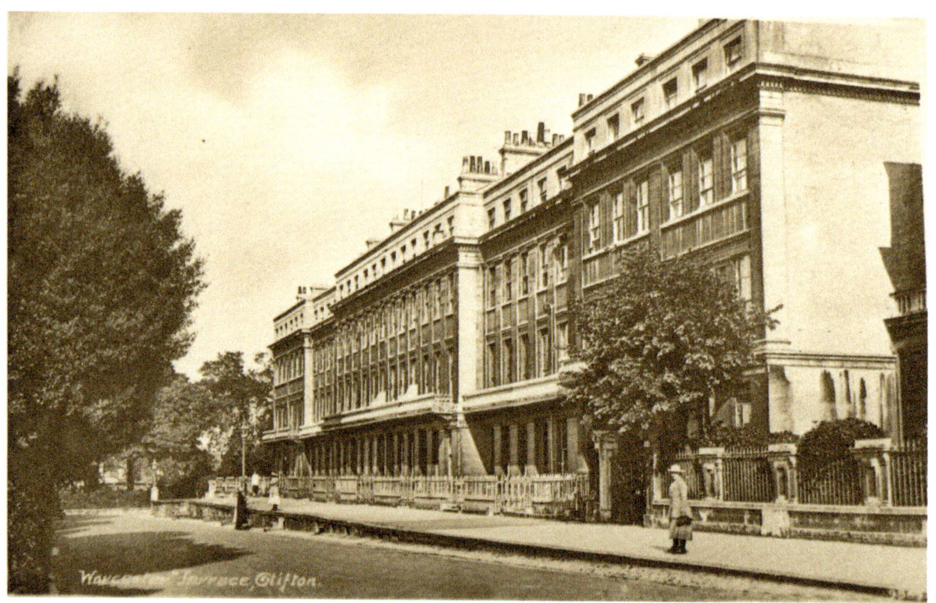

Worcester Terrace, 1990s

Designed by Charles Underwood, Worcester Terrace was built between 1848 and 1853, just after the completion of nearby Vyvyan Terrace. In front of both terraces is a communal garden for the use of residents. They were, and still are private, surrounded by iron railings, with locked gates. There are thirty-eight communal gardens within one square mile. Most remain private, but some, for instance Victoria Square and The Mall Gardens, are now owned by the Bristol City Council and open to the public. Residents help with the planting and some maintenance. The spire of St Peter and Paul's Cathedral can be seen in the background of the new photograph.

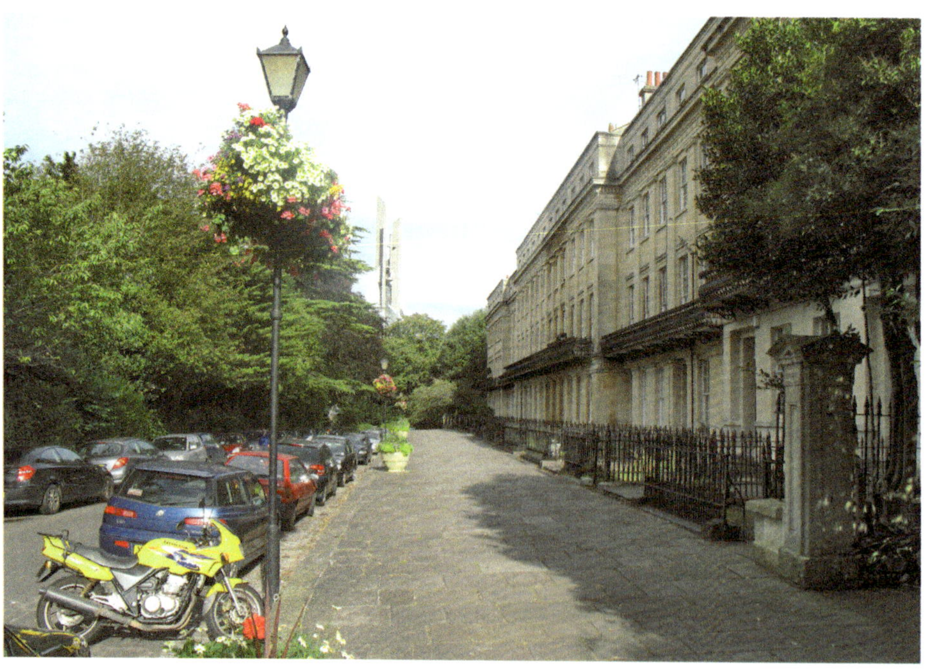

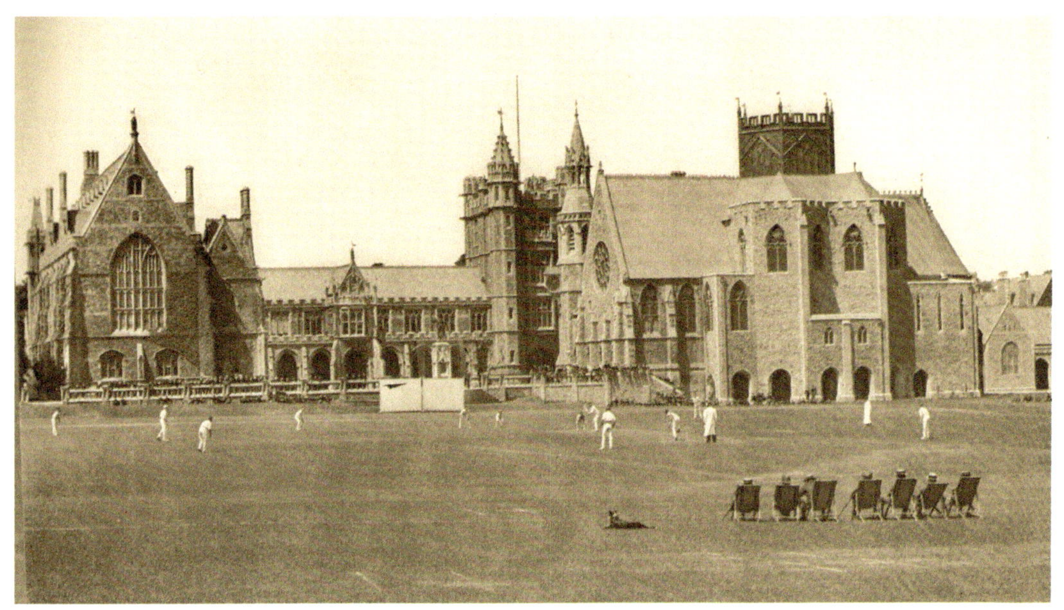

Clifton College, 1860s

Clifton College opened its doors in 1862 with a far-sighted headmaster, the Revd John Percival, in charge of the moral and physical education of Clifton's children. The college has had a number of famous pupils, from Field Marshal Haig (his statue stands outside the school), to John Cleese and Jeffrey Archer. Along with Bristol Grammar School, Queen Elizabeth's Hospital and Clifton High School, it has ensured that Clifton has maintained its reputation for educational excellence.

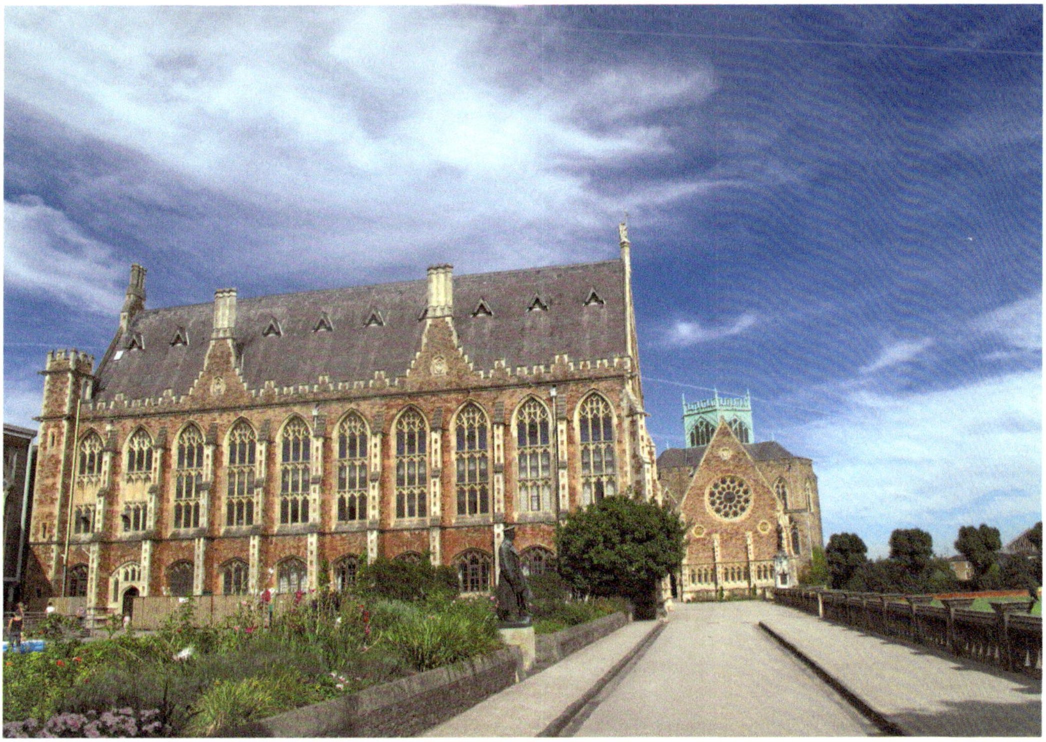

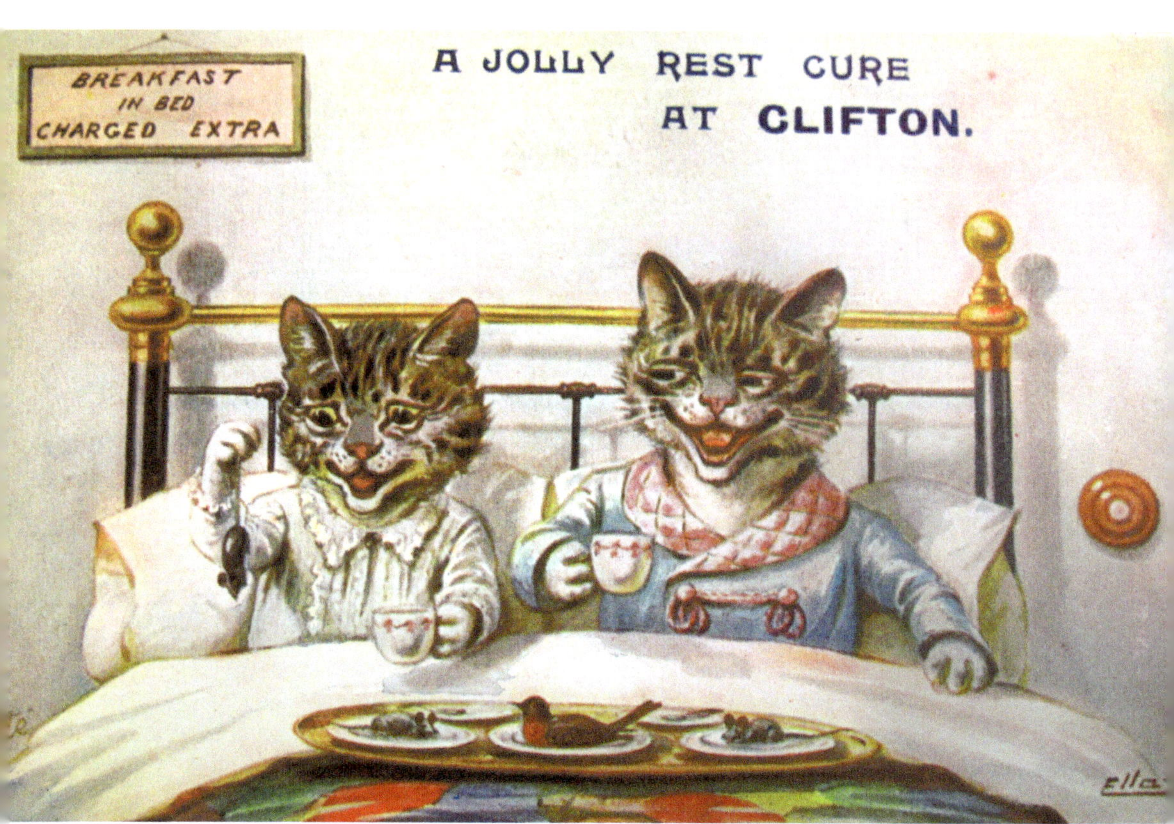

Acknowledgements

The author would like to express his gratitude to Sue Stops, Francis Greenacre, the Clifton and Hotwells Improvement Society, the late Cedric Barker, John and Pat Spiller, John Parke, Peter Craig, the staff at the Bristol Record Office and to the many local authors and historians who have added to the knowledge and appreciation of Clifton through the years. And finally many thanks to my family and Titus the cat.

The following are the reference numbers for the images reproduced from the Vaughan Collection housed at the Bristol Record Office: BRO43207/8 No.: 1; BRO43207/9/7 Nos.: 2, 5, 24, 27, 31, 34, 37, 39, 56; BRO43207/9/11 Nos: 3, 27, 38, 42, 47, 53, 78, 86, 121, 142; BRO43207/9/12 Nos.: 31, 34/4, 41, 42, 83, 131, 144, 160, 173, 185, 188, 204, 208, 245, 247, 252, 254, 257, 258, 264, 264, 267, 282, 307, 318, 320, 336, 395; BRO 43207/12 Nos.: 1/6, 5/10, 5/15, 9/14, 13/9, 40; BRO43207/9/5 No.: 2; BRO43207/9/9 No.: 14; BRO43207/9/29 No.: 2; BRO43207/9/30 Nos.: 16, 100, 108, 249; BRO43207/9/35 Nos. 6, 30, 31, 36, 53, 64, 91, 105, 173, 290, 376, 374.